P9-CQI-148

Learning Base R

Lawrence M. Leemis
Department of Mathematics
The College of William & Mary

Library of Congress Cataloging-in-Publication Data

Leemis, Lawrence M.
     Learning Base R / Lawrence M. Leemis.
     ISBN 978-0-9829174-8-0
     Includes index.
     1. R (Computer program language)
     QA276.45.R3 L44 2016

© 2016 by Lawrence M. Leemis

All rights reserved. No part of this book may be reproduced in any form or by any means, without permission in writing from the publisher.

The author and publisher of this book have used their best efforts in preparing this book. These efforts include the checking of the mathematics and computational techniques for correctness. The author and publisher make no warranty of any kind, expressed or implied, with regard to the mathematics and computational techniques contained in this book. The author and publisher shall not be liable in any event for incidental or consequential damages in connection with, or arising out of, the furnishing, performance, or use of the mathematics or computational techniques contained herein.

Printed in the United States of America

10 9 8 7 6 5 4 3 2 1

ISBN 978-0-9829174-8-0

For Arthur & Ivah

Contents

Preface

R is a free software package that includes a rich set of data structures, computational functions, graphical functions, statistical procedures, programming capability, and much more. This book is designed for novices to R, both those with and without prior programming experience. The emphasis here is on the base capability of R; extended capabilities are introduced in the final chapter.

This text introduces R in small, bite-sized chunks, which take about 15 minutes apiece, on average, to digest. The best way to go through this text is to have R installed and running on a nearby laptop or desktop machine, try each command presented, then experiment a bit with other similar commands. Think of each chapter as a separate R session. All of the commands in this text are available on my homepage at www.math.wm.edu/~leemis in case you would like to save some typing. I have worked with R and its predecessors S and S-Plus for many years, and I have yet to crash the software, so feel free to experiment with reckless abandon.

Two small examples are provided here to illustrate how short R commands involving just a few keystrokes can result in output that would take significant programming in other languages. Consider the single R command

```
> hist(rnorm(143))
```

The greater-than symbol (>) at the beginning of the line is a prompt that awaits an R command from the user. After the R command hist(rnorm(143)) is keyed in and the return key is pressed, R opens a graphics window displaying the histogram shown below.

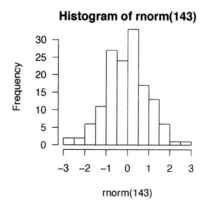

The function name hist is short for "histogram." The argument associated with hist is the data to be plotted in the histogram. Rather than using an actual data set collected in an experiment, the data is given by rnorm(143), which is 143 random variates (the number of random variates was selected arbitrarily) drawn from a standard normal population.

Not surprisingly, the histogram shows a roughly bell-shaped distribution to the data values; its shape is bumpy due to random sampling variability. This random sampling variability decreases as the number of random variates generated increases. There are dozens of default decisions that were made in constructing this histogram. For example, there are 12 cells to hold the data values, the tick marks extend out of the plot, the histogram bars are not shaded, the heights of the bars are the counts of the number of data values falling in the cells, and a main title and axis labels are included. All of these decisions are easily modified to produce a custom plot.

Rather than using simulated data values, the second example uses a real data set. Consider the R command

```
> barplot(VADeaths, beside = TRUE, legend = TRUE)
```

This command produces a bar chart, complete with a legend, of the VADeaths data set built into R. The bar chart appears in a pop-up graphics window and is shown below. Once again, R makes several decisions internally to produce the graphic. R selects a scale for the vertical axis, and plots bars of appropriate heights. R includes tick marks and associated labels. R even found some room in the upper-right-hand corner of the graphic and placed the requested legend there. R chose to shade the interior of the bars in the bar chart. All of these were easily-modified default decisions.

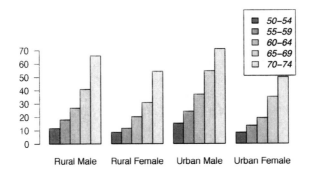

But it is not clear what is in the data set VADeaths. Typing

```
> VADeaths
```

shows the data values and typing

```
> help(VADeaths)
```

gives information concerning the data set, revealing that the heights of the bars are annual death rates per 1000 residents, stratified by age, gender, and domicile, in Virginia in the 1940s.

My thanks goes to Russell Atkinson, Barry Lawson, and Tanujit Dey for ideas and brainstorming, and to Nadia Aly, Daniel Block, Rob Downs, Anthony Finch, Kristina Kelly, Samantha King, Larson Lasek, Arthur Leemis, Bob Lewis, Bob Noonan, Scott Percic, and Andrew Turscak for looking the text over prior to publication. Special thanks to Daniel McGibney and Raghu Pasupathy for class testing the text. I also thank Lindsey Leemis for the handsome cover design. Finally, thanks to the designers and contributors to S, S-Plus, and R, and to Don Knuth for TeX. Any suggestions for the improvement of the text will be gratefully received. Enjoy R!

Williamsburg, VA   *Larry Leemis*
                                                                                             August, 2015

Chapter 1

Introducing R

R is a free language that can easily be downloaded from the internet. Regardless of whether you work in industry, academics, or government, or if you just use the language for personal use, you will always have access to the R language. So why use R? There are at least six answers to this question. First, R is freeware. It can be used on a desktop or a laptop computer. Second, R is capable of performing numerical calculations on scalars, vectors and matrices, and can be used as a high-powered calculator. Third, R has built-in functions for performing probability and statistical calculations, and R can run simulation experiments using these functions. Fourth, R has extensive graphics capabilities so that it can produce production-level graphics. Fifth, R can be used as a programming language. R allows the user to execute several types of loops for iteration and also supports conditional execution of code. Sixth, hundreds of contributors have written R code contained in "packages," which continue to extend the language in the same way that apps have transformed handheld devices.

The R language, originally known as S, was developed in 1976 at Bell Labs by John Chambers and his colleagues. S-Plus is the current commercial version of S. In 1993, the free, open source R language was first developed by Ross Ihaka and Robert Gentleman (notice the common first initial) from the University of Auckland. R and S have a very large overlap of capabilities. If you know one, you essentially know the other. The differences are minor. One advantage to R over S, however, is the number of packages that have been written in R that are capable of extending the base language. These packages can be quite useful in specific niche applications.

The orientation for R is as follows. R is a vector-based language that uses vectors as its primary data structure. R has a command-line orientation rather than a Graphical User Interface (GUI) menu orientation. Although this might seem a bit antiquated at first, the size and capability of the language force this orientation. The focus here will be on the syntax, that is, the rules for issuing R commands. There are plenty of other R books on the market that are much more encyclopedic in nature or cover specific applications. This book is designed to be a quick introduction to the language for R novices. More advanced books on R will be much easier to read once you master the basics presented here.

You will notice that R tends to favor short, abbreviated variable and function names, which is helpful on your fingers in terms of saving keystrokes. It is also a heritage from the C language and the Unix environment that was present at Bell Labs in the 1970s.

The R language can be located by doing a web search on the letter R in a browser. Alternatively, you can use the website `http://www.r-project.org`. Once you get to the website you should pick a mirror site that is near your location and install the binary version. You will need to choose an appropriate platform: Windows, Mac, or Linux. For your first installation, it is probably best to select the default location for installing R. Installing R is similar to installing any other type of software. A license agreement must be accepted and you will want to install the most recent base version of the software. R is a fairly large language, so installing it will typically take a few minutes. On most platforms, an icon with the letter R will appear on your desktop after downloading and installation. To launch R, double-click the R icon on your desktop. This will bring up a window which contains a greater-than prompt, which looks like this:

```
>
```

The prompt indicates that R is waiting for an R command from you. The remainder of this book describes what you can type after the prompt and the associated results. If you type any valid R command at this point and press the return key, R will display the output. If a command is too long for a single line, it is fine to press the return key and continue the command over several lines. There is a + prompt that reminds you that you are completing a command from the previous line. If a command requires significant processing, there will be a time delay for processing before a new prompt appears.

When your R session is finished, you can quit R by typing q(), for quit, at the prompt. A dialog box will open that asks: Save workspace image? [y/n/c]. This determines whether R saves the objects that you have created during the R session for a future R session. After responding to that question, your R session is completed.

Experienced programmers who are used to working with compiled languages may find R's orientation foreign. The practice of submitting a command, viewing the results, then perhaps submitting a subsequent command based on the results is not the way compiled languages are generally used. This orientation is largely a result of the roots of R in exploratory data analysis. One preliminary look at the data often guides subsequent analysis techniques. It is easy to execute a series of R commands that are stored in an external file if the exploratory data analysis approach is not appropriate in a particular setting. Also, R stores its matrices in a column-major orientation, as opposed to the more standard row-major orientation. This is also an artifact of R's roots in exploratory data analysis and the associated data structures required to efficiently store data sets.

R is an interpreted rather than a compiled language, which means that each R command must be interpreted and then executed. Therefore, run times for R code will be a bit slower than comparable code in a compiled language. Some speed pick-up is possible, however, with vector-based programming, which will be described later in the text.

"Comments" are useful for documenting the purpose of a particular R command for yourself or for someone else who might use the code. A comment consists of text that is ignored by R as it processes your R input command. When R encounters the # symbol, it ignores all subsequent input on that line.

One weird trick that can save you some typing is to use the up arrow to repeat a previous command. Every time the up arrow is pressed, the previous R command is displayed. If this command needs to be altered, you can use the destructive backspace, or the nondestructive backspace (the left arrow) to delete or edit R commands. Pressing the enter key executes the original or modified previous R command.

The R language does not have a natural way to sequence the introduction of the various topics. I have decided to sequence the chapters in the following fashion.

- Chapters 2 and 3 introduce elementary arithmetic operations and named storage in R.

- Chapters 4, 5, and 6 introduce three elementary data structures: vectors, matrices, and arrays. In these early chapters, these data structures are filled with numeric elements.

- Chapters 7 and 8 introduce built-in and user-written functions.

- Chapter 9 introduces helpful utilities.

- Chapters 10, 11, and 12 introduce three other types of elements that can be stored in a data structure: complex numbers, character strings, and logical elements.

- Chapters 13 and 14 introduce methods for comparing elements and coercing elements to a particular type.

- Chapters 15 and 16 introduce two advanced data structures: lists and data frames.

- Chapter 17 surveys some data sets that are built into R.

- Chapter 18 introduces functions that interface R with the outside world.

- Chapter 19 introduces functions that are useful in probability calculations.

- Chapters 20 and 21 introduce R's graphical capabilities.

- Chapters 22, 23, and 24 introduce R's programming capabilities.

- Chapter 25 shows how to conduct simulations in R.

- Chapter 26 surveys R's capability for performing statistical inference.

- Chapter 27 introduces linear algebra functions that are built into R.

- Chapter 28 shows how to extend R's base capability by using packages.

You will find R to be a very efficient language for performing both simple and complex calculations. R can be used for analyzing data, performing simulations, performing calculations, etc. The value of a language like R was recognized long ago.

> Civilization advances by extending the number of important operations which we can perform without thinking about them.   —Alfred North Whitehead (1861–1947)

The next chapter introduces R in its simplest form—as a calculator.

Exercises

1.1 Download R from the website `http://www.r-project.org` onto your desktop or laptop computer.

1.2 Visit the comprehensive R archive network (cran) website `http://cran.r-project.org`. Browse some of the online documentation for R.

Chapter 2

R as a Calculator

R can be used as a calculator. This chapter (a) outlines rules associated with the order in which R executes simple arithmetic operations, (b) introduces a function that controls the number of digits that R uses to display the results of a calculation, (c) shows how R handles an extreme calculation like 1/0, and (d) introduces the integer-divide and modulo functions.

In the examples given throughout this text, R commands that you type will be set in monospace font following the > prompt. The response from R will be given on the next line or lines, also set in monospace font. This is exactly what you will see in the R environment.

2.1 Order of operations

We begin with simple arithmetic operations. The order that arithmetic operations are performed is consistent with convention. The PEMDAS convention implies that parentheses get highest priority, followed by exponentiation, followed by multiplication and division, followed by addition and subtraction. The first example of using R in the calculator mode is given below.

```
> 2 + 9 * 4          # PEMDAS; place spaces around operators
[1] 38
```

No equal sign is necessary; pressing the return key serves that role. The response from R is [1] 38, which means that R performed the multiplication before the addition per the PEMDAS convention, giving a result of 38. The [1] that appears before the 38 indicates that the result is a vector of length one. More details concerning vectors will be given in Chapter 4. The [1] can be ignored for now. The text after the # is a comment and has been added to highlight the concept being presented. It is good programming practice to surround the operators with a single space for readability. This is not necessary, however, and it is perfectly acceptable to key in the R command as

```
> 2+9*4              # no spaces around operators; it still works
[1] 38
```

But you could imagine how difficult this would be to read if it was 30 or 40 characters long.

The exponentiation operator is the caret symbol, ^, as illustrated with

```
> 4 + 3 / 10 ^ 2     # exponentiation first, then division, then addition
[1] 4.03
```

Parentheses can be used to alter the order of operations.

```
> 4 + (3 / 10) ^ 2      # division first, then exponentiation, then addition
[1] 4.09
> (4 + 3) / 10 ^ 2      # addition first, then exponentiation, then division
[1] 0.07
> (4 + 3 / 10) ^ 2      # division first, then addition, then exponentiation
[1] 18.49
> ((4 + 3) / 10) ^ 2    # addition first, then division, then exponentiation
[1] 0.49
```

If you accidentally press the return key prior to completing a command, the usual greater than prompt will be replaced by a + prompt, which is R asking you to continue the command.

```
> 2 * 3 -               # + prompt for more input
+ 7                     # completed command 2 * 3 - 7
[1] -1
```

An R command that traverses several lines in this fashion is appropriate for a particularly-long calculation. Now consider computing 1/4.

```
> 1 / 4                 # the display suppresses trailing zeros
[1] 0.25
```

R calculates one-fourth and displays it as the decimal equivalent 0.25, suppressing the trailing zeros. Now consider computing 1/3.

```
> 1 / 3                 # default seven display digits
[1] 0.3333333
```

R must make a decision on how many digits to display. The default in R is to display seven digits. This can be altered, however, as will be shown subsequently.

R does not include commas to separate groups of three digits when displaying the result.

```
> 8 * 10 ^ 3            # exponentiation first
[1] 8000
```

Now consider the calculation of a large number.

```
> 1111111 * 1111111     # no commas on constants; result in scientific notation
[1] 1.234568e+12
```

The result of this calculation is expressed in scientific notation: $1.234568 \cdot 10^{12}$. With only seven digits displayed, it is not possible to know the exact value of the product.

2.2   Number of digits displayed

By default, R displays seven digits, but more digits are stored. As an illustration, the built-in constant π is designated with pi.

```
> pi                    # built in constant
[1] 3.141593
```

The `options` function has several optional arguments, which are placed in parentheses, and separated by commas if there are multiple arguments. One of these arguments controls the number of digits that are displayed when R displays the result of a calculation. The call to the `options` function below with the `digits` argument changes the default of displaying seven digits to displaying ten digits in all subsequent calculations.

```
> options(digits = 10)    # display ten digits
> pi                      # pi to ten digits
[1] 3.141592654
```

R stores constants as floating-point numbers to machine precision internally. The largest number of digits that can be displayed is 22. So asking for 50 digits in `options` results in an "error message" from R.

```
> options(digits = 50)    # display 50 digits
Error in options(digits = 50) :
  invalid 'digits' parameter, allowed 0...22
> options(digits = 22)    # display 22 digits
> pi                      # pi to 22 digits
[1] 3.141592653589793115998
```

Now that more digits are displayed, the previous multiplication can be calculated exactly and will not be displayed in scientific notation.

```
> 1111111 * 1111111       # now exact
[1] 1234567654321
```

Of course a large number raised to a large power will need to be expressed in scientific notation, but this time with more digits displayed.

```
> 789 ^ 10                # expressed in scientific notation
[1] 9.349104886236698188523e+28
```

The exact value displayed for this calculation might be machine dependent.

R users should be aware that some numbers are not stored exactly internally because they are stored internally in binary. For example, the constant 17.046875 is stored exactly by R because it has an exact binary representation. However, the constant $6.02214 \cdot 10^{23}$ is *not* stored exactly in R because it does not have an exact binary representation.

```
> 17.046875               # stored exactly
[1] 17.046875
> 6.02214e23              # not stored exactly
[1] 602213999999999969067008
```

Further details are given in Chapter 9. The constant one divided by seventeen raised to the seventh power is a small number that will also be stored in scientific notation.

```
> 1 / 17 ^ 7              # a small number
[1] 2.437011341604645826792e-09
```

2.3   Undefined calculations

R has special procedures for handling division by zero or taking the square root of a negative number. First, try dividing one by zero.

```
> 1 / 0                 # infinity
[1] Inf
```

R has a reserved character string `Inf` that is used to represent infinity. Calculations involving `Inf` can also be executed.

```
> Inf - Inf             # infinity minus infinity
[1] NaN
```

The output from R in this case is another reserved symbol `NaN`, which stands for "Not a Number." When R calculates the ratio of negative one to zero, it displays negative infinity.

```
> -1 / 0                # negative infinity
[1] -Inf
```

When R encounters the ratio of 0 to 0, it also returns `NaN`.

```
> 0 / 0                 # not a number
[1] NaN
```

The square root of a negative number is also undefined.

```
> (-9) ^ (1 / 2)        # square root of negative nine
[1] NaN
```

2.4   Integer divide and modulo

There are two other operators that are of interest in calculator mode. The first gives the integer part of a fraction.

```
> 37 %/% 5              # integer part of a fraction
[1] 7
```

This operator is often known as "integer divide." The second operator, known as the "modulo" operator, gives the remainder associated with the division of two integers.

```
> 37 %% 5               # modulo (remainder) function
[1] 2
```

   This concludes this brief introduction to R as a calculator. The introduction to R as a calculator is incomplete, however, because calculators have buttons for calculating square roots, logarithms, trigonometric functions, etc. R can perform calculations of this type as well, but the discussion of these topics is postponed until Chapter 7. The table given next summarizes the arithmetic operators, in decreasing priority order, described in this chapter.

operator	description
^	exponentiation
%/%, %%	integer divide, modulo
*, /	multiplication, division
+, −	addition, subtraction

Parentheses can be used to alter the order of operations from the default. R uses `Inf` to represent infinity, which is generated by, for example, $1/0$. R uses `NaN` to represent "not a number," which is generated by, for example, $0/0$.

The next chapter defines the notion of an "object" in R. Using objects is the key to extending the capability of R well beyond that of a calculator.

Exercises

2.1   Write an R command to compute

$$100 \left(1 + \frac{0.05}{12} \right)^{24},$$

which is the value of $100 invested at an annual rate of 5% after two years with monthly compounding.

2.2   What is returned by the following R command? (Guess before computing this in R.)

```
> 5 %% 2
```

2.3   What is the remainder when 3333 is divided by 222?

2.4   Use R to investigate the behavior of $(1 + 1/n)^n$ for large, integer values of n.

Chapter 3

Simple Objects

Using R as a calculator is useful, but its capability is not limited to just operators applied to numeric values. We now define an *object* in R, which is a more general notion. An object is typically called a *variable* in most computer languages, but the designers of R chose the term object in order to highlight their generality as a data structure. Simple named objects that contain a single numeric value are considered in this chapter; more complicated objects will be covered in subsequent chapters.

Objects are identified by their name. Object names typically begin with a letter and can contain letters, numbers, periods, and underscores. So R2D2, Pay.Rate, and Hours_worked are all legitimate object names. Object names are "case sensitive," so Mary, mary, and MARY are three distinct object names. All of the characters in an object name are significant.

The topics considered in this chapter are (a) assigning numeric values to objects, (b) applying arithmetic operators to objects, (c) listing and removing objects, and (d) choosing meaningful object names.

3.1 Assigning numeric values to objects

The = and <- assignment operators assign a numeric value to an object. The two assignment operators are equivalent. The latter has been defined to look a bit like an arrow that points to the left. (No space is allowed between the < and the - when using the arrow-like version of the assignment operator.) The example given below assigns the numeric value 2 to an object named x.

```
> x = 2                    # assign two to the object x
```

The R object x has silently been set to 2. R does not give any confirmation that the assignment has taken place. To confirm the assignment, simply type the name of the object and its value will be displayed.

```
> x                        # display x
[1] 2
```

As was the case when using R as a calculator, a [1] appears to the left of the value in the object x to indicate that this object is a vector of length one. Vectors containing more than one value will be considered in the next chapter.

Next, the object y is set to four and is then displayed by typing its name.

```
> y = 4                          # assign four to y
> y                              # display y
[1] 4
```

Although x and y have been assigned the integer values 2 and 4, R allows objects to also be set to floating point numbers. Using the other R assignment operator, the object z is set to 3.7, and then z is displayed.

```
> z <- 3.7                       # assign 3.7 to z
> z                              # display z
[1] 3.7
```

The assignment operators = and <- take the expression to the right of the assignment operator and place it in the object on the left of the operator. This allows the possibility of the same object appearing on both sides of the assignment operator. Let's say we want to take whatever the current value is in the object x, increase it by one (this operation is known as *incrementing*), and display its updated value. This is accomplished with the commands

```
> x <- x + 1                     # increment x
> x
[1] 3
```

The reason for the arrow-like assignment operator is now apparent. The mathematical equation

$$x = x + 1$$

is not what is occurring with the assignment operation. Rather, we are taking whatever is to the right of the operator, computing it, then placing it into the object given to the left of the assignment operator. The arrow-like version makes the assignment operation and more adequately captures what is happening when an assignment takes place. In this text, we generally use the = assignment operator because it can be typed with fewer keystrokes.

It is possible to assign the same value to several objects simultaneously, as illustrated below.

```
> x = y = z = 5                  # set x, y, and z to 5
```

The objects x, y, and z have had their previous values, namely x = 3, y = 4, and z = 3.7, over-written. They all have the value 5 at this point. Once an object is reassigned in this fashion, the previous value is replaced and cannot be accessed again. Objects have no sense of "memory" in terms of the values that they have previously held.

It is possible to have multiple R commands on a single line by separating the two commands with a semi-colon.

```
> x = 3; y = 4                   # the semi-colon separates the two commands
```

This style is not encouraged because of decreased readability of the R code.

3.2 Arithmetic operations on objects

Once simple objects have been defined, mathematical operations illustrated in the previous chapter can be applied to them. The following examples illustrate addition, multiplication, exponentiation, and the modulo operator applied to x and y.

```
> x + y                 # sum
[1] 7
> x * y                 # product
[1] 12
> x ^ y                 # 3 ^ 4
[1] 81
> y %% x                # y modulo x
[1] 1
```

3.3   Listing and removing objects

During an R session, you might wind up defining several objects. In order to see the names of all of the existing objects, use the `objects` function or the `ls` (list) function (the two functions perform the same task) with no arguments.

```
> ls()                  # display object names
[1] "x" "y" "z"
```

Once you terminate your R session with the `q()` command, these objects will be deleted from memory unless you request R to keep them for the next R session. If you want to clear an object from the current session, this can be done with the `rm` (remove) function using the object name as an argument. For example, to remove the object x, but leave the objects y and z, use the `rm` function.

```
> rm(x)                 # remove (unassign) x
```

Typing x at this point

```
> x                     # the object x no longer exists
Error: object 'x' not found
```

results in an error message indicating that there is no longer an object named x. The `ls` function can be invoked again to confirm that x has indeed been removed.

```
> ls()                  # display object names
[1] "y" "z"
```

If the objects y and z are also removed, then there are no objects at all, and this is reflected with the (not-so-helpful) response `character(0)`.

```
> rm(y, z)              # remove y and z
> objects()             # display object names
character(0)
```

A space is added after the comma in the call to the `rm` function for readability. All of the objects that have been created in the current session can be removed with the command

```
> rm(list = ls())       # remove all objects in current session
```

This is often more efficient than deleting each object individually.

3.4   Selecting meaningful object names

Object names should be chosen carefully. They should succinctly capture the essence of what is contained in the object. Code with well-thought-out object names is self-documenting. Conversely, using object names that don't reflect the purpose of the R objects results in code that is painful to interpret. As an example, let's say that you have $155 in cash on hand. Here are three ways to assign 155 to such an object.

```
> CashOnHand = 155          # meaningful object name using upper case
> cash_on_hand = 155        # meaningful object name using underscore
> cash.on.hand = 155        # meaningful object name using periods
> objects()                 # display object names
[1] "cash_on_hand" "cash.on.hand" "CashOnHand"
```

The first style of object name, illustrated by CashOnHand, is known as "camel case." The second style of object name, illustrated by cash_on_hand, is known as "snake case." The third style of object name, illustrated by cash.on.hand, is sometimes referred to as "dot notation."

When you are writing R code for yourself, the choice between the three variable names is a matter of personal taste. Once a style has been selected, it should be used consistently. Regardless of the style selected, an object name should be chosen in a manner so that someone else who is reading your code (including the future you!) will know the meaning of the contents of the object.

When you are writing R code for others or on a team, it is much more important to adhere to universal conventions when choosing variable names and formatting your code. One such convention is *Google's R Style Guide*, which is available on the internet.

Certain object names should be avoided. Examples include q, which is used for the R quit function described previously, Inf, which is a reserved character string that represents infinity, and if, which has an alternative meaning for conditional execution.

This concludes the introduction to simple named objects in R. The table below summarizes the operators and functions described in this chapter.

operator or function	description
=	assignment
<-	assignment
ls	list objects in current session
objects	list objects in current session
rm	remove objects in current session

The next three chapters cover three fundamental data structures in R: the *vector*, *matrix*, and *array*. These data structures provide mechanisms for organizing and accessing data values. The first of these data structures, vectors, is a natural generalization of the simple objects introduced in this chapter. The simple objects described in this chapter are actually just vectors of length one, so they do not have a special name that describes them.

Exercises

3.1   The Economic Order Quantity model, or EOQ model, gives the optimal order quantity as

$$Q = \sqrt{\frac{2DK}{h}},$$

where D is the annual demand, K is the fixed cost per order, and h is the annual holding cost per item. The EOQ model is used to solve *inventory control* problems and is appropriate when demand for items can be assumed to be constant over time. Write R commands that set the objects D, K, and h to

$$D = 1000, K = 5, \text{ and } h = 0.25$$

and compute the associated value of Q.

3.2 For an initial principal amount P and a nominal annual interest rate r that is compounded n times per year over a span of t years, the final value of a certificate of deposit is

$$F = P\left(1 + \frac{r}{n}\right)^{nt}.$$

Write R commands that set the objects P, r, n, and t to

$$P = 100, r = 0.08, n = 12, \text{ and } t = 3$$

and compute the associated value of F.

Chapter 4

Vectors

The population of Florida, in thousands, during the twentieth century from the United States decennial census is given in the table below.

1900	1910	1920	1930	1940	1950	1960	1970	1980	1990
529	753	968	1,468	1,897	2,771	4,952	6,789	9,746	12,938

The spectacular growth of the population was partially fueled by the invention of air conditioning during the twentieth century. One could easily create ten simple objects in R, perhaps named p00, p10, p20, etc., to hold the ten population values. For a longer list of data values, however, this would be a cumbersome process. There is a more efficient mechanism for storing the ten values. Since the values are all of the same nature (that is, they are all populations), a single object, known as a vector, can hold all ten values. A vector is an ordered sequence of elements of a particular type that can be accessed by an index. The three topics introduced in this chapter are (a) creating a vector, (b) extracting elements of a vector by using subscripts, and (c) performing arithmetic operations on a vector.

4.1 Creating a vector

A vector is a linear arrangement of elements. Four different mechanisms for creating a vector in R are:

- the : operator,
- the c (combine) function,
- the seq (sequence) function, and
- the rep (repeat) function.

These four mechanisms will be presented in the order given above. Each mechanism for creating a vector is useful in various settings. Vectors are an instance of what computer scientists refer to as a *data structure*. In subsequent chapters, other data structures, such as matrices, arrays, lists, and data frames, will be defined. The vector is the primary data structure in R, so mastering it is important before moving on to more complex data structures.

We begin with the : operator for creating a vector. The number that appears to the left of the colon tells R the value in the first element of the vector; the number that appears to the right of the colon tells R the value in the last element of the vector. (A minor exception to this rule is illustrated subsequently.) The absolute difference between successive elements in a vector created with the : operator is one. As a simple example, the R command to create a vector whose elements are the first 10 positive integers is

```
> 1:10                  # a vector of the first ten integers
 [1]  1  2  3  4  5  6  7  8  9 10
```

The 10 elements, which reside in positions 1 to 10, are displayed following the creation of the vector. The elements of a vector can be negative, as illustrated in the creation of a nine-element vector:

```
> -3:5                  # integers from -3 to 5
[1] -3 -2 -1  0  1  2  3  4  5
```

The colon operator increments each successive element by one. If the number to the left of the colon is larger than the number to the right of the colon, R decrements each successive element by one:

```
> 5:-3                  # integers from 5 to -3
[1]  5  4  3  2  1  0 -1 -2 -3
```

There is no limit, other than machine memory, to the length of a vector. The R command to create a vector whose elements are the first 100 positive integers is

```
> 1:100                 # integers from 1 to 100
  [1]   1   2   3   4   5   6   7   8   9  10  11  12  13  14  15  16  17  18
 [19]  19  20  21  22  23  24  25  26  27  28  29  30  31  32  33  34  35  36
 [37]  37  38  39  40  41  42  43  44  45  46  47  48  49  50  51  52  53  54
 [55]  55  56  57  58  59  60  61  62  63  64  65  66  67  68  69  70  71  72
 [73]  73  74  75  76  77  78  79  80  81  82  83  84  85  86  87  88  89  90
 [91]  91  92  93  94  95  96  97  98  99 100
```

The 100 elements of the vector are displayed on one line after another. The reason for the [1] on the display provided by R seen in the previous two chapters now becomes clear. The index of the first element displayed on each line is given in brackets. R displays the vector using a default width of 80 character positions. The format for the display is known as *monospace*, which means that each character displayed assumes the same width on the screen. This is handy for aligning values. The display width can be altered with the options function, which will be described in Chapter 9. The R command above simply echos the value of the vector. It can also be useful to store the vector in an object. So the R command

```
> x = 1:100             # store the integers from 1 to 100 in the vector x
```

stores the first 100 positive integers in the vector named x. The numbers on either side of the colon need not necessarily be integers:

```
> 4.5:25                # won't make it to 25
 [1]  4.5  5.5  6.5  7.5  8.5  9.5 10.5 11.5 12.5 13.5 14.5 15.5 16.5 17.5 18.5
[16] 19.5 20.5 21.5 22.5 23.5 24.5
```

The first element is 4.5, and each subsequent element is one more than the previous element. The 16th element of this vector, for example, contains 19.5.

The colon operator is useful for creating vectors whose elements differ by one. But not all vectors have this property. A more general way of creating vectors is with the c (combine) function, which concatenates its arguments together to form a vector. The syntax for the c function is

$$c(element1, element2, \ldots)$$

The numeric values that are placed inside the parentheses are known generically as *arguments* to the function. So to create a four-element vector that contains the elements 2, −3, 4, and 0, use the R command

```
> c(2, -3, 4, 0)            # a four-element vector
[1]  2 -3  4  0
```

In order to set this vector to the object x, use the assignment operator as in the previous chapter.

```
> x = c(2, -3, 4, 0)        # x is a four-element vector
> x                         # display x
[1]  2 -3  4  0
```

If a data set contains missing observations, R allows you to set these elements of a vector to NA, which stands for "Not Available." This is for leaving a position in a vector for a data value that should be present, but, for some reason, is missing.

```
> y = c(1, NA, -3)          # y is a three-element vector
> y                         # display y
[1]  1 NA -3
```

The : operator and the c function can be used together to form a vector, as illustrated below, where x, y, and the vector -1:3 are concatenated together to form the vector z.

```
> z = c(x, y, -1:3)         # z is the concatenation of x, y, and -1:3
> z                         # display z
 [1]  2 -3  4  0  1 NA -3 -1  0  1  2  3
```

The resulting vector z has $4 + 3 + 5 = 12$ elements.

So far we have used two methods, namely the : operator and the c function, to create vectors. The seq (sequence) function, which is a generalization of the : operator, can also be used to create a vector of numeric values. The syntax for the seq function is

$$seq(from = 1, to = 1, \ldots)$$

The first argument to the seq function is named from, and it has a default value of 1; the second argument is named to, and it also has a default value of 1. There are several options that follow the first two arguments, and that is indicated by the three dots that follow the from and to arguments in the syntax. The from and to arguments can be given without including their names by placing numerical values in the first two positions in a call to the seq function. For example, to create a vector with first element 2, last element 20, and increment by = 2, use

```
> seq(2, 20, by = 2)               # a vector from 2 to 20 by 2
 [1]  2  4  6  8 10 12 14 16 18 20
```

The by argument allows increments other than the $+1$ and -1 increments that are used by the : operator. The next example creates an identical vector as the one in the previous example, but this time uses the argument length.out = 10 to force the vector to be of length 10.

```
> seq(2, 20, length.out = 10)     # a vector from 2 to 20 of length 10
 [1]  2  4  6  8 10 12 14 16 18 20
```

Depending on the setting, sometimes the `by` argument is more useful and sometimes the `length.out` argument is more useful for creating a particular vector. A negative increment with the `seq` function could be coded as

```
> seq(20, 1, by = -3)          # a vector from 20 to 2 by -3
[1] 20 17 14 11  8  5  2
```

A vector of seven elements is created that has last element 2 because the increment of -3 between the elements takes precedence over the vector ending at 1.

The fourth and final method for creating a vector presented here is the `rep` (repeat) function. The syntax for the `rep` function is

$$\text{rep(x, times, ...)}$$

The first argument x is an object to be repeated; the second argument `times` is an object that indicates how many times the first object should be repeated. The first example of `rep` repeats 5 four times.

```
> rep(5, 4)                    # repeat 5 four times
[1] 5 5 5 5
```

The next example repeats the vector consisting of 1, 2, and 3 twice.

```
> rep(1:3, 2)                  # repeat 1:3 two times
[1] 1 2 3 1 2 3
```

The next example repeats the vector consisting of 1, 3, and 5 twice.

```
> rep(seq(1, 5, by = 2), 2)    # repeat (1, 3, 5) two times
[1] 1 3 5 1 3 5
```

The next example repeats two copies of 1, followed by four copies of 5.

```
> rep(c(1, 5), c(2, 4))        # repeat 1 twice and 5 four times
[1] 1 1 5 5 5 5
```

The next example creates a vector that repeats one copy of 1, followed by three copies of 3, followed by five copies of 5.

```
> rep(seq(1, 5, 2), seq(1, 5, 2))  # one 1, then three 3s, then five 5s
[1] 1 3 3 3 5 5 5 5 5
```

Finally, using the `each` argument, each element in the vector in the first argument is repeated four times.

```
> rep(1:3, each = 4)           # four 1s, then four 2s, then four 3s
 [1] 1 1 1 1 2 2 2 2 3 3 3 3
```

4.2   Extracting elements of a vector

Now that we have established four methods for creating a vector, the focus shifts to techniques for accessing the elements of a vector. R uses the index of the position, known as a subscript, to extract a particular element. The syntax for extracting an element or elements from a vector named `VectorName` is

```
VectorName[ subscript(s) ]
```

The brackets signify that one or more elements of the object are to be extracted. The R convention is that positive subscripts include an element and negative subscripts exclude an element. The absolute values of the subscripts run from 1 to the length of the vector, and can be given in any order. (Some other programming languages, notably C, begin subscripts at 0.) To illustrate some basic techniques for extracting elements of a vector, we first establish a six-element vector named x that contains the elements 2, 0, -1, 6, 7, and 8.

```
> x = c(2, 0, -1, 6,          # continue input
+        7, 8)                # x is a six-element vector
> x                           # display x
[1]  2  0 -1  6  7  8
```

Let's say that we would like to extract the third element of the vector. R uses brackets containing the subscript of interest:

```
> x[3]                        # third element of x
[1] -1
```

In order to extract the third through the sixth elements of x, the vector 3:6 is placed in the brackets.

```
> x[3:6]                      # elements 3 through 6
[1] -1  6  7  8
```

There is no requirement that the subscript values be given in sorted order, as they were when x[3:6] were accessed. The R command below extracts the sixth element of x, followed by the third element, followed by the sixth element, followed by the first element.

```
> x[c(6, 3, 6, 1)]            # elements 6, 3, 6, and 1
[1]  8 -1  8  2
```

All of the subscript values thus far have been positive. As noted earlier, negative subscript values are used to exclude elements. For example, to display all elements of x except for the fourth element, use the R command

```
> x[-4]                       # all elements except the 4th
[1]  2  0 -1  7  8
```

To create a vector that consists of all elements of x except for the fourth, fifth, and sixth elements, use the R command

```
> x[-4:-6]                    # all elements except the 4th, 5th, and 6th
[1]  2  0 -1
```

The c function can also be used to selectively exclude elements. For example, to create a vector that consists of all elements of x except for the second and fifth elements, use the R command

```
> x[-c(2, 5)]                 # all elements except the 2nd and 5th
[1]  2 -1  6  8
```

R does not allow the mixing of positive and negative subscripts. The reason for this restriction is that it would be ambiguous as to whether the element with the positive subscript is included before or after removing the element with the negative subscript. An illustration, along with the associated error message, is

```
> x[c(-2, 5)]                          # don't mix positive and negative subscripts
Error in x[c(-2, 5)] : only 0's may be mixed with negative subscripts
```

Subscripts on a vector are best kept as integers. But R is a forgiving language. It will do something sensible if it gets a non-integer subscript. In particular, it will truncate any non-integer subscript toward zero. The example given next takes the subscript 3.3 and truncates it to 3.

```
> x[3.3]                               # R truncates toward zero
[1] -1
```

In the case of using a subscript of 0.8, this will get truncated to zero, and there is no 0 subscript (by convention, R begins its indexing of vectors at 1). In this case, R returns with (not-very-helpful) response numeric(0).

```
> x[0.8]                               # use integer subscripts
numeric(0)
```

Finally, when R encounters the negative subscript -1.8, it truncates toward zero, meaning that the first element of x is excluded.

```
> x[-1.8]                              # use integer subscripts
[1]  0 -1  6  7  8
```

Non-integer subscripts are a bad idea because they often produce inadvertent errors in R commands. Just because you can use non-integer subscripts does not mean that you should.

This section on using subscripts to extract elements of a vector ends with a short, but slightly more complicated example. The R reserved word NULL is used to denote a vector with no elements. The first R command below creates such a vector named x; the second R command displays x; the third R command sets the first, third, fifth, seventh, and ninth elements to 11, 12, 13, 14, and 15, respectively.

```
> x = NULL                             # set x to a vector with no elements
> x                                    # display x
NULL
> x[seq(1, 9, 2)] = 11:15              # fill elements with odd subscripts only
> x                                    # display x
[1] 11 NA 12 NA 13 NA 14 NA 15
```

Since the elements with even subscripts have not yet been assigned values, R places NAs (for Not Available) in those positions. There is a subtle but important distinction between NA and NULL. An object defined to be NULL has no elements; an element defined to be NA corresponds to a placeholder for a missing data value.

4.3   Vector arithmetic

The last topic concerning vectors is *vector arithmetic*. Vectors can be added, subtracted, multiplied, etc. It is interesting that the : operator fits into the middle of the precedence of operators. From highest to lowest, the precedence order of the operators encountered thus far is

- parentheses via (and),

- exponentiation via ^,

- vector creation via :,

- integer divide and modulo via %/% and %%,

- multiplication and division via * and /,

- addition and subtraction via + and -.

Operators of the same precedence are evaluated from left to right. The first example adds three to every element of a vector that consists of the first ten positive integers.

```
> (1:10) + 3                    # add 3 to each element of the vector
 [1]  4  5  6  7  8  9 10 11 12 13
```

The parentheses around 1:10 were not necessary here. Since the : operator has a higher priority than the + operator, the parentheses could have been dropped and the command would have executed in exactly the same fashion with

```
> 1:10 + 3                      # precedence of : vs +
 [1]  4  5  6  7  8  9 10 11 12 13
```

Each element of a vector can be multiplied by a constant

```
> 1:10 * 7                      # multiply each element by 7
 [1]  7 14 21 28 35 42 49 56 63 70
```

or divided by a constant

```
> 1:10 / 20                     # divide each element by 20
 [1] 0.05 0.10 0.15 0.20 0.25 0.30 0.35 0.40 0.45 0.50
```

The parentheses are necessary when it is desired to place the first ten perfect cubes in a vector.

```
> (1:10) ^ 3                    # the first ten perfect cubes
 [1]    1    8   27   64  125  216  343  512  729 1000
```

If you omit the parentheses in this command, a vector containing the first 1000 positive integers will be displayed. It is important to know the precedence of operations well in order to avoid subtle bugs that can arise in your R code. In order to create a vector containing the first ten powers of 2, the vector of the first ten integers is placed in the exponent.

```
> 2 ^ (1:10)                    # the first ten powers of 2
 [1]    2    4    8   16   32   64  128  256  512 1024
```

Although the : operator has been used to create vectors in the previous few examples, the c, seq, and rep functions can also be used:

```
> 2 ^ c(2, -3, 4, 0)            # various powers of 2
 [1]  4.000  0.125 16.000  1.000
```

Vector arithmetic can also be applied to named variables. After setting x to a vector of elements -1, 0, and 1, the first example given next illustrates element-wise division. Then a second vector y is created whose elements are four times the elements of x. Next, the product of the two vectors x and y is another vector with elements that are the element-wise products (which is *not* the dot product from mathematics). Finally, the last R command illustrates element-wise exponentiation.

```
> x = c(-1, 0, 1)              # define x
> x / x                        # ratio of x to x
[1]   1 NaN   1
> y = 4 * x                    # define y to be (-4, 0, 4)
> x * y                        # product taken element-wise
[1] 4 0 4
> y ^ x                        # element-wise exponentiation
[1] -0.25  1.00  4.00
```

The final concept introduced in vector arithmetic is known as *recycling*. Begin by defining a vector z which is of length 6.

```
> z = c(y, y)                  # z has length 6
> z                            # display z
[1] -4  0  4 -4  0  4
```

Now if we attempt to raise z, a vector of length 6, to the power x, a vector of length 3, what is R to do? The decision made by the designers of R is to *recycle* the values in the shorter vector, which means that the six values in the resulting vector are

$$(-4)^{-1} \qquad 0^0 \qquad 4^1 \qquad (-4)^{-1} \qquad 0^0 \qquad 4^1.$$

So the result of raising z to the x power is

```
> z ^ x                        # recycle the values once you run out
[1] -0.25  1.00  4.00 -0.25  1.00  4.00
```

Finally, if the lengths of the two vectors being combined are not multiples of one another, R will go ahead and recycle, but it will also give you a warning message telling you that the longer vector is not a multiple of the shorter vector, just to make sure that the intended operation has indeed occurred.

```
> y ^ c(1, 2, 3, 9)            # lengths of the vectors are not multiples
[1]      -4       0      64 -262144
Warning message:
In y^c(1, 2, 3, 9) :
  longer object length is not a multiple of shorter object length
```

The resulting vector has elements

$$(-4)^1 \qquad 0^2 \qquad 4^3 \qquad (-4)^9.$$

This ends the introduction to the important topic of vectors. A vector can be thought of as a linear arrangement of elements of a particular type (numeric values in this chapter) that can be accessed via one or more subscripts. A vector is the primary data structure in R. The elements of vectors will be generalized in subsequent chapters to allow non-numeric elements. The table given next summarizes the operators and functions described in this chapter.

operator or function	description
:	generate a regular sequence (whose adjacent elements differ by 1)
c	combine values to form a vector
seq	generate a regular sequence
rep	repeat elements of a vector

Subscripts are used for accessing particular elements of a vector. The subscripts are placed in brackets [ ].

In the next chapter, numeric values will be placed in a rectangular arrangement in a data structure known as a matrix.

Exercises

4.1 Use the `rep` function to create a vector that has the following elements:

$$2.7 \quad 8.0 \quad 3.0 \quad 2.7 \quad 8.0 \quad 3.0.$$

4.2 Use the `seq` function with the `by` argument to create a vector that has the following elements:

$$0.0 \quad 0.4 \quad 0.8 \quad 1.2 \quad 1.6 \quad 2.0.$$

4.3 What is returned by the following R commands? (Guess before computing this in R.)

```
> primes = c(2, 3, 5, 7, 11, 13, 17, 19, 23, 29)
> composites = c(4, 6, 8, 9, 10)
> primes[composites]
```

4.4 What is returned by the following R command?

```
> seq(3, 28, by = 11) %/% 4
```

4.5 Use the `seq` function with the `length.out` argument to create a vector that has the following elements:

$$0.0 \quad 0.5 \quad 1.0 \quad 1.5 \quad 2.0.$$

4.6 What is returned by the following R commands?

```
> x = c(2, 0, -5, 7)
> x[-2.8]
```

4.7 What is returned by the following R command?

```
> 3 ^ rep(0:2, 1:3)
```

4.8 Write an R command that uses `rep` to create the vector with elements

$$1 \ 2 \ 3 \ 4 \ 2 \ 3 \ 4 \ 5 \ 3 \ 4 \ 5 \ 6 \ 4 \ 5 \ 6 \ 7$$

4.9 Use the `:` operator and vector arithmetic to create a vector whose first element is 0, last element is 4, and difference between adjacent elements is 0.05.

4.10 Assign the vector x to the first eight positive integers. Show that the three R commands

```
> x[6:8]
> x[c(6:8)]
> x[-c(-6:-8)]
```

all yield identical results.

4.11 Write an R command that calculates n^n for $n = 1, 2, \ldots, 10$.

Chapter 5

Matrices

A matrix is a rectangular arrangement of numbers. Mathematicians tend to write matrices in the following fashion:

$$\begin{bmatrix} 3 & 5 & 0 & 7 \\ 8 & 0 & 3 & -1 \\ -31 & 1 & 5 & 5 \end{bmatrix}.$$

Convention dictates that the *dimensions* of a matrix are given by the number of rows followed by the number of columns. When stating the dimensions of a matrix, a $\times$ is usually used to separate the number of rows and the number of columns. So the dimensions of the matrix given above are 3×4. The elements of a matrix can be positive, negative, or zero. Although the elements in the 3×4 matrix above are all integers, matrices often contain real numbers. The formal study of matrices generally occurs in a college-level mathematics course called *linear algebra*.

The three topics introduced in this chapter are (a) creating a matrix, (b) extracting elements of a matrix by using subscripts, and (c) performing arithmetic operations on a matrix. The discussion of operations on matrices, such as multiplying two matrices, inverting a matrix, or finding the eigenvalues of a matrix, is postponed until Chapter 27.

5.1   Creating a matrix

The three mechanisms for creating a matrix in R described in this chapter are:

- the matrix function,

- the rbind (row bind) function, and

- the cbind (column bind) function.

These three mechanisms will be presented in the order given above. In this chapter, we assume that the elements of a matrix are numeric values. This assumption will be relaxed in subsequent chapters.

Matrices can be created in R with the matrix function. The syntax for the matrix function is

```
matrix(data = NA, nrow = 1, ncol = 1, byrow = FALSE, dimnames = NULL)
```

The defaults associated with the named arguments are given in the syntax. The first argument indicates that NA, for Not Available, is the default if no data is supplied. The data vector contains the numeric values that will be contained in the elements of the matrix. The second and third arguments indicate that the default dimensions for a matrix are 1×1, that is, there is just one row and one column. The fourth argument, byrow, indicates that the matrix will *not* be created in a row-wise fashion by default, which is to say it will be created in a column-wise fashion. As was the case with NA, NULL, and Inf, the strings TRUE and FALSE, which can be abbreviated with just T and F, are reserved words in R. The fifth and final argument in the syntax for invoking the matrix function, dimnames, indicates that there will not be any row and column names by default. The first application of the matrix function creates a 2×3 matrix whose elements are the first six positive integers. The byrow and dimnames arguments are defaulted, which means that the integers will be entered into the matrix in a column-wise fashion, and there are no labels on the rows and columns.

```
> matrix(1:6, nrow = 2, ncol = 3)        # a 2 by 3 matrix
     [,1] [,2] [,3]
[1,]   1    3    5
[2,]   2    4    6
```

The fact that 1:6 appeared as the first argument in the call to matrix indicates that the first six positive integers will serve as the elements of the matrix. R displays the matrix in a rectangular format, and uses [1,] and [2,] to denote the first and second rows. Likewise, R uses [,1], [,2], and [,3] to denote the first, second, and third columns. Had row and column labels been specified using the dimnames argument, they would appear in these positions to the left of the matrix elements (the row names) and above the matrix elements (the column names). As a second example, let the *positions* of the second and third arguments denote the number of rows and the number of columns, but this time the elements are placed in the matrix by row because of the byrow = TRUE argument.

```
> matrix(1:6, 2, 3, byrow = TRUE)        # a 2 by 3 matrix
     [,1] [,2] [,3]
[1,]   1    2    3
[2,]   4    5    6
```

A 2×3 matrix is again produced, but the integers are positioned into elements by row. The next example illustrates how recycling works in the matrix function. Only a single data value, namely zero, appears as the first argument. The zero is recycled and is placed in all six positions of the resulting 2×3 matrix.

```
> matrix(0, 2, 3)                        # a 2 by 3 matrix of zeros
     [,1] [,2] [,3]
[1,]   0    0    0
[2,]   0    0    0
```

Recycling makes sense when the product of the two dimensions, which is $2 \cdot 3 = 6$ here, is a multiple of the number of elements in the data vector, which is 1 here. When this is not the case, R will still recycle the values in the data vector, but it will also print a warning message because this might not be what you intended. Consider the case when data is a vector of length four, but there are six elements in the matrix.

```
> matrix(seq(1, 7, 2), 3, 2)             # a 3 by 2 matrix with recycling
     [,1] [,2]
[1,]   1    7
[2,]   3    1
[3,]   5    3
```

```
Warning message:
In matrix(seq(1, 7, 2), 3, 2) :
  data length [4] is not a sub-multiple or multiple of the number of rows [3]
```

The number of elements in the matrix, which is $3 \cdot 2 = 6$, is not a multiple of the length of the data vector, which is 4, which results in the warning message. The c (combine) function that was introduced in the previous chapter to create vectors can be generalized to the rbind and cbind functions, which are introduced in the next two paragraphs.

A second way to create a matrix is to use the rbind (row bind) function. The syntax for the rbind function is

$$rbind(\ldots)$$

where the ... represents the names of the objects that will be pasted together as rows to form a matrix. The number of arguments to rbind is not fixed and there are no default values. The first example binds three vectors, each of length five, together as rows to form a 3×5 matrix.

```
> rbind(1:5, 2:6, 3:7)                    # row-bind pastes objects as rows
     [,1] [,2] [,3] [,4] [,5]
[1,]    1    2    3    4    5
[2,]    2    3    4    5    6
[3,]    3    4    5    6    7
```

As with the matrix function, rbind will recycle elements when the lengths of the vectors do not match.

```
> rbind(1:8, 1:2)                         # shorter vector gets recycled
     [,1] [,2] [,3] [,4] [,5] [,6] [,7] [,8]
[1,]    1    2    3    4    5    6    7    8
[2,]    1    2    1    2    1    2    1    2
```

In this case, the length of the longer vector is a multiple of the length of the shorter vector, so no warning message is displayed.

A third way to create a matrix is to use the cbind (column bind) function. The cbind function is analogous to the rbind function. The syntax for the cbind function is

$$cbind(\ldots)$$

where the ... represents the names of the objects that will be pasted together as columns to form a matrix. The R commands below bind the two vectors x and y together as columns to form a 2×2 matrix.

```
> x = 1:2                                 # first column
> y = 8:9                                 # second column
> z = cbind(x, y)                         # column-bind pastes objects as columns
> z                                       # display z
     x y
[1,] 1 8
[2,] 2 9
```

Because the cbind function used the objects named x and y as arguments, these object names were used as column names when the resulting matrix z was displayed. The rbind and cbind functions have been illustrated here for binding vectors together to form a matrix. These functions can also be used to bind matrices together, or to bind a combination of matrices and vectors together.

5.2   Extracting elements of a matrix

Now that three ways of creating a matrix have been established, the focus shifts to techniques for accessing the elements of a matrix. As in the case of vectors, subscripts are used to pluck elements of interest from a matrix. The syntax for extracting an element or elements from a matrix named MatrixName is

MatrixName[row.subscript(s), col.subscript(s)]

The brackets again signify that one or more elements of the matrix are to be extracted. Placing the row subscript(s) first and the column subscript(s) second is consistent with convention. The R convention that positive subscripts include elements and negative subscripts exclude elements also applies to matrices. To illustrate some basic techniques for extracting elements of a matrix, we first establish a 2×3 matrix named x that contains the first six positive integers.

```
> x = matrix(1:6, 2, 3, byrow = TRUE)   # x is a 2 by 3 matrix
> x                                      # display x
     [,1] [,2] [,3]
[1,]   1    2    3
[2,]   4    5    6
```

The R command that accesses the (2, 1) element of x is given below.

```
> x[2, 1]                                # second row, first column of x
[1] 4
```

An entire row or column can be accessed by simply leaving the appropriate subscript out. The R command below, for example, extracts the first column of x as a two-element vector.

```
> x[ , 1]                                # first column of x
[1] 1 4
```

Likewise, the following R command extracts the second row of x as a three-element vector.

```
> x[2, ]                                 # second row of x
[1] 4 5 6
```

As was the case with vectors, it is also possible to have a vector of subscripts for the rows, the columns, or both. To extract the second row and the second and third columns, use

```
> x[2, 2:3]                              # 2nd row, 2nd and 3rd columns of x
[1] 5 6
```

To extract a 2×2 matrix of the first and second rows and the second and third columns, use

```
> x[1:2, 2:3]                            # 1st and 2nd row, 2nd and 3rd columns
     [,1] [,2]
[1,]   2    3
[2,]   5    6
```

The same result with fewer keystrokes could have been achieved by just stating that the first column should be eliminated:

```
> x[ , -1]                          # eliminate the first column
     [,1] [,2]
[1,]    2    3
[2,]    5    6
```

Although counter-intuitive, R allows a matrix to be indexed with just a single subscript. If the single subscript 3 is applied to x, the element containing 2 is extracted.

```
> x[3]                              # third element of x (column-major)
[1] 2
```

The elements in a vector are stored internally in R in what is known to computer scientists as a *column-major* storage convention, which is to say that they are stored by column. The third element encountered in x in this case is the element in the $(1, 2)$ position, which contains 2.

5.3   Matrix arithmetic

The final topic concerning matrices is arithmetic operations. The demonstration matrix will again be x.

```
> x                                 # display x
     [,1] [,2] [,3]
[1,]    1    2    3
[2,]    4    5    6
```

When a constant is added to a matrix, every element of the matrix is increased by the value of the constant, resulting in a matrix with the same dimensions as x.

```
> x + 7                             # add 7 to every element of x
     [,1] [,2] [,3]
[1,]    8    9   10
[2,]   11   12   13
```

The matrix x, however, remains the same. Likewise for subtraction. When multiplying a matrix by a constant, each element of the matrix gets multiplied by the constant.

```
> 7 * x                             # multiply every element of x by 7
     [,1] [,2] [,3]
[1,]    7   14   21
[2,]   28   35   42
```

Raising a matrix to a power results in each element of the matrix being raised to that particular power. This convention is not consistent with the notion of "matrix multiplication" from linear algebra, which will be addressed in Chapter 27.

```
> x ^ 2                             # square every element of x
     [,1] [,2] [,3]
[1,]    1    4    9
[2,]   16   25   36
```

When an operator like the modulo function is applied to a matrix, the operator is applied to each element individually.

```
> x %% 2                             # every element of x modulo 2
     [,1] [,2] [,3]
[1,]   1    0    1
[2,]   0    1    0
```

The subscripting on matrices can be used to selectively modify selected elements of a matrix. Once again, we use x as the demonstration matrix.

```
> x                                  # display x
     [,1] [,2] [,3]
[1,]   1    2    3
[2,]   4    5    6
```

You can set the elements in the first column of x to zero with

```
> x[ , 1] = 0                        # zero out the first column
> x                                  # display x
     [,1] [,2] [,3]
[1,]   0    2    3
[2,]   0    5    6
```

The second row of x is set to -1 with

```
> x[2, ] = -1                        # second row set to -1
> x                                  # display x
     [,1] [,2] [,3]
[1,]   0    2    3
[2,]  -1   -1   -1
```

Setting the $(1, 2)$ and $(2, 1)$ elements of x to 17 can be accomplished by the following two R commands.

```
> x[1, 2] = 17                       # set upper left
> x[2, 1] = 17                       # set lower right
> x                                  # display x
     [,1] [,2] [,3]
[1,]   0   17    3
[2,]  17   -1   -1
```

This is a fine way to proceed for a tiny matrix like x with only six elements. But this would not be practical if x were a 100×100 matrix and several dozen elements needed to be altered. R has a more efficient way to attack such a problem. Let's say that the goal is to set the values of the $(1, 2)$ and $(2, 1)$ elements of x to 19 in an efficient manner that would apply easily to a much larger matrix. The first R command below sets the rows of a 2×2 matrix named index to the target subscripts. The second command displays the contents of the index matrix. The third command shows that when the index matrix is used as an argument in x, the current values of the $(1, 2)$ and $(2, 1)$ elements of x are displayed. The fourth command sets these values to 19, and the fifth command displays the updated matrix x.

```
> index = matrix(c(1:2, 2:1), 2, 2)  # define a matrix of subscripts
> index                              # the rows contain target subscripts
     [,1] [,2]
```

```
[1,]    1    2
[2,]    2    1
> x[index]                          # display targeted values in x
[1] 17 17
> x[index] = 19                     # set target values to 19
> x                                 # display x
      [,1] [,2] [,3]
[1,]    0   19    3
[2,]   19   -1   -1
```

This chapter has focused only on creating matrices and accessing their elements. There are dozens of operations that can be performed on matrices. The discussion of those operations has been postponed to Chapter 27, which is titled "Linear Algebra." The table given below summarizes the functions described in this chapter.

function	description
matrix	create a matrix
rbind	combine objects by rows
cbind	combine objects by columns

Subscripts are used for accessing particular elements of a vector. The subscripts are placed in brackets [,]. Subscripts listed before the comma correspond to rows; subscripts listed after the comma correspond to columns.

The previous chapter introduced *vectors*, which can be thought of as one-dimensional arrangements of numeric values. This chapter has introduced *matrices*, which can be thought of as two-dimensional arrangements of numeric values. The next chapter introduces *arrays*, which can be thought of as arrangements of numeric values in three or more dimensions.

Exercises

5.1 Using the *minimum number of keystrokes*, write a single R command that constructs the matrix A given below.

$$A = \begin{bmatrix} 5 & 6 & 7 & 8 & 9 \\ 12 & 12 & 12 & 12 & 12 \\ 81 & 64 & 49 & 36 & 25 \\ 2 & 8 & 4 & 7 & 3 \end{bmatrix}.$$

5.2 Write R commands that create a 2×4 matrix named x that contains the integers $11, 12, \ldots, 18$ arranged in a column-wise fashion. Then use subscripts that extract the elements that exclude the first row and include the first and fourth columns.

5.3 Let A and B be the following 3×2 matrices:

$$A = \begin{bmatrix} 1 & 4 \\ 2 & 5 \\ 3 & 6 \end{bmatrix} \qquad B = \begin{bmatrix} 7 & 10 \\ 8 & 11 \\ 9 & 12 \end{bmatrix}.$$

Write R commands to create the matrices A and B using the matrix function, then combine A and B to create two new matrices with the rbind and cbind functions.

5.4   A *one-step transition matrix* has elements that are between 0 and 1, row sums that equal 1, and the same number of rows and columns. Write an R command to create the 2×2 one-step transition matrix A with elements given by

$$A = \begin{bmatrix} 0.8 & 0.2 \\ 0.3 & 0.7 \end{bmatrix}.$$

5.5   Write a single R command that creates a sequence of one 1, two 2s, three 3s, and four 4s, and places them in a 2×5 matrix named b in a row-wise fashion. This command should use as few keystrokes as possible.

Chapter 6

Arrays

This chapter introduces the array data structure in R, which is the next logical step after introducing vectors and matrices. There is a geometric interpretation of the progression of data structures surveyed so far.

- Chapter 3 introduced *simple objects* that can assume just a single numeric value. These objects are analogous to *points* in geometry.

- Chapter 4 introduced *vectors* that can assume a number of numeric values arranged linearly. Vectors are analogous to *lines* in geometry.

- Chapter 5 introduced *matrices* that can assume a number of numeric values arranged in a rectangular fashion. Matrices are analogous to *planes* in geometry.

- This chapter introduces *arrays* that can assume a number of numeric values arranged in a fashion that requires three or more subscripts to access an individual element. Arrays in three dimensions are analogous to *rectangular solids* in geometry.

The figure below shows an array in three dimensions. The front face of the array is a matrix, but there are several layers of identically-dimensioned matrices lying just behind the first matrix. An element in such a matrix can be accessed by three subscript values: the first is the row number, the second is the column number, and the third is, for lack of a better term, the layer number.

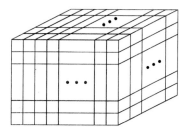

The three topics introduced in this chapter are (a) creating an array, (b) extracting elements of an array by using subscripts, and (c) performing arithmetic operations on an array.

6.1   Creating an array

Arrays can be created in R with the `array` function, which has the following syntax.

$$array(data = NA, \ dim, \ dimnames = NULL)$$

The `array` function is a generalization of the `matrix` function. The first argument is the vector `data`, which contains the elements that will populate the array. As with the `matrix` function, the default for `data` is NA. The second argument `dim` is a vector of integer elements that establishes the largest indexes in each dimension. As was the case with vectors and matrices, these subscript values begin at 1. The third argument `dimnames` can be used to place labels on the various dimensions of the array. The first example of the use of the `array` function creates an array of zeros (recycling is used) to form a $3 \times 5 \times 2$ array.

```
> array(0, dim = c(3, 5, 2))     # 3 x 5 x 2 array of zeros
, , 1

     [,1] [,2] [,3] [,4] [,5]
[1,]    0    0    0    0    0
[2,]    0    0    0    0    0
[3,]    0    0    0    0    0

, , 2

     [,1] [,2] [,3] [,4] [,5]
[1,]    0    0    0    0    0
[2,]    0    0    0    0    0
[3,]    0    0    0    0    0
```

R displays each of the two layers separately in the same fashion it would display a matrix. Above the first layer is the heading `, , 1` and above the second layer is the heading `, , 2`, which indicates the value of the third subscript associated with each layer. The next R command sets the object named `a` to a $2 \times 3 \times 4$ array containing the first 24 positive integers.

```
> a = array(1:24, c(2, 3, 4))    # set a to a 2 x 3 x 4 three-dimensional array
> a                              # display a
, , 1

     [,1] [,2] [,3]
[1,]    1    3    5
[2,]    2    4    6

, , 2

     [,1] [,2] [,3]
[1,]    7    9   11
[2,]    8   10   12

, , 3
```

```
      [,1] [,2] [,3]
[1,]   13   15   17
[2,]   14   16   18

, , 4

      [,1] [,2] [,3]
[1,]   19   21   23
[2,]   20   22   24
```

The elements are placed into a in a column-wise fashion.

6.2 Extracting elements of an array

The focus shifts to techniques for accessing the elements of an array. As in the case of vectors and matrices, subscripts are used to pluck elements of interest from an array. The syntax for extracting an element or elements from an array with three dimensions named `ArrayName` is

```
ArrayName[ row.subscript(s), column.subscript(s), layer.subscript(s) ]
```

The brackets again signify that one or more elements of the array are to be extracted. This syntax generalizes to arrays with more than three dimensions. The R convention that positive subscripts include elements and negative subscripts exclude elements also applies to arrays. An empty index signifies that the full range is to be taken. The $2 \times 3 \times 4$ array a will be used to illustrate some basic techniques for extracting elements of an array. To access a single element in the array a, simply specify the appropriate row number, column number, and layer number:

```
> a[1, 2, 3]                     # an element in a
[1] 15
```

In order to access the third layer of a, give empty subscripts for the row and column, and then specify 3 as the layer number:

```
> a[ , , 3]                      # the third layer in a
      [,1] [,2] [,3]
[1,]   13   15   17
[2,]   14   16   18
```

In order to extract the 2×2 sub-matrix consisting of the first two columns of the third layer of a, ranges should be placed on the row and column subscripts:

```
> a[1:2, 1:2, 3]                 # two by two matrix in the third layer in a
      [,1] [,2]
[1,]   13   15
[2,]   14   16
```

In order to extract the first row and all columns of the fourth layer of a, use an empty subscript for the columns. The resulting data structure will be a vector.

```
> a[1, , 4]                      # first row, all columns, fourth layer of a
[1] 19 21 23
```

Negative subscripts are used to exclude elements. To extract the vector that excludes the first row, includes the second column, and excludes the third layer, use

```
> a[-1, 2, -3]               # no row 1, second columns only, no layer 3
[1]   4 10 22
```

As was the case with vectors and matrices, negative and positive subscripts cannot be mixed within one particular dimension. Finally, this last example of subscripting excludes the second row, includes the second and third columns, and includes the first and fourth layers, resulting in a 2×2 matrix.

```
> a[-2, 2:3, c(1, 4)]        # no row 2, columns 2 and 3, layers 1 and 4
      [,1] [,2]
[1,]    3   21
[2,]    5   23
```

Once again, the column-major storage convention for these elements is apparent from the way that they are arranged in the 2×2 matrix. Even though subscripting has been used here to extract elements from an array, the results can also be assigned to an object using the = or <- operators.

6.3   Array arithmetic

Arithmetic operations are performed on arrays in an element-wise fashion. These operations are applied to arrays in an analogous fashion to their application to vectors and matrices. A single illustration begins by defining a 40-element $2 \times 10 \times 2$ array named b. Next, the integer-divide operation %/% is applied to each element of b, and the result is displayed.

```
> b = array(0:39, c(2, 10, 2))  # b is a 40-element array
> b %/% 4                        # integer divide element-wise
, , 1

     [,1] [,2] [,3] [,4] [,5] [,6] [,7] [,8] [,9] [,10]
[1,]    0    0    1    1    2    2    3    3    4     4
[2,]    0    0    1    1    2    2    3    3    4     4

, , 2

     [,1] [,2] [,3] [,4] [,5] [,6] [,7] [,8] [,9] [,10]
[1,]    5    5    6    6    7    7    8    8    9     9
[2,]    5    5    6    6    7    7    8    8    9     9
```

This completes the discussion of arrays. Although the discussion in this chapter has been limited to arrays with three dimensions, the syntax associated with the extension to more than three dimensions proceeds in an analogous fashion. Only one function has been introduced in this chapter, the array function, which creates an array. Subscripts contained in brackets are used to access particular elements in an array in an analogous fashion to a vector or a matrix.

Vectors, matrices, and arrays have been populated with elements that are numeric values in the past three chapters to simplify the introduction of these data structures. But these objects can be populated with other types of elements, such as complex numbers, Boolean values, or character strings. Details concerning such elements will be given in subsequent chapters.

Now that vectors, matrices, and arrays have been established as some of the basic data structures in R, we formally introduce *functions*, many of which can be applied to any of the data structures encountered thus far. The next chapter surveys functions that are built into R; the chapter after that shows how you can write your own R functions. Functions give R a capability that goes well beyond that of a calculator.

Exercises

6.1 True or false: A matrix is a special case of an array.

6.2 Write an R command that assigns the elements of the $3 \times 3 \times 2$ array named x to the first 18 positive integers using the default input convention. Next, write an R command that extracts the elements of x in a fashion that includes the second and third rows, excludes the second column, and includes the second layer.

6.3 The $3 \times 4 \times 5$ array a is filled with numeric values. The R command

```
> b = a[c(1, 3), -c(1, 4), 3:5]
```

sets b to a $2 \times 2 \times 3$ array that includes the first and third rows, excludes the first and fourth columns, and includes the third, fourth, and fifth layers of a. Write an R command that accomplishes this same operation using the smallest number of keystrokes.

Chapter 7

Built-In Functions

There are hundreds of functions built into R, which takes its capability far beyond that of a handheld calculator. These functions range from simple numerical operations, such as the square root function sqrt, to functions that perform complicated statistical and graphical operations. We have already encountered several of these functions, such as c, matrix, and cbind. This chapter introduces several dozen more functions that are built into R. If R does not have a function to perform an operation that is of interest, you have the option of writing your own function. Guidelines for writing a custom function will be given in the next chapter. The topics covered in this chapter are (a) syntax, arguments, and elementary functions, (b) functions for truncating and rounding, (c) functions for sorting, ordering, and ranking, (d) functions that determine the properties of an object, and (e) functionals.

7.1 Syntax, arguments, and elementary functions

The general syntax for calling (invoking) a function, either built into R or written by you, named FunctionName, is

```
FunctionName(argument1, argument2, ... )
```

As was the case with object names, the name of the function and the arguments are both case sensitive. Typing the name of the function (without the arguments) at the R command prompt allows you to see its source code. The arguments to the function are contained in parentheses and are separated by commas. R identifies these arguments by one of two mechanisms: by *name* or by *position*. In addition, some R functions have *default* argument values, which are assumed if a particular argument is omitted in a call to the function.

This section surveys some elementary functions that are built into R. This is only a sampling, however, of all of the functions R has to offer. It is only the tip of the iceberg. Other functions can be found via a web search or by using some of the help capabilities outlined in Chapter 9.

The discussion concerning functions that are built into R begins with the first function encountered back in Chapter 1: the q function that is used to quit an R session. Typing the function name q at the R command prompt echos the source code.

```
> q                     # the quit function q has three arguments
function (save = "default", status = 0, runLast = TRUE)
.Internal(quit(save, status, runLast))
```

```
<bytecode: 0x1034a7838>
<environment: namespace:base>
```

The first line of output is the most helpful of the four. It tells us that the q function has three arguments named save, status, and runLast. Furthermore, the first line also tells us that the default values for these three arguments are save = "default", status = 0, and runLast = TRUE. When the q function is called with an empty argument list, the default values for the arguments are assumed, for example

```
> q()                   # use the defaults
```

sets the three arguments to save = "default", status = 0, and runLast = TRUE. The first argument to the q function, namely save, can be set to the character string "no" by placing the character string in the first position (which defaults all subsequent arguments) or by explicitly setting the save argument to "no". The next two R commands are equivalent; both quit an R session without saving any objects created during that session.

```
> q("no")               # save argument is "no"
> q(save = "no")        # save argument is "no"
```

If, on the other hand, you want to save the objects that were created during the current R session, you could use

```
> q(save = "yes")       # save objects created for next session
```

Now consider the third argument to q, which is runLast. Some searching on the web reveals that this argument concerns whether or not to execute functions named .Last and .Last.sys upon exiting R. The argument can assume the values TRUE or FALSE. The default value for runLast is TRUE. The next two R commands are equivalent. The first sets runLast to FALSE based on its *position*; the second sets runLast to FALSE explicitly.

```
> q( , , FALSE)         # don't run .Last() and .Last.sys() on exiting
> q(runLast = FALSE)    # don't run .Last() and .Last.sys() on exiting
```

The next group of functions that are introduced will be applied to a vector named x. Begin by setting x to a four-element vector containing 2, −3, 0, and 8 via the c function.

```
> x = c(2, -3, 0, 8)    # a vector of data values
> x                     # display x
[1]  2 -3  0  8
```

The group of R commands given next produces various summary measures concerning the vector x. The comments should help illuminate what the function does. Some of these functions return a single numeric value, such as sum and max, while others return a vector, such as cumsum and range.

```
> sum(x)                # sum of the elements of x
[1] 7
> sum(x ^ 2)            # sum of the squares of the elements of x
[1] 77
> cumsum(x)             # cumulative sum
[1]  2 -1 -1  7
> prod(x)               # product
[1] 0
```

```
> cumprod(x)           # cumulative product
[1]   2 -6  0  0
> min(x)               # minimum
[1] -3
> max(x)               # maximum
[1] 8
> cummin(x)            # cumulative minimum
[1]   2 -3 -3 -3
> cummax(x)            # cumulative maximum
[1] 2 2 2 8
> diff(x)              # difference between adjacent elements
[1] -5  3  8
> diff(x, lag = 2)     # lag 2 differences
[1] -2 11
> mean(x)              # sample arithmetic mean
[1] 1.75
> median(x)            # sample median
[1] 1
> var(x)               # sample variance
[1] 21.58333
> sqrt(var(x))         # sample standard deviation
[1] 4.645787
> sd(x)                # sample standard deviation
[1] 4.645787
> range(x)             # range
[1] -3  8
> diff(range(x))       # maximum element of x minus the minimum element of x
[1] 11
```

Many built-in functions, for example sum and mean, accept the additional argument na.rm = TRUE, which ignores elements containing NA. R functions may be embedded, or composed, in the same manner that the mathematical functions $f(x)$ and $g(x)$ are composed as $f(g(x))$. In the R commands above, the sqrt and var functions are composed as sqrt(var(x)) in order to compute the standard deviation of the elements in the vector x. Alternatively, the sd function computes the standard deviation with a single function call.

The formulas that R uses for the sample mean and sample variance are

$$\bar{x} = \frac{1}{n} \sum_{i=1}^{n} x_i \qquad \text{and} \qquad s^2 = \frac{1}{n-1} \sum_{i=1}^{n} (x_i - \bar{x})^2,$$

where $x_1, x_2, \ldots, x_n$ denote the data values and n denotes the sample size. The sample standard deviation s is the positive square root of the sample variance, and is calculated with the sd function. The median function selects the middle sorted value if there are an odd number of elements in the vector, and averages the two middle sorted values if there are an even number of elements in the vector.

A very crude histogram, which is known as a "stem-and-leaf plot," can be generated with the stem function:

```
> stem(x)              # stem and leaf plot
```

```
The decimal point is 1 digit(s) to the right of the |
-0 | 3
 0 | 02
 0 | 8
```

Some R functions accept two arguments. To illustrate, we assign the four elements of the vector y to $-1, 5, 9$, and 4.

```
> y = c(-1, 5, 9, 4)    # another vector of data values
> y                     # display y
[1] -1  5  9  4
```

The vector x still contains the elements 2, -3, 0 and 8. The next four functions can be called with two arguments, which are typically vectors of equal length. R supports recycling in the usual fashion for the pmin and pmax functions when the length of the two vectors differs.

```
> pmin(x, y)           # pairwise minimum
[1] -1 -3  0  4
> pmax(x, y)           # pairwise maximum
[1] 2 5 9 8
> var(x, y)            # sample covariance between x and y
[1] -4.916667
> cor(x, y)            # sample correlation between x and y
[1] -0.2573085
```

The pmin and pmax functions take two vectors as arguments and compute the pairwise minimum and pairwise maximum of the values in the two vectors. When the var function is called with two arguments, it calculates the sample covariance between the elements $x_1, x_2, \ldots, x_n$ of the first vector and the elements $y_1, y_2, \ldots, y_n$ of the second vector using the formula

$$q = \frac{1}{n-1} \sum_{i=1}^{n} (x_i - \bar{x})(y_i - \bar{y}).$$

The cor function calculates the sample correlation between the elements $x_1, x_2, \ldots, x_n$ of the first vector and the elements $y_1, y_2, \ldots, y_n$ of the second vector using the formula

$$r = \frac{1}{n-1} \sum_{i=1}^{n} \left(\frac{x_i - \bar{x}}{s_x}\right)\left(\frac{y_i - \bar{y}}{s_y}\right),$$

where s_x and s_y are the sample standard deviations of the elements in the two vectors.

In many applications, a mathematical transformation is required. R provides a wide array of functions to calculate common transformations, such as the square root function sqrt, to more obscure transformations, such as the inverse hyperbolic cosine function acosh. These functions can be applied to simple objects consisting of a single numeric value, vectors, matrices, or arrays. The vector x is set to the elements $-1, 0, 1, 2$, and will be used as an illustration in some of the examples.

```
> x = -1:2             # a vector
> x                    # display x
[1] -1  0  1  2
```

When the transformations are applied to a vector, matrix, or array, they are applied in an element-wise fashion. This results in readable and computationally efficient code. Warning messages are displayed when an illegal operation, such as taking the square root of a negative number or taking the logarithm of a nonpositive number, is input.

```
> sqrt(9)              # square root
[1] 3
> sqrt(1:10)           # square root
 [1] 1.000000 1.414214 1.732051 2.000000 2.236068 2.449490 2.645751 2.828427
 [9] 3.000000 3.162278
> sqrt(1:10)[2]        # the second element of the vector
[1] 1.414214
> print(sqrt(1:10), digits = 3)
 [1] 1.00 1.41 1.73 2.00 2.24 2.45 2.65 2.83 3.00 3.16
> sqrt(x)              # square root
[1]      NaN 0.000000 1.000000 1.414214
Warning message:
In sqrt(x) : NaNs produced
> abs(x)               # absolute value
[1] 1 0 1 2
> sign(x)              # sign (returns -1, 0, or 1)
[1] -1  0  1  1
> log(x)               # log base e (natural logarithm)
[1]      NaN     -Inf 0.0000000 0.6931472
Warning message:
In log(x) : NaNs produced
> log10(1000)          # log base 10
[1] 3
> log2(32)             # log base 2
[1] 5
> logb(49, 7)          # log base 7
[1] 2
> log(Inf)             # log base e (natural logarithm)
[1] Inf
> exp(x)               # e ^ x
[1] 0.3678794 1.0000000 2.7182818 7.3890561
> cos(pi)              # argument in radians
[1] -1
> cos(180)             # argument still in radians
[1] -0.5984601
> atan(1)              # inverse tangent (arctangent)
[1] 0.7853982
> pi / 4               # 45 degrees in radians
[1] 0.7853982
> sinh(2)              # hyperbolic sin:  sinh(x) = (exp(x) - exp(-x)) / 2
[1] 3.62686
> acosh(3)             # inverse hyperbolic cosine (hyperbolic arccosine)
[1] 1.762747
> factorial(x)         # x! (not defined for negative integers)
[1] NaN   1   1   2
Warning message:
In gamma(x + 1) : NaNs produced
> factorial(3.7)       # not limited to just integer arguments
```

```
[1] 15.43141
> gamma(1:5)              # the gamma function:  gamma(x) = (x - 1)!
[1]  1  1  2  6 24
> gamma(4.7)             # any real argument except nonpositive integers
[1] 15.43141
> choose(52, 5)          # combinations:  the number of 5-card poker hands
[1] 2598960
```

The `choose` function given above calculates the number of five-card poker hands that can be dealt from a 52-card deck as

$$\binom{52}{5} = \frac{52!}{5!47!} = 2,598,960.$$

These are known in combinatorics as "combinations."

7.2   Truncating and rounding

There are a group of R functions that can be used for truncating and rounding. The `floor` function, also known as the *greatest integer function*, maps a real number to the greatest previous integer. The most common mathematical notation for the floor of a real number x is $\lfloor x \rfloor$. For example,

$$\lfloor 3.7 \rfloor = 3 \qquad \lfloor 6 \rfloor = 6 \qquad \lfloor -3.14 \rfloor = -4 \qquad \lfloor -8 \rfloor = -8.$$

The `ceiling` function, commonly denoted in mathematics by $\lceil x \rceil$, maps a real number to the least subsequent integer, for example,

$$\lceil 3.7 \rceil = 4 \qquad \lceil 6 \rceil = 6 \qquad \lceil -3.14 \rceil = -3 \qquad \lceil -8 \rceil = -8.$$

The `trunc` (truncate) function simply removes the digits to the right of the decimal point for a real-valued argument. The `round` function rounds its argument to a specified precision. Finally, the `signif` (significance) function is used to display a real-valued argument to a specified number of digits. These functions will be illustrated for the two-element vector x defined below.

```
> x = c(289.333, 4.9) # redefine x
> x                    # display x
[1] 289.333   4.900
> floor(x)             # floor function
[1] 289   4
> ceiling(x)           # ceiling function
[1] 290   5
> trunc(x)             # truncate removes digits right of the decimal point
[1] 289   4
> round(x)             # round to nearest integer
[1] 289   5
> round(x, 1)          # round to nearest 10 ^ (-1)
[1] 289.3   4.9
> round(x, -2)         # round to nearest 10 ^ 2
[1] 300   0
> signif(x, 4)         # display to four significant digits
[1] 289.3   4.9
```

7.3   Sorting, ordering, and ranking

There are a number of R functions that sort, order, and rank numeric values. The rev (reverse) function reverses the order of the elements. The order function gives the permutation of the subscripts
that results in a sorted vector. The rank function operates similarly, but averages the ranks for tied
observations. These functions are illustrated for a vector x.

```
> x = c(2, 0, -3, 2)     # a vector of data values
> x                      # display x
[1]  2  0 -3  2
> rev(x)                 # reverse the order of the elements
[1]  2 -3  0  2
> unique(x)              # unique elements
[1]  2  0 -3
> sort(x)                # sort into ascending order
[1] -3  0  2  2
> sort(x, decreasing = TRUE)   # sort into descending order
[1]  2  2  0 -3
> order(x)               # ordering permutation via subscripts
[1] 3 2 1 4
> rank(x)                # ordering permutation via subscripts adjusted for ties
[1] 3.5 2.0 1.0 3.5
```

The sort function places missing values (NAs) at the end of the returned vector by default. This can
be altered by setting the na.last argument to FALSE to place the missing values at the beginning of
the returned vector or setting the na.last argument to NA to remove the missing values.

As an illustration of the application of these sorting functions, consider an automobile company
that has eight plants that manufacture the same car. The cost per car manufactured at the eight plants,
in thousands of dollars, is given in the vector named cost. The associated monthly capacity of the
eight plants, in thousands of cars, is given in the vector named ncar. The cumulative number of cars
that can be manufactured, ordered by the cost of manufacturing the cars (lowest cost first), can be
generated by using the cumsum and order functions.

```
> cost = c(12.4, 11.7, 13.5, 13.1, 12.0, 12.8, 11.6, 13.3)
> ncar = c(30.3, 24.7, 16.8, 30.0, 14.0, 33.0, 22.1, 29.4)
> cumsum(ncar[order(cost)])
[1]  22.1  46.8  60.8  91.1 124.1 154.1 183.5 200.3
```

7.4   Properties of an object

R has a group of built-in functions that determine certain properties of an object. To illustrate these
functions, set x to a vector, y to a matrix, and z to an array.

```
> x = 1:8                    # x is a vector
> y = matrix(1:8, 2, 4)      # y is a 2 x 4 matrix
> z = array(1:8, c(2, 2, 2)) # z is a 2 x 2 x 2 array
```

The first function, class, returns a character string (which will be enclosed in quotes) that describes
the type of data structure associated with a particular object.

```
> class(x)                    # x is a vector
[1] "integer"
> class(y)                    # y is a matrix
[1] "matrix"
> class(z)                    # z is an array
[1] "array"
```

Rather than returning "vector" for x, class instead indicates that the vector is comprised of integers. The next function, mode, returns the nature of the elements that comprise the object.

```
> mode(x)                     # x contains numeric elements
[1] "numeric"
> mode(y)                     # y contains numeric elements
[1] "numeric"
> mode(z)                     # z contains numeric elements
[1] "numeric"
```

Since each of the three objects consists of the first eight positive integers, the mode function returns "numeric" in each case. The related function typeof will return "integer" for all three of the objects because each consists of integer-valued elements. If non-integer elements were present, typeof would return "double".

Occasions often arise in which it is useful to know the size of an object. The built-in functions that can be used to determine the size of an object are:

- the length function returns the number of elements in an object,

- the nrow / ncol functions return the number of rows / columns in a matrix or an array,

- the dim function returns the dimensions of a matrix or array as a vector.

The vector x, matrix y, and array z each consist of 8 elements, so the length function returns 8 for each.

```
> length(x)                   # extract the number of elements in x
[1] 8
> length(y)                   # extract the number of elements in y
[1] 8
> length(z)                   # extract the number of elements in z
[1] 8
```

The nrow and ncol functions can be applied to matrices and arrays.

```
> nrow(y)                     # extract the number of rows in y
[1] 2
> ncol(y)                     # extract the number of columns in y
[1] 4
> nrow(z)                     # extract the number of rows in z
[1] 2
> ncol(z)                     # extract the number of columns in z
[1] 2
```

The dim function can be used to fetch the dimensions of a matrix.

```
> dim(y)                      # extract the dimensions of y
[1] 2 4
> dim(z)                      # extract the dimensions of z
[1] 2 2 2
```

In addition to returning the size of an object, the `length` and `dim` functions can also be used to *alter* the size of an object. The example that follows coerces the elements of a vector into an array with dimensions supplied to `dim`. Seeing `dim` on the left-hand side of an assignment operator will seem counterintuitive, but the versatile `dim` function can both get and set the dimensions of an object. When doing so in the example below, it is important to remember that when R populates the array, the first subscript (the row number in the example) moves fastest and the last subscript (the layer number in the example) moves slowest.

```
> b = 24:1                    # b is a 24-element vector
> b                           # display b
 [1] 24 23 22 21 20 19 18 17 16 15 14 13 12 11 10  9  8  7  6  5  4  3  2  1
> dim(b) = c(4, 3, 2)         # transform b to a 4 x 3 x 2 array
> b                           # display b
, , 1

     [,1] [,2] [,3]
[1,]   24   20   16
[2,]   23   19   15
[3,]   22   18   14
[4,]   21   17   13

, , 2

     [,1] [,2] [,3]
[1,]   12    8    4
[2,]   11    7    3
[3,]   10    6    2
[4,]    9    5    1
```

The functions described in this section are helpful in determining properties of an object. The `str` (structure) function can be used to capture several properties of an object at once. It provides a compact summary of the data structure associated with an object, for example,

```
> str(b)                      # display the structure of b
 int [1:4, 1:3, 1:2] 24 23 22 21 20 19 18 17 16 15 ...
```

The display indicates that the elements of b are integers, the data structure is a three-dimensional $4 \times 3 \times 2$ array, and the first few elements are displayed.

7.5   Functionals

There is a family of functions that includes a function as an argument. The term "functional" is sometimes used to describe functions of this type. One particular type of functional comes from what is known as the *apply* family. These functionals can effectively perform looping (looping is a programming topic that is introduced in Chapter 23). The next three paragraphs describe three representative functionals. There are plenty of others.

Consider the sapply function, whose first argument X is a vector and whose second argument FUN is a function that is to be applied to the first argument. This is one of the most elementary functionals from the apply family. The factorials of the first four positive integers is computed with

```
> sapply(1:4, factorial)      # 1!, 2!, 3!, 4!
[1]  1  2  6 24
```

Even though this requires more keystrokes than the more compact

```
> factorial(1:4)              # 1!, 2!, 3!, 4!
[1]  1  2  6 24
```

the benefits to using a functional will be apparent with the next example.

As a second example, consider the apply function, whose first argument X is a matrix (or more generally an array), whose second argument MARGIN specifies the subscripts over which the function will be applied (1 for rows, 2 for columns, and c(1, 2) for both rows and columns), and whose third argument FUN is a function that is to be applied to the elements of the matrix. In the example below, x is set to a 3×4 matrix, the row means are calculated, the column products are calculated, and the square roots of each element are calculated.

```
> x = matrix(1:12, 3, 4)      # set x to a 3 by 4 matrix containing 1:12
> x                           # display x
     [,1] [,2] [,3] [,4]
[1,]    1    4    7   10
[2,]    2    5    8   11
[3,]    3    6    9   12
> y = apply(x, 1, mean)       # find the row means
> y                           # display y
[1] 5.5 6.5 7.5
> z = apply(x, 2, prod)       # find the column products
> z                           # display z
[1]    6  120  504 1320
> apply(x, c(1, 2), sqrt)     # apply sqrt over rows and columns
           [,1]     [,2]     [,3]     [,4]
[1,] 1.000000 2.000000 2.645751 3.162278
[2,] 1.414214 2.236068 2.828427 3.316625
[3,] 1.732051 2.449490 3.000000 3.464102
```

As a third example of a functional, consider the sweep function, whose first argument x is a matrix or an array, whose second argument MARGIN specifies the subscripts over which the function will be applied (1 for rows, 2 for columns, and c(1, 2) for both rows and columns), whose third argument STATS gives the summary statistic to be swept out in the calculation, and whose fourth argument FUN gives the function to be used to carry out the sweep. To illustrate, consider again the matrix x from the previous example. We would like to use sweep to find the largest element in each row, then divide the elements in each row by the largest element in the row. The apply function identifies the largest element in each row:

```
> apply(x, 1, max)            # identify the maximum elements in each row
[1] 10 11 12
```

The largest element in the first row is 10; the largest element in the second row is 11; the largest element in the third row is 12. Now the sweep function will be used to divide each element of x by the largest element in its row.

```
> sweep(x, 1, apply(x, 1, max), '/')   # divide each row by its maximum element
          [,1]      [,2]       [,3] [,4]
[1,] 0.1000000 0.4000000 0.7000000   1
[2,] 0.1818182 0.4545455 0.7272727   1
[3,] 0.2500000 0.5000000 0.7500000   1
```

The division operator must be enclosed in backquotes.

This ends the survey of built-in functions in the base distribution of **R**. There are many other functions that have not been surveyed here, and even more that can be accessed using the packages that are introduced in the last chapter. The table below summarizes the functions that were introduced in this chapter in approximately the same order as they appeared. The characterization of these functions by the number of arguments ignores optional arguments.

function	description
sum, prod, min, max, mean, median, var, sd	single-argument functions that typically return a single value
cumsum, cumprod, cummin, cummax, diff, range	single-argument functions that typically return a vector
stem	stem-and-leaf plot
pmin, pmax var, cor	multi-argument functions that return a single object
sqrt, abs, sign, log, exp	mathematical transformations
cos, atan, sinh, acosh	trigonometric functions
factorial, gamma, choose	gamma function and friends
floor, ceiling, trunc, round, signif	rounding and truncation
rev, unique, sort, order, rank	sorting, ordering, and ranking
class, mode, typeof, length, nrow, ncol, dim, str	properties of objects
sapply, apply, sweep	functionals

Many of the arguments to these functions have default values that are used when the argument is omitted. Type ls(pos = 3) and ls(pos = 9), for example, to list the names of the hundreds of functions that are built into the base distribution of **R**. (The pos parameter on the ls function specifies the target environment, which corresponds to groupings of the functions.) The `getAnywhere` function can be used to view the code associated with a built-in function. For example, `getAnywhere('median.default')` displays the code associated with the `median` function.

This ends this long chapter on functions that are built into R. Although the combined capability of these functions is extensive, you will encounter applications in which you need to write a custom function to perform a particular task. The next chapter shows you how you can write your own functions in R.

Exercises

7.1 Write a single R command that calculates: $\sin\left(e^4 + \sqrt{\arccos(1/3)}\right)$.

7.2 What is returned by the following R commands? (Guess before computing this in R.)

```
> x = c(pi, 4 / 3, 7)
> round(x, 2)
```

7.3 What is returned by the following R commands?

```
> x = (1:10) ^ 2
> diff(range(x))
```

7.4 What is returned by the following R commands?

```
> x = 1:4
> y = 4:1
> pmax(x, y)
```

7.5 What is returned by the following R commands?

```
> x = 1:4
> cumsum(x)
```

7.6 What is returned by the following R commands?

```
> x = c(1, 1, 1, -1, -1, -1, NA)
> y = c(0, 1, 4,  0, -1, NA,  1)
> x / sqrt(y)
```

7.7 What is returned by the following R commands?

```
> x = seq(1, 7, by = 3)
> sum(x ^ 2) / length(x)
```

7.8 What is returned by the following R command?

```
> sqrt(max(9:-3))
```

7.9 Let x be a vector of length three or greater that contains numeric elements. Write a single R command that calculates the sample mean of all of the elements of x except the smallest and largest.

7.10 Write an R command that creates a 2×3 matrix named x that contains the first six positive integers entered row-wise into the matrix. Display x. Then write another R command that uses the `dim` function to change the dimensions of x to a 3×2 matrix. Display the updated matrix x.

7.11 Write two R commands that calculate

$$\sum_{i=1}^{15} \left(\frac{2^i}{i!} - \frac{\cos(3i)}{i^4} \right).$$

7.12 Write two R commands that calculate

$$\prod_{x=4}^{12} \left| \frac{x(x-1)(x-2)}{(x-3)!} + \frac{\arctan x}{x^2} \right|.$$

7.13 Write a single R command that calculates

$$\frac{3}{4} + \left(\frac{3}{4} \cdot \frac{5}{6} \right) + \left(\frac{3}{4} \cdot \frac{5}{6} \cdot \frac{7}{8} \right) + \cdots + \left(\frac{3}{4} \cdot \frac{5}{6} \cdot \frac{7}{8} \cdots \cdot \frac{49}{50} \right).$$

7.14 Write a single R command that calculates e^e.

7.15 Write a single R command that calculates $1^3 + 2^3 + \cdots + 100^3$.

7.16 Write a single R command that creates a vector with elements

$$\left(5, \frac{5^2}{2!}, \frac{5^3}{3!}, \ldots, \frac{5^{10}}{10!} \right)$$

using a minimum number of keystrokes.

7.17 Write a single R command that calculates

$$\sum_{i=3}^{8} \sum_{j=2}^{9} \frac{i^2}{7+4j}.$$

7.18 The two-element vector named `point1` contains the x-coordinate and the y-coordinate of a point on the Cartesian coordinate system. Likewise for `point2`. Write a single R command that calculates the quantity of interest requested below.

   (a) Calculate the distance between the two points, where "distance" is interpreted as the Euclidean distance, the distance "as the crow flies," or the L_2 norm.

   (b) Calculate the rectilinear distance between the two points, where the "rectilinear distance" is interpreted as the "Manhattan distance," "taxicab norm," or the L_1 norm.

7.19 Experiment with the `Sys.sleep` function using a single argument, a small integer, to determine its purpose.

7.20 Compose two R functions so as to count the number of distinct elements in a vector named x.

7.21 An unsorted 99-element vector named x contains all but one of the first 100 positive integers. Write a single R command that determines the missing integer.

Chapter 8

User-Written Functions

The previous chapter outlined functions that are built into the R language. But you will likely encounter applications in which an appropriate function is not available. R gives you the capability to write your own functions for such applications. This chapter gives the syntax and some examples of writing simple R functions. More sophisticated functions can be written after covering the programming topics in Chapters 22–24. When a user-written function is saved at the end of an R session, it can be used in subsequent R sessions. An important purpose of user-written R functions is to decompose complex programming tasks into smaller pieces, thus decreasing the chances of an error.

The syntax for defining a user-written function named `FunctionName` is

```
FunctionName = function(argument1, argument2, ...)  {  }
```

where the curly braces contain the R commands associated with the function. If the entire function can be written on a single line, the curly braces are not necessary; the R command is simply written after the argument list. Most functions, however, require multiple lines, so there is typically a left-hand curly brace on the first line of the function and a right-hand curly brace on the last line of the function. You choose the name of the function and the name of the arguments using the usual naming rules for objects, for example these names are case sensitive. Typing the name of the function (without the arguments) at the R command prompt allows you to see its source code. The arguments to the function are contained in parentheses and are separated by commas. You have the option of establishing *default* argument values, which are assumed if certain arguments are omitted in a call to the function. It is acceptable for a function to have no arguments. There are certain function names that should be avoided because they perform other roles in R, such as `c`, `q`, `if`, `while`, etc. As was the case with object names, it is helpful to choose function names that adequately and succinctly reflect the purpose of the function.

R's style of using the assignment operator (= or <-) to define a function is unlike most programming languages. One upside to this approach is that a user-written function is an object, just like a vector, matrix, or array. Typing `ls()` or `objects()` displays the names of the user-written functions along with all of the other objects.

The syntax for calling (invoking) a user-written function is exactly the same as calling a function that is built into R. To call a function named `FunctionName`, use

```
FunctionName(argument1, argument2, ...  )
```

The topics considered in this chapter are (a) elementary functions, (b) scoping, the rules that govern the way that R looks up the value of an object, and (c) variable number of arguments.

8.1 Elementary functions

As an elementary first example of a user-written function, consider a function that cubes its argument. We will name this function cube. There is currently no such function with that name in R, but, to be on the safe side, begin by typing cube to see if there is an existing object or function named cube.

```
> cube                        # check for a built-in function named cube
Error: object 'cube' not found
```

Seeing that the name cube is "available," we can begin writing the function.

```
> cube = function(x) x ^ 3    # write the function
```

This function is so short that the curly braces were not necessary. R silently accepts the new function. Next, type the name of the function to see that it has been successfully included.

```
> cube                        # display the code
function(x) x ^ 3
```

All looks good so far. The next step is to test the function.

```
> cube(2)                     # 2 ^ 3
[1] 8
```

Success! Now try a bigger argument.

```
> cube(10)                    # 10 ^ 3
[1] 1000
```

It seems as though cube will work for constants, although it would be prudent to test it with some negative values and some non-integers. Next, try a vector as an argument in cube.

```
> cube(1:10)                  # first ten perfect cubes
 [1]    1    8   27   64  125  216  343  512  729 1000
```

Our cube function works in exactly the same fashion as, for example, the sqrt function. It works in an element-wise fashion. Next, try placing a matrix into cube.

```
> cube(matrix(1:8, 2, 4))     # cube each element in a matrix
     [,1] [,2] [,3] [,4]
[1,]    1   27  125  343
[2,]    8   64  216  512
```

Each element of the matrix is cubed as desired. Notice in this case that reversing the order of the calls to cube and matrix in the R command results in the same 2 × 4 matrix.

```
> matrix(cube(1:8), 2, 4)     # matrix of the cubes
     [,1] [,2] [,3] [,4]
[1,]    1   27  125  343
[2,]    8   64  216  512
```

Finally, using an array as an argument in cube also works.

```
> cube(array(1:24, c(2, 3, 4))) # cube each element in an array
, , 1

     [,1] [,2] [,3]
[1,]    1   27  125
[2,]    8   64  216

, , 2

     [,1] [,2] [,3]
[1,]  343  729 1331
[2,]  512 1000 1728

, , 3

     [,1] [,2] [,3]
[1,] 2197 3375 4913
[2,] 2744 4096 5832

, , 4

     [,1]  [,2]  [,3]
[1,] 6859  9261 12167
[2,] 8000 10648 13824
```

So now cube has been established as a function that accepts a single argument, which can be a single numeric value, a vector of numeric values, a matrix of numeric values, or an array of numeric values. The function cube is still an object, but its mode is function:

```
> mode(cube)              # the mode of cube is function
[1] "function"
```

The cube function required a single argument. The next function will require two arguments. The hyp (short for hypotenuse) function, with arguments a and b, returns the length of the hypotenuse of a right triangle with leg lengths a and b. As before, begin by typing hyp at the command prompt to make sure that an object named hyp currently does not exist.

```
> hyp                     # check for a built-in function named hyp
Error: object 'hyp' not found
```

The error message assures us that hyp is available for use, so we can move forward with writing the function. Although the hyp function could be written as a single-line function, the curly braces will be used to enclose the R commands that comprise the function. The first line defines hyp as a function of two arguments, a and b. R responds with the continuation prompt + to indicate that, having encountered the opening curly brace on the previous line, it is expecting more R commands to follow. The second line sets a *local object* named temp to the sum of the squares of a and b. The local object temp will not be known outside of the function hyp. The third line calculates the length of the hypotenuse as the square root of the local object temp. The last line is the curly brace, and R knows that this is the end of the user-written hyp function, so it responds with the usual > prompt. By default, the value returned by a function is the final expression evaluated. In this case, `sqrt (temp)` is returned. (The default returned value can be modified with the `return` function, which will be illustrated subsequently.)

```
> hyp = function(a, b) {        # use { } for multiple line function
+   temp = a ^ 2 + b ^ 2        # temp is known as a "local" object
+   sqrt(temp)                  # returned value using sqrt function
+ }                            # closing curly brace
```

Typing `hyp` at the prompt will echo the contents of the `hyp` function (including comments):

```
> hyp                          # display the code
function(a, b) {               # use { } for multiple line function
  temp = a ^ 2 + b ^ 2         # temp is known as a "local" object
  sqrt(temp)                   # returned value using sqrt function
}
```

Now it is time to test the `hyp` function. First, try the famous 3–4–5 triangle.

```
> hyp(3, 4)                    # 3, 4, 5 triangle
[1] 5
```

Success! Next, try `hyp` on the not-quite-as-famous 5–12–13 triangle.

```
> hyp(5, 12)                   # 5, 12, 13 triangle
[1] 13
```

Finally, test `hyp` to see that it will handle a non-integer hypotenuse length.

```
> hyp(1, 1)                    # 1, 1, sqrt(2) triangle
[1] 1.414214
```

At this point, we are reasonably sure that the `hyp` function is working properly for two constant values as arguments for the length of the legs. But what if `hyp` is given two vectors as arguments? The results below show the vector that is returned for three pairs of triangle leg lengths.

```
> hyp(c(2, 3, 4), c(3, 4, 5))   # three hypoteni
[1] 3.605551 5.000000 6.403124
```

This ends the discussion of the `hyp` function.

The functions `cube` and `hyp` are objects just like any vector, matrix, or array that has been created during the current R session. Typing `ls()` or `objects()` reveals that `cube` and `hyp` are objects in the current session, but `temp` is not because it is local to `hyp`. With any user-written function such as `cube` or `hyp`, you must explicitly save the function at the end of your R session, or else it will be swept away with any other objects that are not saved.

The next user-written function concerns the calculation of the balance in a bank account with annual compounding. An initial deposit P held for n years at annual interest rate r compounded annually yields a balance

$$F = P(1+r)^n.$$

A user-written function named `balance` will calculate the value of F and illustrate the notion of *default arguments*, which are assumed values for the arguments if no values are specified. First, check to see if the name `balance` is already assumed by an object or another function.

```
> balance                       # check for built-in function named balance
Error: object 'balance' not found
```

It is available, so we can write the function balance with three arguments, deposit, rate, and years, which assume the roles of *P*, *r*, and *n* in the formula. In addition, the arguments will assume the *default values* $P = \$1000$, $r = 0.05$, and $n = 30$. (It is acceptable to set some, but not all of the arguments to default values.) If balance is called without specifying one or more of these arguments, the arguments will assume the default values.

```
> balance = function(deposit = 1000, rate = 0.05, years = 30) {
+    return(deposit * (1 + rate) ^ years)
+ }
```

There is a new function call that is being made in the body of the function—the return function. In cube and hyp, R returned the value computed on the last line of the function. The return function is more explicit in that the value of its argument will be returned by the function. You may have several calls to the return function within a function. Execution in the function ceases when the first return is encountered. Typing balance displays the function.

```
> balance                       # display the code
function(deposit = 1000, rate = 0.05, years = 30) {
  return(deposit * (1 + rate) ^ years)
}
```

Calling balance with the default arguments of $1000 invested for 30 years at 5% interest,

```
> balance()                     # call with default arguments
[1] 4321.942
```

results in a balance of $4321.94. If the initial deposit is decreased to $100, the interest rate is decreased to 4%, and the term is increased to 150 years, the call to balance yields

```
> balance(100, 0.04, 150)       # call with ordered arguments
[1] 35892.27
```

Finally, if the deposit amount and term are defaulted, but the rate is set to 2%, the appropriate call to balance is

```
> balance(rate = 0.02)          # call with 2% annual interest rate
[1] 1811.362
```

8.2   Scoping

When writing the hyp function, a local object named temp was used. This section considers the *scope of objects* in R: local vs. global. An intuitive way of thinking about a function is that it is an insulated environment that cannot be accessed from outside of the function. It communicates with the outside world via its arguments, which are the input to the function, and its returned values, which are output from the function. This arrangement ensures that activity within the function only changes objects that are *local* to the function. This is a one-way relationship, however, because a function can access objects defined outside of the function.

The next example considers a user-written function that will be named setxtotwo, which (surprise!) sets x to two. The function will have no arguments. First, check to see if an object named setxtotwo is in use.

```
> setxtotwo                      # check for built-in function named setxtotwo
Error: object 'setxtotwo' not found
```

The object name `setxtotwo` is available, so the next step is to write the function. The function requires just a single R command, so

```
> setxtotwo = function() x = 2  # this function appears to set x to two
> setxtotwo                      # display the code
function() x = 2
```

defines and echos the function. Now it is time to test the function. The code below sets x to 3, displays x, calls `setxtotwo`, and then again displays x.

```
> x = 3                          # set x to three
> x                              # display x
[1] 3
> setxtotwo()                    # call the function
> x                              # display x
[1] 3
```

It appears that `setxtotwo` failed to set x to two. This often shocks and befuddles those new to computing. What occurred here is that the global version of x gets set to 3, then the version of x that is local to the function `setxtotwo` (which is separate from the global version of x) gets set to 2, which means that the global version of x never gets changed. The *scope* of the object x used in the function `setxtotwo` is *local* to the function.

Functions can call other functions. We have already encountered this when the user-written function `hyp` called the built-in function `sqrt`. The example in the next set of R commands creates two functions named `inside` and `outside` that illustrate one user-written function calling another user-written function, along with the associated local vs. global object issues.

```
> inside                         # check for a built-in function named inside
Error: object 'inside' not found
> outside                        # check for a built-in function named outside
Error: object 'outside' not found
> inside = function() 2 * x      # the function inside doubles x
> outside = function() {         # the function outside ...
+    x = 17                      # sets x to 17 ...
+    inside()                    # calls inside ...
+ }                              # and concludes
> x = 4                          # set x to 4
> outside()                      # call the function outside
[1] 8
> x                              # display x
[1] 4
```

When the `inside` function is called within the `outside` function, it finds the global value of x, which has been set to 4. This is why the call to `outside` returns 8. The global version of x, however, never gets altered. The lesson here is to be careful regarding the status—local vs. global—of objects when writing and calling functions.

8.3   Variable number of arguments

As a final example of a user-written function in R, consider the case of a function that has a variable number of arguments. For example, sometimes it can be called with three arguments, but other times it can be called with eight arguments. The function `mean.of.objects` will calculate the arithmetic average of the elements in the data structures passed in its arguments. R uses `...` to signify an unknown number of arguments whose names do not match other arguments. The `mean.of.objects` function can be written in a single line, so the curly braces are not necessary. The `exists` function is used initially (rather than typing the proposed function name as we have earlier in this chapter) to determine whether the object `mean.of.objects` exists. Its argument must be a character string enclosed in quotes.

```
> exists("mean.of.objects")
[1] FALSE
> mean.of.objects = function(...) mean(c(...))
> x = 1                         # x is a scalar (vector with one element)
> y = 2:3                       # y is a vector
> z = matrix(4:9, 2, 3)         # z is a 2 x 3 matrix
> mean.of.objects(x, y, z)      # function call
[1] 5
```

The first argument passed to `mean.of.objects`, x, is a vector of length 1; the second argument, y, is a vector of length 2; the third argument, z, is a 2×3 matrix. These three arguments are passed to the c function. This function has no difficulty handling a mix of data structures in the example given above.

This ends the brief introduction to user-written functions. One practical topic that has not yet been addressed is how to modify a function. One rather inefficient way is to simply key the function back in from scratch, which will overwrite the existing version of the function. But there is a much better way. The `fix` function brings up a dialog box containing the function to be edited, which is a much more efficient way to edit a function consisting of multiple R commands. To edit the function named hyp, for example, simply type

```
> fix(hyp)
```

which brings up the appropriate dialog box. Altering the function in the dialog box, and subsequently closing the dialog box redefines the function. The versatile `fix` function is not just limited to altering the commands within a function. It can also be used to alter the elements of a vector, matrix, or array, as well as altering the elements of a list (introduced in Chapter 15) or a data frame (introduced in Chapter 16). The function or data structure must subsequently be saved at the end of the R session for the alterations to become permanent.

Only three new functions were presented in this chapter, and they are listed in the table below.

function	description
return	return a value from a function
exists	determine whether an object exists
fix	invoke an editor to alter an existing object

The next chapter, titled "Utilities," pulls together some useful utility functions that can be helpful during an R session.

Exercises

8.1 Write a one-line function named `reverse` with a single argument x that reverses the order of the elements in the vector x.

8.2 Write a function named `my.cos` with two arguments. The first argument is named `angle` and the second argument is named `degrees`, which has a default value of `FALSE`. Test your function with the R commands `my.cos(pi / 2)` and `my.cos(90, degrees = TRUE)`.

8.3 Write a function named `cube.root` that calculates the cube root(s) of its argument. Test your function with the R command

```
> cube.root(c(-8, 8, 729, 1000000))
```

8.4 Consider the sample data values $x_1, x_2, \ldots, x_n$ and the associated sample order statistics $x_{(1)}, x_{(2)}, \ldots, x_{(n)}$. The *sample truncated mean* (also known as the *sample trimmed mean*) is a measure of central tendency defined as

$$\bar{x} = \frac{x_{(k+1)} + x_{(k+2)} + \cdots + x_{(n-k)}}{n - 2k}.$$

This is the arithmetic average of the data values with the k lowest and k highest observations removed. The truncated mean is less sensitive to outliers than the arithmetic mean and is hence known as a *robust estimator*. This estimator is used in sports that are evaluated by a panel of n judges in which the lowest and highest scores ($k = 1$) are discarded. Likewise, the truncated mean is used in calculating the London Interbank Offered Rate (LIBOR) when $n = 18$ interest rates are collected, and the lowest four and highest four interest rates ($k = 4$) are discarded. Assuming that $k < n/2$, write an R function named `tmean` with two arguments x and k that calculates the sample truncated mean of the elements in the vector x discarding the k lowest and k highest observations. Test your code with the R commands

```
> tmean(c(9.4, 9.6, 9.1, 9.5, 9.3), 1)
> tmean(1:18, 4)
```

8.5 Let $x_1, x_2, \ldots, x_n$ be the $n > 2$ elements in a vector x. Write an R function named `movave` with a single argument x that returns a vector of length $n - 1$ whose elements are the moving averages

$$\frac{x_1 + x_2}{2}, \frac{x_2 + x_3}{2}, \frac{x_3 + x_4}{2}, \ldots, \frac{x_{n-1} + x_n}{2}.$$

Test your function for some sample vectors used as arguments.

8.6 Let $x_1, x_2, \ldots, x_n$ denote the elements of the vector x. Write an R function named `L2` with a single vector argument x that calculates the L_2 norm

$$\sqrt{x_1^2 + x_2^2 + \cdots + x_n^2}.$$

Test your function with the R commands

```
> L2(c(3, 4))
> L2(c(1, 1, 1))
```

8.7   Let $x_1, x_2, \ldots, x_n$ denote the elements of the vector x. Write an R function named Lp with a vector argument x and an integer argument p that calculates the p-norm

$$\left(\sum_{i=1}^{n} |x_i|^p \right)^{1/p}.$$

Test your function with the R commands

```
> Lp(c(3, 4), 2)
> Lp(c(1, 1, 1), 3)
```

8.8   The built-in R function mean calculates the sample mean $\bar{x}$. Write R functions named hmean, gmean, and qmean that calculate the sample harmonic mean, geometric mean, and quadratic mean defined by

$$h = \left(\frac{1}{n} \sum_{i=1}^{n} \frac{1}{x_i} \right)^{-1} \qquad g = \left(\prod_{i=1}^{n} x_i \right)^{1/n} \qquad q = \sqrt{\frac{1}{n} \sum_{i=1}^{n} x_i^2},$$

where $x_1, x_2, \ldots, x_n$ are the data values. Test your functions with a vector of data values of your choice and verify the inequality

$$\min\{x_1, x_2, \ldots, x_n\} \le h \le g \le \bar{x} \le q \le \max\{x_1, x_2, \ldots, x_n\}.$$

8.9   Let $x_1, x_2, \ldots, x_n$ be the n elements in the R vector x. Write an R function named mad (for *mean absolute deviation*) with a single argument x that calculates

$$\sum_{i=1}^{n} |x_i - \bar{x}|,$$

where $\bar{x}$ is the sample mean.

8.10   Write an R function named fifth with a single vector argument x that calculates and returns the sample mean of the 5th, 10th, 15th, ... elements of x. You may assume that x has at least five elements.

8.11   The rectangular coordinate system uses x, the signed horizontal distance from the origin, and y, the signed vertical distance from the origin, to describe the point (x, y). The polar coordinate system, on the other hand, uses r, the signed distance from the origin, and θ, the signed angle measured counterclockwise from the polar axis, to describe the point (r, θ). Assume that θ is measured in radians.

(a)   Write an R function named polar2rect with arguments r and theta that returns a two-element vector that contains the rectangular coordinates associated with the point (r, θ) in the polar coordinate system.

(b)   Write an R function named rect2polar with arguments x and y that returns a two-element vector that contains the polar coordinates associated with the point (x, y) in the rectangular coordinate system.

8.12   Write a one-line function named fourth that raises its argument to the fourth power. Then apply the formals, body, and environment functions to fourth in order to isolate the arguments to the function, the R code that comprises the function, and the location of the objects used in the function.

Chapter 9

Utilities

This is an opportune time to introduce some helpful utilities that are built into R. These utilities can be used to customize the environment for a particular R session, provide documentation for an operator or a function, and provide assistance concerning roundoff issues. So the topics considered in this chapter are (a) managing the workspace, (b) getting help, and (c) floating point representations.

9.1   Managing the workspace

The first function investigated is history. This function is helpful for finding, and perhaps repeating or modifying, a previous command. When history is called without any arguments, it gives a listing of the previous 25 R commands.

```
> history()                          # history of previous commands
```

The output has been suppressed. It might be necessary to press the q key (for quit) in order to exit history and return to the command prompt. Typing

```
> history(100)                       # history of previous 100 commands
```

displays the previous 100 R commands. If you are interested in seeing just those commands that contain the character string abs, for example, use the pattern argument in the call to history.

```
> history(pattern = "abs")           # history of previous commands with "abs"
```

Again, the output is suppressed.

The options function was introduced in Chapter 2 as a mechanism for controlling the number of digits displayed. But it can do so much more. To set the number of display digits to 17, for example, use the digits argument.

```
> options(digits = 17)               # display 17 digits of output  (default 7)
```

To control the width of the output that is displayed by R, use the width argument.

```
> options(width = 99)                # display 99 characters wide (default 80)
```

R will fit the display into 99 character positions. The width of the window associated with your R session, measured in character positions, also figures into the width of the display. The warn argument in the `options` function allows you to control the handling of warning messages. A negative `warn` argument means all warnings are ignored; a zero `warn` argument, the default, means warnings are buffered until the top-level function returns; a `warn` argument of one means warnings are printed as they occur; a `warn` argument greater than one means warnings are turned into errors. For example,

```
> options(warn = 4)                 # sets warning level (default 0)
```

sets the `warn` argument to 4. You are not limited to the > prompt for an R command and the + prompt for continuing an R command. To change the prompt to >>, for example, use the `prompt` argument in the `options` function.

```
> options(prompt = ">> ")           # prompt is now >>
```

The continue prompt can be changed from the default + to `continue:`, for example, by using the `continue` argument in `options` function.

```
>> options(continue = "continue: ") # continue prompt is now continue:
```

An illustration of what a simple R command looks like with the two new prompts is

```
>> 2 + 3 -
continue: 7
[1] -2
```

Finally, the `scipen` argument on the `options` function can be used to favor or avoid displaying a number using scientific notation. Positive values bias the display mechanism away from scientific notation and negative values bias the display mechanism towards scientific notation.

```
>> options(scipen = 999)            # avoid scientific notation
>> 0.000000001                      # roundoff issues
[1] 0.00000000100000000000000001
>> options(scipen = -999)           # force scientific notation
>> 193
[1] 1.93e+02
```

The roundoff problem is apparent in the number displayed in the first calculation. More detail concerning roundoff will be given later in this chapter. This section is just a quick survey of some of the environmental control capabilities in R. But what if you want more information about the arguments and capability of the `options` function, or any other function? That is the topic of the next section, which outlines how help can be accessed in R.

9.2   Getting help

Since R is free (open source) software, it must be self-documenting. There is no live help nor is there a phone number to call. Inside of R and outside of R, there is significant documentation for questions or problems that might arise. This section considers three topics: standard help queries, generating examples and demonstrations, and internet-based help.

There is a built-in R function named `help` that can be used to get documentation on an object (such as the built-in constant `pi`), operator (such as the modulo function `%%`), or function (such as the standard deviation function `sd`). Returning to the default command prompt, a call to `help` to learn about the `sd` function yields a large store of information.

```
> help(sd)                    # help page for the sd (standard deviation) function

sd                    package:stats                    R Documentation

Standard Deviation
```

Description:

    This function computes the standard deviation of the values in x. If
    na.rm is TRUE then missing values are removed before computation
    proceeds.

Usage:

    sd(x, na.rm = FALSE)

Arguments:

      x: a numeric vector or an R object which is coercible to one by
         as.vector(x, "numeric").

   na.rm: logical. Should missing values be removed?

Details:

    Like var this uses denominator n - 1.

    The standard deviation of a zero-length vector (after removal of NAs
    if na.rm = TRUE) is not defined and gives an error. The standard
    deviation of a length-one vector is NA.

    Prior to R 2.14.0, sd(dfrm) worked directly for a data.frame dfrm.
    This is now defunct and you are expected to use sapply(dfrm, sd).

See Also:

    var for its square, and mad, the most robust alternative.

Examples:

    sd(1:2) ^ 2

The help page shows that the sd function is in a package named stats, and has two arguments, x,
a vector of numeric values, and na.rm, a logical argument with a default of FALSE that controls the
treatment of elements of x containing NA. At the bottom of the help page is an example of the use of
sd. If you would like to save a few keystrokes, typing

```
> ?sd                    # alternative way to access help page
```

brings up the very same help page. In order to get help on an operator, the operator must be placed in quotes. For example, to get help on the addition operator, type

```
> help("+")          # help on the addition operator
```

The output has been suppressed. In order to bring up the help page on subscripting, type

```
> help("[")          # help on subscripting
```

In order to bring up the help page on the built-in object pi, type

```
> help(pi)           # help on pi
```

(A similar approach applies to the built-in data sets that will be introduced in Chapter 17.)

R also allows you to search the entire help system for a particular string with the help.search function.

```
> help.search("median")  # search the help system for "median"
```

```
Help files with alias or concept or title matching median using fuzzy
matching:

stats::mad            Median Absolute Deviation
stats::median         Median Value
stats::medpolish      Median Polish of a Matrix
stats::runmed         Running Medians - Robust Scatter Plot Smoothing
stats::smooth         Tukey's (Running Median) Smoothing
stats::smoothEnds     End Points Smoothing (for Running Medians)


Type '?PKG::FOO' to inspect entries 'PKG::FOO', or 'TYPE?PKG::FOO' for
entries like 'PKG::FOO-TYPE'.
```

Every entry in the help system that contains the string of characters median, regardless of case, will appear. If you would like to save a few keystrokes, typing

```
> ??median           # alternative way to access help.search
```

brings up the same list.

Another helpful function is apropos, which gives a list of all objects that contain a particular string. For example,

```
> apropos("median")     # find all objects containing the string "median"
[1] "median"         "median.default"
```

returns a vector of the two character strings "median" and "median.default", which both contain the string "median".

Sometimes an entire manual page on an object, operator, or function is more than is necessary. Oftentimes just a simple example or two is preferred to a manual page. The example function takes care of such a situation. If, for instance, you would like to see examples of the median function, just type

```
> example(median)          # examples of the median function

median> median(1:4)        # = 2.5 [even number]
[1] 2.5

median> median(c(1:3, 100, 1000))   # = 3 [odd, robust]
[1] 3
```

The example function temporarily modifies the prompt to include the function of interest, then gives two examples of calculating the sample median of an even and odd number of observations. To generate examples of using the modulo operator (and the related integer-divide operator), type

```
> example("%%")            # examples of using the modulo operator %%

%%> x <- -1:12

%%> x + 1
 [1]  0  1  2  3  4  5  6  7  8  9 10 11 12 13

%%> 2 * x + 3
 [1]  1  3  5  7  9 11 13 15 17 19 21 23 25 27

%%> x %% 2 #-- is periodic
 [1] 1 0 1 0 1 0 1 0 1 0 1 0 1 0

%%> x %/% 5
 [1] -1  0  0  0  0  0  1  1  1  1  1  2  2  2
```

R executes five examples in this case.

In some situations, it is helpful to view a demonstration of one of R's capabilities. The command

```
> demo()                   # list demonstration topics
```

gives a list of demonstration topics that can be run with a subsequent call to demo with a specific value for its argument. To view a demonstration of some of the graphics capability in R, for example, type

```
> demo(graphics)           # run demonstration of graphics capability
```

There is even more help available on the internet concerning R. One obvious option is to use a search engine to hunt for a topic of interest. A second option is the use the help.start function. Typing

```
> help.start()             # launch help page with hyperlinks
```

will bring up a browser window containing R's online documentation. The R command

```
> RSiteSearch("sd")        # search R site for help on a topic
```

searches the R website for information concerning the sd function. Finally, the main website for R http://www.r-project.org contains dozens of links to various sites that can be helpful.

9.3 Floating point representations

Understanding how computers store numbers internally is important for understanding how overflow and roundoff can adversely impact certain numerical calculations. Consider the number 12.75. In decimal, which is also known as base ten, the place-value method that we use to write numbers means that 12.75 can be written as

$$1 \cdot 10^1 + 2 \cdot 10^0 + 7 \cdot 10^{-1} + 5 \cdot 10^{-2}.$$

As is the case with most computer languages that operate on a digital computer, numeric values are stored internally in *binary*. Binary, also known as base 2, is a number system that consists entirely of the digits 0 and 1. Instead of writing the decimal number 12.75 in terms of powers of 10, it can be written in binary as powers of 2 as

$$1 \cdot 2^3 + 1 \cdot 2^2 + 0 \cdot 2^1 + 0 \cdot 2^0 + 1 \cdot 2^{-1} + 1 \cdot 2^{-2}.$$

Hence, the decimal 12.75 is written in binary as 1100.11. The binary representation is the way that R stores the number internally, although this conversion is transparent to the user because numbers are input into R in decimal and displayed in decimal. The conversion between the two number systems is done automatically. But not all numbers can be stored exactly in R. As an example, consider 1/3. On a calculator that uses decimal to store 1/3 with a finite number of digits, it can only be stored approximately:

```
> 1 / 3                        # approximate in decimal (base 10)
[1] 0.3333333
```

Next consider the fraction 11/4. This can be stored exactly in decimal as 2.75 and can also be stored exactly in binary as 10.11.

```
> 11 / 4                       # exact in base 10 and in base 2
[1] 2.75
```

You won't get into any trouble using $11/4 = 2.75$ in R because its binary representation is exact. This is not the case with $2/5 = 0.4$. Even though this fraction can be stored exactly in decimal, it is not exact in binary. Typing it into R as

```
> 2 / 5                        # exact in base 10 but approximate in base 2
[1] 0.4
```

does not reveal the trouble that is lurking behind the scenes. The binary representation of 0.4 is repeating: 0.0110011001100110011.... This means that 0.4 cannot be stored exactly internally in R. Here are two examples of the kind of trouble that you can get into when working with the seemingly harmless $2/5 = 0.4$. Consider the two R commands below. The first command sets the vector x to the first 14 positive integers. The second command creates a vector that should contain all zeros (check the algebra).

```
> x = 1:14                     # first fourteen integers
> 2.5 * (x * 0.4) - x          # should be a vector of zeros
 [1] 0.000000e+00 0.000000e+00 4.440892e-16 0.000000e+00 0.000000e+00
 [6] 8.881784e-16 8.881784e-16 0.000000e+00 0.000000e+00 0.000000e+00
[11] 0.000000e+00 1.776357e-15 0.000000e+00 1.776357e-15
```

So it looks like this is just a byzantine way to set the 14-element vector to all zeros. But the approximate internal representation of 0.4 in binary results in some nonzero values cropping up at seemingly random positions in the resulting vector. There is nothing that can be done to prevent this problem, which is known to computer scientists as roundoff error. R does have a function, however, named zapsmall, that can be used to replace numbers that are near zero with zero. It effectively zaps the digits that are far away from the decimal point. Be careful using zapsmall, however, because the definition of being "near zero" is arbitrary, although it can be altered with an additional optional argument. As a final example, consider adding up the troublemaker 2/5 one million times. If all goes well, the sum should be 400,000.

```
> sum(rep(2 / 5, 1000000))       # 2 / 5 + 2 / 5 + ... + 2 / 5 = 400,000
[1] 4e+05
```

All appears to be well. But again there is trouble lurking below the surface. If the number of digits displayed by R is now set to 22 and the same command is executed, the output shows some stray digits.

```
> options(digits = 22)           # maximum precision
> sum(rep(2 / 5, 1000000))       # 2 / 5 + 2 / 5 + ... + 2 / 5 = 400,000
[1] 400000.0000000034924597
```

All of those tiny differences between 2/5 exactly and its approximate binary representation get added repeatedly, and these values show up as digits in the results of the computation.

This concludes the discussion of various utilities in R. The table below summarizes the functions described in this chapter.

function	description
history	display previous commands
options	set options to alter R calculations and display
help	display R documentation
help.search	search help system for a string
apropos	search objects for a string
example	execute an example
demo	execute a demonstration
RSiteSearch	search R website for a string
zapsmall	remove extraneous digits

Three data structures—vectors, matrices, and arrays—have been introduced at this point. Thus far, these data structures have been populated exclusively with numeric values. That is about to change. Many applications require R to store character data (such as eye color) or logical values (true or false) in a data set. The next three chapters introduce three new types of elements that can populate the elements of a vector, matrix, or array. These new types of elements are *complex variables*, *character strings*, and *logical elements*.

Exercises

9.1 Use the options function to set the number of digits displayed to three, the width of the display to 40, and avoid scientific notation. Then use the cos function to display the cosine of the first ten positive integers to three digits.

9.2   Run the `help` function on the `round` function. How many arguments does the `round` function accept?

9.3   Three functions (actually *functionals* because one of their arguments is itself a function) that are useful in numerical problems are `uniroot`, which finds the numerical solution to an equation, `optimise`, which finds the value associated with the minimum or maximum of a function, and `integrate`, which finds the area under a function.

  (a) Use the `help` function to learn about `uniroot` and use it to solve $x = e^{-x}$.

  (b) Use the `help` function to learn about `optimise` and use it to find the value of x that minimizes $g(x) = x + e^{-x}$.

  (c) Use the `help` function to learn about `integrate` and use it to find the area under the function $h(x) = (\sin x)/x$ between $x = 0$ and $x = \pi$, that is,

$$\int_0^\pi \frac{\sin x}{x}\, dx.$$

9.4   Write the floating-point binary representation of the decimal fraction $\frac{19}{8}$.

9.5   Convert the binary number 101111100 to octal (base 8).

9.6   Convert the binary number 101.1001 to decimal.

9.7   What is returned by the following R command? (Hint: R uses only about 9 binary digits to store the exponent for holding a number in scientific notation.)

```
> 9 ^ 999999
```

Chapter 10

Complex Numbers

So far, we have considered various data structures (vectors, matrices, and arrays) that have been populated by numeric elements, and the associated functions that act on the elements in these data structures. This chapter introduces a second type of element that can populate a data structure, namely a complex number. Two other types of elements, namely character strings and logical elements, are introduced in the two chapters that follow this one. The topics considered in this chapter are (a) defining a complex number, (b) operations on complex numbers, and (c) vectors, matrices, and arrays of complex numbers.

10.1 Defining a complex number

In mathematics, a *complex number* has the form

$$z = a + bi,$$

where i is known as the *imaginary unit*, satisfying $i^2 = -1$, a is known as the real part of z, and b is known as the complex part of z. Complex numbers are added, subtracted, multiplied, and divided in R in exactly the same fashion as in mathematics. Since i is also available as an ordinary object name, it will not be recognized by R

```
> i                        # R doesn't recognize i alone ...
Error: object 'i' not found
```

However, if a 1 is placed directly before i, R recognizes it as the imaginary unit and displays it in the special format that R has chosen for complex numbers, which does not include spaces around operators.

```
> 1i                       # ... but it recognizes 1i
[1] 0+1i
```

To check and see whether the imaginary unit indeed satisfies the equation $i^2 = -1$, the imaginary unit 1i can be squared in the usual fashion

```
> 1i ^ 2                   # i ^ 2
[1] -1+0i
```

The complex number $z = 5 - 6i$, for example, can be assigned to an object named z with

```
> z = 5 - 6i              # set z to 5 - 6i
> z                       # display z
[1] 5-6i
```

The `complex` function can also be used to define a complex number. The `real` and `imaginary` arguments define a and b for a complex number of the form $z = a + bi$. So z from the previous illustration could also have been defined with

```
> z = complex(real = 5, imaginary = -6)
> z
[1] 5-6i
```

The `real` and `imaginary` arguments can also be assigned vectors in order to create a vector with elements that are complex numbers.

10.2   Operations on complex numbers

Standard mathematical operations, such as addition, subtraction, multiplication, division, and exponentiation, can be applied to complex numbers, as illustrated by the following series of examples.

```
> 7 * z                   # multiply z by 7
[1] 35-42i
> z ^ 2                   # square z
[1] -11-60i
> z ^ 100                 # raise z to the 100 power
[1] 1.729487e+89+6.48594e+88i
> 1 / z                   # take the reciprocal of z
[1] 0.08196721+0.098360066i
> (1 + 2i) + (3 + 4i)     # add two complex numbers
[1] 4+6i
> (1 + 2i) - (3 + 4i)     # subtract two complex numbers
[1] -2-2i
> (1 + 2i) * (3 + 4i)     # multiply two complex numbers
[1] -5+10i
> (1 + 2i) / (3 + 4i)     # divide two complex numbers
[1] 0.44+0.08i
```

There is also a group of utility functions that extract information about a complex number, perform a calculation on a complex number, or transform a complex number. The `mode` function returns a character string that describes the elements comprising the object. The `Re` function extracts the real part of an complex number. The `Im` function extracts the imaginary part of an complex number. The `Conj` function returns the complex conjugate of its argument. (Recall that the complex conjugate of a complex number $a + bi$ is the complex number $a - bi$.) The `Mod` function returns the modulus of a complex number. (Recall that the modulus of a complex number $a + bi$ is $\sqrt{a^2 + b^2}$.) Finally, the `Arg` function returns the argument of a complex number. (Recall that the argument of a complex number is the measure of the angle, in radians, with the positive real axis in the counterclockwise direction in the complex plane.)

```
> z = complex(real = 3, imaginary = -4)
> z                         # display z
```

```
[1] 3-4i
> mode(z)                 # mode of the element(s) in z
[1] "complex"
> Re(z)                   # real part of z
[1] 3
> Im(z)                   # imaginary part of z
[1] -4
> Conj(z)                 # conjugate of z
[1] 3+4i
> Mod(z)                  # modulus of z
[1] 5
> Arg(z)                  # argument of z, -pi < Arg(z) <= pi
[1] -0.9272952
> z * Conj(z)             # multiply complex numbers
[1] 25+0i
```

10.3   Vectors, matrices, and arrays of complex numbers

So far, complex numbers have all been placed in a vector of length one. As was the case with numeric values, complex numbers can also be placed in vectors, matrices, and arrays. The complex function is used to create a six-element vector of complex numbers with

```
> z = complex(real = 3:8, imaginary = 8:3)  # vector of complex numbers
> z                       # display z
[1] 3+8i 4+7i 5+6i 6+5i 7+4i 8+3i
```

The first two elements of z can be multiplied using subscripting in the usual fashion.

```
> z[1] * z[2]             # multiply the first two elements of the vector z
[1] -44+53i
```

This is checked via

$$(3+8i)(4+7i) = 12+21i+32i+56i^2 = -44+53i.$$

Complex numbers can be placed in a 2×4 matrix in an analogous fashion.

```
> z = matrix(complex(real = 1:8, imaginary = 8:1), 2, 4)
> z                       # display z
     [,1] [,2] [,3] [,4]
[1,] 1+8i 3+6i 5+4i 7+2i
[2,] 2+7i 4+5i 6+3i 8+1i
```

The sum of the complex elements in the first row of z and the product of the complex elements in the second column of z are found with

```
> sum(z[1, ])            # first row sum
[1] 16+20i
> prod(z[ , 2])          # second column product
[1] -18+39i
```

This ends the discussion concerning creating and performing operations on complex numbers in R. The table below summarizes the functions described in this chapter.

function	description
complex	define a complex number
Re	extract the real part of a complex number
Im	extract the imaginary part of a complex number
Conj	find the conjugate of a complex number
Mod	find the modulus of a complex number
Arg	find the argument of a complex number

The next chapter introduces another type of element that can populate one of R's data structures: a character string.

Exercises

10.1   Write a single R command that calculates the product of the complex numbers $2 - 3i$ and $3 + 4i$. Check the correctness of the result by hand.

10.2   What is returned by the following R command? Check the correctness of the result by hand.

```
> (2 - 3i) ^ 2
```

10.3   Write R commands that calculate $(1 - i)^n$, where $i = \sqrt{-1}$, for $n = 4, 8, 16, 20, 24$. Use the results to write a general mathematical expression for $(1 - i)^n$, where n is a multiple of 4.

10.4   Write R commands to create a 5×5 matrix named w whose elements are complex numbers. The real part of each element is the row number; the imaginary part of each element is the column number. Compute the matrix that results from multiplying each element of w by its conjugate.

Chapter 11

Character Strings

Data structures, such as vectors, matrices and arrays, have elements that have thus far been assumed to be either numeric or complex values. This chapter introduces a third possibility for these elements: character strings.

A single character in R is stored in memory in eight consecutive bits, which computer scientists call a "byte." A *bit* is a binary digit. There are $2^8 = 256$ different sequences of eight bits, and the meaning of these 256 possibilities are defined by the American Standard Code for Information Interchange, which is abbreviated by ASCII. The 26 lower-case letters, the 26 upper-case letters, and dozens of symbols are defined as particular strings of eight bits in ASCII. A single such letter or symbol is known as a "character." A sequence of characters is known as a "character string."

This chapter introduces character strings in R. The topics considered in this chapter are (a) simple character strings, (b) automatic coercion, (c) built-in strings, (d) string manipulation, (e) names, and (f) factors.

11.1   Simple character strings

Placing one or more characters in single or double quotes constitutes a character string. In order to assign the string "R" to the object x and display the value of x, type

```
> x = "R"                                # a character: ASCII 01010010
> x                                      # display x
[1] "R"
```

The [1] is again displayed because x is a vector of length one consisting of a single element that has been assigned the string "R". Using single quotes to assign the string 'S' to x is done in the same fashion:

```
> x = 'S'                                # a character: ASCII 01010011
> x                                      # display x
[1] "S"
> nchar(x)                               # character count
[1] 1
```

R displays strings surrounded by double quotes, regardless of whether they are entered with single or double quotes. The nchar function accepts a string as its argument and returns the number of characters in the string, which in this case is one. Strings with multiple characters are input in the same fashion:

```
> x = "Hello world!"                # a string of characters
> x                                 # display x
[1] "Hello world!"
> nchar(x)                          # character count
[1] 12
```

This time the nchar function returns 12, which is a count of the characters in the string "Hello world!" (not including the quotes, but including the space and the exclamation point). The substr (substring) function allows a portion of a string to be extracted.

```
> substr(x, start = 2, stop = 10)   # substring function
[1] "ello worl"
```

Occasions might arise in which you would like to have a quotation mark or apostrophe within a character string. Placing a backslash before the quotation mark or apostrophe is the way to accomplish this. When nchar is called in the example below, it counts the apostrophe as just a single character.

```
> x = "I can\'t go there"          # a string of characters
> x                                 # display x
[1] "I can't go there"
> nchar(x)                          # character count
[1] 16
```

Octal (base 8) is a compact way to write a binary number. Beginning a string with a backslash indicates an octal number in a string. The octal number 007 (binary 000000111) corresponds to the chime sound on a laptop or desktop computer. So one way to sound this chime is to use the cat (concatenate) function to output this particular octal code:

```
> x = "\007"                        # bell sound as octal ASCII code
> cat(x)                            # ring the bell
```

The upper-case R is binary code 001010010 in ASCII, which is octal 122. Calling the print function below prints R as a one-element vector that consists of a character string as an element, but calling the cat function just prints the letter R (not as a vector and without the quotation marks).

```
> x = "\122"                        # letter R as octal ASCII code
> print(x)                          # prints the object x
[1] "R"
> cat(x)                            # display R
R
```

Finally, calling the cat function to generate a tab, followed by the letter R, followed by a newline results in

```
> cat("\t", x, "\n")                # tab then display R then newline
   R
```

11.2 Automatic coercion

R does not allow you to mix data types within the data structures that have been introduced so far. For example, you cannot mix numeric values, complex values, and strings together in a vector. (There is a data structure known as a *list*, introduced in Chapter 15, which allows this mixing.) If you do mix these data types, R will perform what is known as "automatic coercion," and it will coerce the elements to all have the same type. In setting x to a vector of strings and numeric values, for example, R will coerce all values to be strings:

```
> x = c("R", 4.7, 3, -8, 6.02e23, pi)    # mixed data types; auto. coercion
> x                                       # display x
[1] "R"              "4.7"              "3"              "-8"
[5] "6.02e+23"       "3.14159265358979"
```

Coercing numerics to be character strings is more sensible than coercing character strings to be numerics (for example, it is not clear what numerical value should be assigned to "Hello world!"). Applying the nchar function to the vector x results in the following six counts:

```
> nchar(x)                               # character count
[1]  1  3  1  2  8 16
```

Applying the substr function with start = 2 and stop = 4 (the arguments are referenced by position here) to the x vector results in

```
> substr(x, 2, 4)                        # substring function
[1] ""      ".7"  ""      "8"    ".02" ".14"
```

11.3 Built-in objects of character strings

R contains some built-in objects consisting of character strings as elements that can often be useful as labels in graphics. The objects letters and LETTERS, for instance, are each 26-element vectors that contain the lower-case and upper-case letters.

```
> letters                                # lower-case letters
 [1] "a" "b" "c" "d" "e" "f" "g" "h" "i" "j" "k" "l" "m" "n" "o" "p" "q" "r"
[19] "s" "t" "u" "v" "w" "x" "y" "z"
> LETTERS                                # upper-case letters
 [1] "A" "B" "C" "D" "E" "F" "G" "H" "I" "J" "K" "L" "M" "N" "O" "P" "Q" "R"
[19] "S" "T" "U" "V" "W" "X" "Y" "Z"
```

A specific letter can be accessed using a subscript in the usual fashion:

```
> LETTERS[18]                            # one upper-case letter
[1] "R"
```

Two other vectors of built-in strings are month.name and month.abb, which contain the months of the year and their abbreviations.

```
> month.name                             # month names
 [1] "January"   "February"  "March"     "April"     "May"       "June"
 [7] "July"      "August"    "September" "October"   "November"  "December"
> month.abb                              # month abbreviations
 [1] "Jan" "Feb" "Mar" "Apr" "May" "Jun" "Jul" "Aug" "Sep" "Oct" "Nov" "Dec"
```

The 50 United States and their abbreviations are contained in state.name and state.abb.

```
> state.name                            # U.S. state names
 [1] "Alabama"        "Alaska"         "Arizona"        "Arkansas"
 [5] "California"     "Colorado"       "Connecticut"    "Delaware"
 [9] "Florida"        "Georgia"        "Hawaii"         "Idaho"
[13] "Illinois"       "Indiana"        "Iowa"           "Kansas"
[17] "Kentucky"       "Louisiana"      "Maine"          "Maryland"
[21] "Massachusetts"  "Michigan"       "Minnesota"      "Mississippi"
[25] "Missouri"       "Montana"        "Nebraska"       "Nevada"
[29] "New Hampshire"  "New Jersey"     "New Mexico"     "New York"
[33] "North Carolina" "North Dakota"   "Ohio"           "Oklahoma"
[37] "Oregon"         "Pennsylvania"   "Rhode Island"   "South Carolina"
[41] "South Dakota"   "Tennessee"      "Texas"          "Utah"
[45] "Vermont"        "Virginia"       "Washington"     "West Virginia"
[49] "Wisconsin"      "Wyoming"
> state.abb                             # U.S. state abbreviations
 [1] "AL" "AK" "AZ" "AR" "CA" "CO" "CT" "DE" "FL" "GA" "HI" "ID" "IL" "IN"
[15] "IA" "KS" "KY" "LA" "ME" "MD" "MA" "MI" "MN" "MS" "MO" "MT" "NE" "NV"
[29] "NH" "NJ" "NM" "NY" "NC" "ND" "OH" "OK" "OR" "PA" "RI" "SC" "SD" "TN"
[43] "TX" "UT" "VT" "VA" "WA" "WV" "WI" "WY"
```

Most of the functions that have been encountered previously can be applied to strings. The example below illustrates using the sort and c functions.

```
> sort(c(LETTERS, letters))            # not ASCII ordering
 [1] "a" "A" "b" "B" "c" "C" "d" "D" "e" "E" "f" "F" "g" "G" "h" "H" "i" "I"
[19] "j" "J" "k" "K" "l" "L" "m" "M" "n" "N" "o" "O" "p" "P" "q" "Q" "r" "R"
[37] "s" "S" "t" "T" "u" "U" "v" "V" "w" "W" "x" "X" "y" "Y" "z" "Z"
```

11.4   Character string manipulation

There are several functions that are designed specifically for manipulating strings. Many of the illustrations given here will be applied to the vectors animals and adj, which are defined with

```
> animals = c("pig", "cow", "gnu")     # a vector of animal names
> animals                              # display animals
[1] "pig" "cow" "gnu"
> adj = c("pink", "brown", "lonely")   # a vector of adjectives
> adj                                  # display adjectives
[1] "pink"     "brown"     "lonely"
```

The toupper function replaces all lower case letters with upper case letters. The tolower function acts in the opposite fashion.

```
> toupper(animals)                     # convert to upper case
[1] "PIG" "COW" "GNU"
> tolower(LETTERS)                     # convert to lower case
 [1] "a" "b" "c" "d" "e" "f" "g" "h" "i" "j" "k" "l" "m" "n" "o" "p" "q" "r"
[19] "s" "t" "u" "v" "w" "x" "y" "z"
```

The substr (substring) function, introduced earlier, is another that is specifically targeted for character strings.

```
> substr(animals, 1, 2)                    # substring function
[1] "pi" "co" "gn"
> substr(animals[2], 2, 3)                 # substring function
[1] "ow"
```

The strsplit (string split) function allows a character string to be split into several pieces. The second argument determines the character at which the string should be split.

```
> strsplit("9-1-1", "-")                   # split the string; returns a list
[[1]]
[1] "9" "1" "1"
```

The paste function can be used to paste character strings together. Notice the creative use of the sep (separator) and collapse arguments to create new strings from individual strings.

```
> paste("big", animals)                    # paste strings together
[1] "big pig" "big cow" "big gnu"
> paste(adj, animals)                      # paste strings together
[1] "pink pig"    "brown cow"    "lonely gnu"
> paste(adj, " ", animals, "s", sep = "")  # separator is null string
[1] "pink pigs"    "brown cows"    "lonely gnus"
> paste(adj, " ", animals, "s", sep = "", collapse = ", ")
[1] "pink pigs, brown cows, lonely gnus"
```

Recycling is used with strings in a similar fashion to numeric values. The strings associated with x_1, y_2, z_3, x_4, y_5, and z_6, for example, are generated with

```
> paste(c("x", "y", "z"), 1:6, sep = "")   # recycle
[1] "x1" "y2" "z3" "x4" "y5" "z6"
```

The sub (substitute) function can be used to substitute the first occurrence of one string for another.

```
> sub("best", "worst", "It was the best of times.")   # pattern matching
[1] "It was the worst of times."
```

The gsub (global substitute) function can be used to substitute all occurrences of one string for another. The sprintf function returns a character vector that combines text and the values of place values.

```
> sprintf("%s %d by %d gives %d", "Multiplying", 3, 4, 3 * 4)   # substitute
[1] "Multiplying 3 by 4 gives 12"
```

The grep function is a pattern matching and replacement function. In the example below, a search is made in the vector month.name for the character string "ary". This string occurs in January and February, so grep returns the positions in the month.name vector, namely positions 1 and 2.

```
> grep("ary", month.name)                  # search for "ary"
[1] 1 2
```

This example can be taken one step further. If one desires the abbreviations associated with a month whose name contains the character string "ary", simply type

```
> month.abb[grep("ary", month.name)]        # month abbrev. for "ary" months
[1] "Jan" "Feb"
```

The notion of a "regular expression" is supported in R. To find the indexes associated with months *beginning* with the letter J, for example, prepend a ^ to the search string.

```
> grep("^J", month.name)                     # month names that start with J
[1] 1 6 7
```

The indexes for January, June, and July are returned. To find the indexes of month names *ending* with the string "ber", for example, append a $ to the search string.

```
> grep("ber$", month.name)                   # month names that end with ber
[1]  9 10 11 12
```

The indexes for September, October, November and December are returned. A thorough knowledge of the vast topic of regular expressions can be useful for cleaning up strings that might contain coding errors in a large data set.

11.5   Names

Data structures often possess additional attributes, which are also known as *metadata*. One useful attribute that is often applied to vectors is known as a *name*. A name can be attached to each element of a vector upon creation. Consider the case of setting a vector named a to the elements 1, 2, and 17, and these elements are given the names x, y, and z.

```
> a = c(x = 1, y = 2, z = 17)                # create the vector named a
> a                                          # display a
 x  y  z
 1  2 17
> names(a)                                   # display names of a
[1] "x" "y" "z"
```

When the vector a is displayed, the names associated with the elements are given above the elements. It is possible to name some, but not all of the elements in a vector. The names of the elements that are not named are set to the empty vector "". The names function is called to get the names associated with the vector a. The names are displayed as character strings. It is also possible to set the names attribute after a vector is created. As an illustration, recall the Florida population numbers given at the beginning of Chapter 4. The code below places those populations (in thousands) in the vector named flapop. The versatile names function can be used to both get and set the names. In the example below, the names function sets the names associated with flapop to 1900, 1910, ..., 1990.

```
> flapop = c(529, 753, 968, 1468, 1897, 2771, 4952, 6789, 9746, 12938)
> names(flapop) = seq(1900, 1990, 10)        # census years
> flapop                                     # display flapop
 1900  1910  1920  1930  1940  1950  1960  1970  1980  1990
  529   753   968  1468  1897  2771  4952  6789  9746 12938
> names(flapop)                              # display names of flapop
 [1] "1900" "1910" "1920" "1930" "1940" "1950" "1960" "1970" "1980" "1990"
```

If, instead, we want only the last two digits of the years as names, then the names function can be assigned a vector of the appropriate character strings.

```
> names(flapop) = c("00", "10", "20", "30", "40", "50", "60", "70", "80", "90")
> flapop                              # display flapop
   00    10    20    30    40    50    60    70    80    90
  529   753   968  1468  1897  2771  4952  6789  9746 12938
> names(flapop)                       # display names of flapop
 [1] "00" "10" "20" "30" "40" "50" "60" "70" "80" "90"
```

11.6 Factors

The roots of **R** are in statistics, so it is natural that **R** would have some special ways of storing data. Data can be grouped into two very broad categories: numeric data and non-numeric data. Examples of numeric data include the population of Florida in 1950 and the cholesterol level of a patient. Examples of non-numeric data include the gender of a patient and the species of a particular bird. Statisticians often further subdivide non-numeric data as ordinal and categorical data. Both of these types of data are assumed to be limited to just a finite set of possible values, but ordinal data have a natural ordering. The term *levels* is used to describe the possible values in the finite set. Examples of ordinal data include:

- The speed of a treadmill is set at one of the levels *slow, medium,* or *fast.*

- The service at a store is rated as *poor, fair, good,* or *excellent.*

- An economist classifies GDP growth at the levels *negative, low,* or *high* by establishing arbitrary interval boundaries.

Examples of categorical data include:

- The eye color of a person is at one of the levels *blue, brown, green,* or *other.*

- The gender of a patient is *male* or *female.*

- A basketball player's position is either a *guard, forward,* or *center.*

R has a special way of storing character strings for non-numeric data known as a *factor.* Although a factor seems quite similar to a vector of character strings, it is stored differently internally and it obeys different rules. Consider an experiment in which you record the eye color of six subjects, considering only the outcomes *blue, brown, green,* and *other.* The results of the experiment are placed in the vector of character strings named eyes1. Next, the table function is called to display the counts of the various eye colors in the vector.

```
> eyes1 = c("green", "blue", "brown", "brown", "other", "blue")
> table(eyes1)                            # display the counts in eyes1
eyes1
 blue brown green other
    2     2     1     1
```

Next, the same vector of eye colors is passed as an argument into the factor function to create a factor named eyes2. Again the table function is called to display the counts of the various eye colors.

```
> eyes2 = factor(c("green", "blue", "brown", "brown", "other", "blue"))
> table(eyes2)                               # display the counts in eyes2
eyes2
 blue brown green other
    2     2     1     1
```

At this point it seems to be the case that a vector of character strings and a factor are identical. But this is not the case. Hidden below the surface is the fact that factors are stored in a different format internally and therefore have different properties. The elements of a factor, for example, can only assume a finite number of values. To check this, begin by displaying eyes1, then calling the class, mode, and levels functions to see these important attributes of eyes1.

```
> eyes1                                      # display eyes1
[1] "green" "blue"  "brown" "brown" "other" "blue"
> class(eyes1)                               # eyes1 is a vector of strings
[1] "character"
> mode(eyes1)                                # the elements are strings
[1] "character"
> levels(eyes1)                              # the levels function fails
NULL
```

The elements of the eyes1 vector are displayed as character strings. The class and mode functions reveal that eyes1 is a vector of character strings. The levels function returns the levels attribute of its argument. This vector of character strings has no such levels attribute, so it returns NULL. Now apply those same functions to the factor eyes2.

```
> eyes2                                      # display eyes2
[1] green blue  brown brown other blue
Levels: blue brown green other
> class(eyes2)                               # eyes2 is a factor
[1] "factor"
> mode(eyes2)                                # the elements are numeric
[1] "numeric"
> levels(eyes2)                              # eyes2 has four levels
[1] "blue"  "brown" "green" "other"
```

In this case, the factor eyes2 is displayed, without the surrounding quotation marks, along with its levels. The class function indicates that eyes2 is a factor. Surprisingly, the elements of eyes2 are stored in numerical form. This means that the string manipulation functions cannot be applied to the elements of eyes2 in its current form. The levels function returns the levels of the factor in alphabetical order, although that can be altered by using the levels argument in the factor function. (This will be illustrated subsequently.) Next, try assigning the fourth element of eyes1 to the character string "hazel".

```
> eyes1[4] = "hazel"                         # set fourth element to "hazel"
> eyes1                                      # display eyes1
[1] "green" "blue"  "brown" "hazel" "other" "blue"
```

This works fine. Now try that same operation on eyes2.

```
> eyes2[4] = "hazel"                         # set fourth element to NA
```

```
Warning message:
In '[<-.factor'('*tmp*', 4, value = "hazel") :
  invalid factor level, NA generated
> eyes2                                      # display eyes2
[1] green blue  brown <NA>  other blue
Levels: blue brown green other
```

Problems arise in this case because `"hazel"` is not on the list of levels that were created when the `factor` function was first called. It could have been added by including the `labels` argument in the original call to `factor`.

Now consider an ordinal, rather than a categorical data set. A treadmill test is administered to ten subjects, and the speed of the treadmill is at one of three levels: slow, medium, and fast. The natural ordering of these three levels means that a factor with ordered levels is appropriate. The first R command below sets the vector `speeds` to the ten treadmill speeds. The second R command calls the `factor` function with the additional arguments `levels`, `labels`, and `ordered`. The factor `treadmill` is displayed, and then the `table` function is called.

```
> speeds = c("M", "M", "M", "F", "S", "F", "M", "F", "M", "M")
> treadmill = factor(speeds, levels = c("S", "M", "F"),
+                    labels = c("Slow", "Medium", "Fast"), ordered = TRUE)
> treadmill                              # display treadmill
 [1] Medium Medium Medium Fast   Slow   Fast   Medium Fast   Medium Medium
Levels: Slow < Medium < Fast
> table(treadmill)                            # treadmill has three levels
treadmill
  Slow Medium   Fast
     1      6      3
```

The output shows that setting the `ordered` argument to `TRUE` results in the ordering of the values as `Slow < Medium < Fast` as desired. The call to the `table` function reflects this ordering.

This concludes the brief overview of the important topic of character strings. Although the examples given in this chapter have been entirely applied to vectors, character strings are not limited to just elements of vectors. A 2×3 matrix of strings, for example, can be established using the `matrix` function in the usual fashion:

```
> matrix(c(adj, animals), 2, 3, byrow = TRUE) # 2 x 3 matrix of strings
     [,1]   [,2]    [,3]
[1,] "pink" "brown" "lonely"
[2,] "pig"  "cow"   "gnu"
```

Similarly, a $2 \times 4 \times 3$ array of month abbreviations (with recycling) can be created using the `array` function:

```
> array(month.abb, c(2, 4, 3, 2))              # 2 x 4 x 3 array of months
, , 1

     [,1]  [,2]  [,3]  [,4]
[1,] "Jan" "Mar" "May" "Jul"
[2,] "Feb" "Apr" "Jun" "Aug"
```

```
, , 2

     [,1]   [,2]   [,3]   [,4]
[1,]  "Sep"  "Nov"  "Jan"  "Mar"
[2,]  "Oct"  "Dec"  "Feb"  "Apr"


, , 3

     [,1]   [,2]   [,3]   [,4]
[1,]  "May"  "Jul"  "Sep"  "Nov"
[2,]  "Jun"  "Aug"  "Oct"  "Dec"
```

The table below summarizes the functions described in this chapter.

function or string	description
nchar	count the number of characters
substr	extract substring
print	display arguments
cat	display arguments
letters	vector of lower-case letters
LETTERS	vector of upper-case letters
month.name	vector of month names
month.abb	vector of month abbreviations
state.name	vector of state names
state.abb	vector of state abbreviations
toupper	convert to upper case
tolower	convert to lower case
strsplit	split string
paste	paste (concatenate) strings
sub	substitute one string for another
sprintf	format string
grep	pattern match for a string
names	get or set names
factor	create a factor
table	display a table of counts
levels	get or set the levels of a factor

There are now three options for populating the elements of a vector, matrix, or array. They can be populated with numeric values, complex values, or character strings. The next chapter introduces a fourth option: logical elements.

Exercises

11.1   Create a $2 \times 3 \times 2$ array named `abb` of U.S. state abbreviations. Then use the `substr` function to create a second $2 \times 3 \times 2$ array named `abb1` which contains just the first letters of each string in `abb`.

11.2 Discrete-event simulations involve a simulation clock, entities that pass through a system, attributes associated with the entities, and a calendar of future events. Consider a coffee shop with a single server. Currently, Arthur is being served at simulated time 57 minutes. Waiting in line behind Arthur, in order, are Bob, Charise, and Daniel. The event calendar contains, in order, the arrival of Emma at time 60, and the end of service of Arthur at time 62. The current state of the coffee shop is captured by the five R commands

```
> time     = 57
> coffee   = c("Arthur", "Bob", "Charise", "Daniel")
> arrival  = c(50, 52, 55, 56)
> calendar = c(60, 62)
> event    = c("arrival", "end.of.service")
```

The object named `time` contains the simulated time. The vector named `coffee` contains the names of the customers currently in the coffee shop as character strings, ordered by their position in the queue. The vector named `arrival` contains the arrival times of the customer currently being served (in this case Arthur), and the customers currently waiting in line. The vector named `calendar` contains the times of future events. The associated vector named `event` contains the names of the future events.

(a) Write the R commands that update the data structures to process the arrival of Emma at time 60, and schedule the arrival of Flip at time 64.

(b) Write the R commands that update the data structures to process the end of service of Arthur at time 62, and schedule the end of service of Bob at time 66.

Chapter 12

Logical Elements

So far, we have considered three modes for elements of objects: `numeric`, `complex`, and `character`. This chapter introduces a fourth option, a `logical` element, which assumes the values TRUE or FALSE. Logical elements are known in some computer languages as Boolean, named after English mathematician George Boole. The TRUE value can be abbreviated as T and the FALSE value can be abbreviated as F. The two topics considered in this chapter are (a) operations on logical elements, and (b) using logical elements as subscripts.

12.1 Operations on logical elements

We begin the discussion of logical elements by assigning the single-element vector x to the logical value TRUE.

```
> x = TRUE              # logical
> x
```

Although T and F can be used as abbreviations for TRUE and FALSE, respectively, typing out TRUE and FALSE is the safer choice. The illustration below will show that TRUE is not a valid object name, but T is.

```
> TRUE = 17              # set TRUE to 17
Error in TRUE = 17 : invalid (do_set) left-hand side to assignment
> TRUE                   # TRUE remains TRUE
[1] TRUE
> T = 17                 # set T to 17
> T                      # display T
[1] 17
> rm(T)                  # remove the object T
```

Since TRUE is a reserved word in R, but T is not, using TRUE consistently reduces the probability of an error (bug) in your R code. The same thinking applies to F and FALSE. The final R command removes the object T, which restores its former status as an abbreviation for TRUE.

Now set the object x to a six-element vector whose elements are `logical`, but this time use the T abbreviation for TRUE and the F abbreviation for FALSE.

```
> x = c(T, F, T, F, T, F)      # x is a vector of logical elements
> x                            # display x
[1]  TRUE FALSE   TRUE FALSE   TRUE FALSE
> mode(x)                      # the elements of x are logical
[1] "logical"
> length(x)                    # x has six elements
[1] 6
```

R has several operators and functions that can be applied to logical elements. These operators and functions will be illustrated using the vector x. The any and all functions return a single logical value (a vector of length one) depending whether *any* or *all* of the elements in its argument are TRUE.

```
> any(x)                       # are there any TRUE elements in x?
[1] TRUE
> all(x)                       # are all the elements in x TRUE?
[1] FALSE
```

These functions are analogous to determining the value of the structure function for a parallel and series system in reliability theory.

The first operator that can be applied to a data structure consisting of logical elements is the *not* operator. The syntax associated with the *not* operator is to type an exclamation point (!) just prior to the object, for example,

```
> !x                           # not x
[1] FALSE   TRUE FALSE   TRUE FALSE   TRUE
```

returns FALSE values for all TRUE elements in x and returns TRUE values for all FALSE elements in x.

The next set of operators are *and* and *or*. These operators are analogous to intersection (∩) and union (∪) in set theory. These operators act on two vectors, so first define another six-element vector of logical elements named y with

```
> y = c(TRUE, TRUE, TRUE, FALSE, FALSE, FALSE)      # y is a vector of logicals
> y                            # display y
[1]  TRUE  TRUE  TRUE FALSE FALSE FALSE
```

The syntax for the *and* operator is an ampersand (&) between the two vectors. This version of the *and* operator is vectorized, so it will make pairwise comparisons of the elements of each vector. When each comparison is made, if both logical elements are TRUE, then TRUE is returned. Otherwise FALSE is returned.

```
> x & y                        # x and y (vectorized and operator)
[1]  TRUE FALSE   TRUE FALSE FALSE FALSE
```

Stated in another fashion, the *and* operator returns TRUE if and only if both of the corresponding elements are TRUE. The syntax for the *or* operator is a pipe (|) between the two vectors. This version of the *or* operator is also vectorized, so it will make pairwise comparisons of the elements of each vector. When each comparison is made, if both logical elements are FALSE, then FALSE is returned. Otherwise TRUE is returned.

```
> x | y                        # x or y (vectorized or operator)
[1]  TRUE  TRUE  TRUE FALSE  TRUE FALSE
```

Stated in another fashion, the *or* operator returns TRUE if and only if one or both of the elements are TRUE.

There are non-vectorized versions of *and* and *or* given by `&&` and `||`. They are typically used for comparing one-element vectors. The reason that they exist is that they are optimized in the sense that they will not evaluate the second operand if the first operand determines the outcome of the operation. If the non-vectorized versions are given vectors, they only compare the first elements of each vector:

```
> x && y              # x and y (non-vectorized and operator)
[1] TRUE
> x || y              # x or y (non-vectorized or operator)
[1] TRUE
```

Automatic coercion also applies to logical elements. The command below first asks R to subtract 1 (a numeric element) from y (a vector of logical elements). The y vector will be coerced into a vector of numeric elements, with TRUE being replaced by 1 and FALSE being replaced by 0. Next, the vectorized *or* operator is applied to x (a six-element vector of logical elements) and the six-element vector of numeric elements that had just been computed in the portion of the command in parentheses. In this case, the numeric elements of the y - 1 vector get coerced to logical values (nonzero becomes TRUE and zero becomes FALSE), and the *or* operator works in the usual fashion.

```
> x | (y - 1)              # nonzero TRUE, zero FALSE (automatic coercion)
[1]  TRUE FALSE  TRUE  TRUE  TRUE  TRUE
```

The automatic coercion of logical values to numeric values applies to functions as well. Four examples of automatic coercion applied to the sum, mean, range, and diff functions follow.

```
> sum(x)              # FALSE is 0; TRUE is 1 (automatic coercion)
[1] 3
> mean(x)             # sample mean (fraction of TRUEs)
[1] 0.5
> range(x)            # sample range
[1] 0 1
> diff(x)             # differences
[1] -1  1 -1  1 -1
```

12.2   Using logical elements as subscripts

In Chapter 4, subscripting was introduced as a way to extract certain elements of a vector by placing a vector of subscripts between brackets, for example, x[2:4] returns the second, third, and fourth elements of x. Logical elements can also be used for subscripting. As an illustration, begin by setting the vector z to the first six positive integers.

```
> z = 1:6              # first six integers
```

The vector x, which currently contains TRUE, FALSE, TRUE, FALSE, TRUE, FALSE, can be used as subscripts. A TRUE value means that the element should be included and a FALSE value means that the element should be excluded. So

```
> z[x]                 # logical vector used for subscripting
[1] 1 3 5
```

displays the odd-numbered elements. As another illustration, let's say we want to change all of the elements in z with odd-numbered subscripts to 8. This can be accomplished with

```
> z[x] = 8                # set z elements associated with TRUE in x to 8
> z                       # display z
[1] 8 2 8 4 8 6
```

Finally, to subtract one from the first three elements of z can be accomplished with

```
> z[y] = z[y] - 1         # subtract 1 from the z elements with TRUE in y
> z                       # display z
[1] 7 1 7 4 8 6
```

This ends the discussion of elements that assume logical values. The table below summarizes the operators and functions described in this chapter.

operator or function	description
any	any TRUE values?
all	all TRUE values?
!	not operator (vectorized)
&	and operator (vectorized)
|	or operator (vectorized)
&&	and operator (not vectorized)
||	or operator (not vectorized)

Logical values can also be used as subscripts when indexing values in a vector. The elements associated with subscripts that are TRUE are accessed.

We have now encountered five different data types for the elements that constitute an object: NULL, numeric, complex, character, and logical. These elements can reside in a vector, matrix, or array. This is a good time to review these data types. In addition, another data type, integer, is introduced. Although it is not used as much as the other data types, an integer can be defined by appending an upper-case L to an integer. When an element is defined to be an integer, it will be stored internally with a single bit devoted to the sign of the integer, and the remaining bits used to store the magnitude of the integer. When an element is defined to be a numeric, it will be stored internally as a floating point or double value. The table below lists the six data types, ordered by the increasing amount of information that they contain.

data type	description
NULL	the NULL (empty) object
logical	logical (Boolean) value
integer	integer value
numeric	numeric value
complex	complex value
character	character string

These six data types are illustrated in the calls to the class function, which returns a character string containing the data type.

```
> class(NULL)                # NULL
[1] "NULL"
> class(TRUE)                # logical element
[1] "logical"
> class(3L)                  # integer element
[1] "integer"
> class(3)                   # numeric element
[1] "numeric"
> class(3 + 4i)              # complex element
[1] "complex"
> class("yak")               # character element
[1] "character"
```

The next chapter takes up a topic that is closely related to logical elements: how the elements of data structures can be compared using relational operators.

Exercises

12.1   Write a one-line function named oddjob with a single argument x that returns the elements in odd-numbered positions in the vector x.

12.2   Write a description of the purpose of the xor (exclusive or) function based on results of the R command

```
> xor(c(FALSE, FALSE, TRUE, TRUE), c(FALSE, TRUE, FALSE, TRUE))
```

Chapter 13

Relational Operators

The relational operators $>$, $\geq$, $<$, $\leq$, $=$, and $\neq$ can be used to compare objects. These relational operators return the logical values TRUE or FALSE. The relational operators considered here are implemented in R as

>   >=   <   <=   ==   !=

The double equals == is used for testing equality because the single equals = has already been used for assigning values to the elements of objects. The relational operators are vectorized so that they can be applied element-wise to the objects under consideration. The two topics considered in this chapter are (a) relational operators applied to objects, and (b) conditional execution.

13.1 Relational operators applied to objects

Although the illustrations used in this chapter are applied to vectors, they are easily adapted for more complicated data structures, such as matrices or arrays. To illustrate the use of relational operators, begin by defining a vector x that contains four numeric elements:

```
> x = c(2, -3, 0, 8)        # a vector of numeric elements
> x                         # display x
[1]  2 -3  0  8
```

Next, to check whether any of the elements of x assume the value 7, type

```
> x == 7                    # which elements in x, if any, equal 7?
[1] FALSE FALSE FALSE FALSE
```

The value 7 is effectively recycled, and the equality operator == returns a vector of four FALSE elements because none of the elements of x equal 7. In the same fashion, to check whether any elements in x are equal to 8, type

```
> x == 8                    # which elements in x equal 8?
[1] FALSE FALSE FALSE  TRUE
```

The last element in x is 8, so a TRUE is returned in that position.

The discussion concerning floating point representations from Chapter 9 also applies to relational operators. The == operator tests whether the values stored internally are identical. Consider the R commands

```
> sqrt(3) * sqrt(3)          # the square root of 3 squared is 3
[1] 3
> sqrt(3) * sqrt(3) == 3    # test for equality
[1] FALSE
```

What happened? The square root of 3, which is irrational, does not have an exact binary representation, so although $\sqrt{3} \cdot \sqrt{3}$ *rounds* to 3, it might not be equal to 3 in its binary representation. This was the case in the computation above. The alternative all.equal function includes a tolerance when testing for equality.

```
> all.equal(sqrt(3) * sqrt(3), 3)
[1] TRUE
```

This returns the intuitive result. The tolerance argument can be adjusted in the all.equal function if necessary.

The "not equal" operator is an explanation point before the =, as indicated below.

```
> x != 0                     # which elements in x are nonzero?
[1]  TRUE  TRUE FALSE  TRUE
```

In this case, the first, second, and fourth elements of x are nonzero, resulting in the vector of logical values displayed. To determine which elements of the vector x are negative, type

```
> x < 0                      # which elements in x are negative?
[1] FALSE  TRUE FALSE FALSE
```

Only the second element is negative. The logical vectors that are generated by the relational operators can be manipulated in the same manner as any other vectors. For example, using the c function

```
> c(x == 0, x != 0)          # vector of eight logical elements
[1] FALSE FALSE  TRUE FALSE  TRUE  TRUE FALSE  TRUE
```

concatenates the two four-element vectors of logical elements together to form an eight-element vector of logical elements. The next R command locates all of the positions of the negative elements in x and replaces their values with 17:

```
> x[x < 0] = 17              # set all negative elements in x to 17
> x                          # display x
[1]  2 17  0  8
```

In this case, the logical values are used as subscripts as they were in the previous chapter. Although all of the examples in this chapter use relational operators to compare numeric values, they can also be applied to strings. To compare the strings "C" and "R", for example, type

```
> "C" < "R"                  # is "C" less than "R"?
[1] TRUE
```

The internal representations of these two strings are compared, and the value for "C" is less than the value for "R", so TRUE is returned.

Relational operators can also be applied to two named objects in a component-wise fashion. Begin by assigning the four-element numeric vector y the values 1, 4, 2, and 5.

```
> y = c(1, 4, 2, 5)          # another vector of numeric elements
> y                          # display y
[1] 1 4 2 5
```

The vectors x (which currently contains the elements 2, 17, 0, 8) and y can be compared in an element-wise fashion with

```
> x > y                    # which elements of x are greater than y
[1]  TRUE  TRUE FALSE   TRUE
```

In this case, the vectors x and y were of the same length. If this is not the case, then R recycles the values in the shorter vector in the usual fashion. In a minor extension of this example, you can display the elements of x in which the corresponding element of x is greater than the associated element of y with

```
> x[x > y]                 # elements of x in which x is greater than y
[1]   2 17   8
```

If you would like to take those elements associated with x > y and multiply each of the associated elements of the x vector by 4, type

```
> x[x > y] = x[x > y] * 4  # multiply elements of x such that x > y by four
> x                        # display x
[1]   8 68   0 32
```

The which function is useful for defining the index values that satisfy a particular logical relationship. The which function accepts a vector of logical elements as an argument and returns the *indexes* of all TRUE values in the vector, not the values of the elements themselves. The R command

```
> which(x < 5)             # indexes of elements in x that are less than 5
[1] 3
```

indicates that the third element of x (x currently contains the numeric values 8, 68, 0, 32) is the only element that is less than 5. Notice that the x < 5 portion of this R command creates a vector of four logical elements, and the which function then returns the index or indexes of the TRUE elements in the vector. As a second example, which determines the indexes of those values of x that are less than the sample mean:

```
> which(x < mean(x))       # indexes of elements in x that are less than xbar
[1] 1 3
```

Finally, the following R commands assign the four-element vectors name, age, and va to elements that are character strings, numeric values, and logical values, respectively, then finds the names of all people under the age of 21 who live in Virginia.

```
> name = c("Joe", "Ian", "Liz", "Ali")  # vector of names
> age  = c(19, 21, 18, 20)              # vector of ages
> va   = c(TRUE, FALSE, TRUE, FALSE)    # vector of virginia resident statuses
> name[age < 21 & va]                   # names of young virginians
[1] "Joe" "Liz"
```

This example combines operators on logical elements from last chapter and relational operators from this chapter with subscripting to produce efficient, vectorized calculations. In this example, R had to choose between the relational operator < and the and operator & in terms of precedence. R chose to execute the < before the &. The table that follows gives the precedence rules for the operators that we have encountered thus far, with the operator with highest precedence ranked first; exceptions to these precedences can be accomplished by adding parentheses.

operator	description
[ ]	subscripting
^	exponentiation operator
–	unary minus
:	vector creation
%/%, %%	integer-divide and modulo operators
*, /	multiplication and division operators
+, –	addition and subtraction operators
>, >=, <, <=, ==, !=	relational operators
!	*not* operator
&, &&, |, ||	*and* and *or* operators
=, <-	assignment operators

13.2   Conditional execution via `ifelse`

Now that relational operations have been introduced, the versatile `ifelse` function can be discussed. The `ifelse` function provides a compact mechanism for *conditional execution* in some programming situations. The syntax for `ifelse` is

`ifelse(test, yes, no)`

where `test` is an object that can be coerced to a logical value, `yes` contains the return values for elements of `test` that evaluate to TRUE, and `no` contains the return values for elements of `test` that evaluate to FALSE. Typically, the test argument will be an expression involving a relational operator, which will return logical values. The returned object from `ifelse` will have the same shape as `test`. If the three objects that are arguments of `ifelse` have different lengths, R will recycle the shorter vectors in the usual fashion. This section consists of five elementary applications of the `ifelse` function. A more general treatment of the topic of conditional execution is given in Chapter 22.

A simple example of the use of `ifelse` to indicate whether elements of a vector are nonnegative or negative is

```
> x = c(2, -7, 0, 9, 3.3)  # a vector of five numeric elements
> ifelse(x >= 0, "nonnegative", "negative")
[1] "nonnegative" "negative"    "nonnegative" "nonnegative" "nonnegative"
```

The second argument in the call to `ifelse` is returned when the condition x >= 0 is TRUE; the third argument in the call to `ifelse` is returned when the condition is FALSE. Since the vector x has length 5, and the second and third arguments to the `ifelse` function are vectors of character strings of length 1, recycling is used. So x >= 0 is equivalent to a vector with the five elements TRUE, FALSE, TRUE, TRUE, TRUE, which results in the vector of character strings returned by the `ifelse` function.

As a second example, if the magnitude of an element of x exceeds 5, then the character string `"largemag"` is returned; otherwise the character string `"smallmag"` is returned.

```
> x = c(2, -7, 0, 9, 3.3)  # a vector of five numeric elements
> ifelse(abs(x) > 5, "largemag", "smallmag")
[1] "smallmag" "largemag" "smallmag" "largemag" "smallmag"
```

The `abs(x) > 5` portion of the commands returns FALSE, TRUE, FALSE, TRUE, FALSE, which results in the vector of character strings returned by the `ifelse` function.

The third example illustrates embedding the `ifelse` function within a call to `ifelse`. Let's say we want to replace every element in x that is less than −5 with −5, and every element in x that is greater than 5 with 5.

```
> x = c(2, -7, 0, 9, 3.3)   # a vector of five numeric elements
> ifelse(x < -5, -5, ifelse(x > 5, 5, x))
[1]  2.0 -5.0  0.0  5.0  3.3
```

(Leaving a space between < and - in the condition is crucial for avoiding invoking the assignment operator <-, which would alter the outcome of the command.) The outside call to `ifelse` accounts for elements of x that are less than −5; the inside call to `ifelse` accounts for elements of x that are greater than 5. This operation could also have been performed with the more succinct R commands

```
> x = c(2, -7, 0, 9, 3.3)   # a vector of five numeric elements
> pmax(pmin(x, 5), -5)      # left truncate at -5 and right truncate at 5
[1]  2.0 -5.0  0.0  5.0  3.3
```

These R commands execute significantly faster than the solution that uses embedded calls to the `ifelse` function. A more thorough discussion of execution speed is postponed until Chapter 23.

The fourth example of the use of the `ifelse` function involves suppressing warning messages. Using the vector -1:2 as an argument in `sqrt` results in a warning message.

```
> x = -1:2                 # x is a vector with elements -1, 0, 1, 2
> sqrt(-1:2)               # the square roots of -1, 0, 1, 2
[1]      NaN 0.000000 1.000000 1.414214
Warning message:
In sqrt(-1:2) : NaNs produced
```

A `NaN` value is generated any time the square root encounters a negative value, which results in a warning message. The `ifelse` function can be called inside of the call to `sqrt` in order to suppress the associated warning.

```
> sqrt(ifelse(x >= 0, x, NaN))
[1]      NaN 0.000000 1.000000 1.414214
```

This produces an identical result, but without the warning message.

As a fifth and final example, the `ifelse` function can be used in writing functions. Let's say we want a function named `my.sign` that accepts an object consisting of numerical elements as a parameter and returns an object of the same size with negative elements replaced by −1, positive elements replaced by 1, and elements containing 0 left in place. First, check to see if an object named `my.sign` exists.

```
> exists("my.sign")        # does the object named my.sign exist?
[1] FALSE
```

It does not, so the object name `my.sign` is available. The `my.sign` function uses embedded `ifelse` calls to achieve its purpose.

```
> my.sign = function(x) ifelse(x > 0, 1, ifelse(x == 0, 0, -1))
```

Now to test the function to see if it works. Begin with a vector as an argument.

```
> x = -1:2                  # x is a vector with elements -1, 0, 1, 2
> x                         # display x
[1] -1  0  1  2
> my.sign(x)                # apply the my.sign function to x
[1] -1  0  1  1
```

It behaves appropriately for this particular x. Now try a matrix as an argument.

```
> y = matrix(-2:3, 2, 3)    # y is a 2 x 3 matrix with integer elements
> y                         # display y
     [,1] [,2] [,3]
[1,]   -2    0    2
[2,]   -1    1    3
> my.sign(y)                # apply the my.sign function to y
     [,1] [,2] [,3]
[1,]   -1    0    1
[2,]   -1    1    1
```

The my.sign function returns a matrix with the same dimensions, but elements replaced as specified. The my.sign function encompasses the capability of the built-in sign function.

This concludes the discussion of relational operators. The table given in this chapter lists the six relational operators >, >=, <, <=, ==, and != and places them in their precedence hierarchy among other operators. The next chapter takes up a topic that we have already encountered—coercion—and moves it from automatic coercion to coercion by design.

Exercises

13.1 Let x be a vector containing numerical elements, each of which is a positive integer. Write a single line of R code that replaces each element that is a perfect square with zero.

13.2 What is returned by the following R commands?

```
> month.len = c(31, 28, 31, 30, 31, 30, 31, 31, 30, 31, 30, 31)
> month.abb[month.len < 30]
```

13.3 What is returned by the following R commands?

```
> x = seq(1, 9, length.out = 5)
> y = -1:3
> x[x <= y ^ 2]
```

13.4 Suppose that x is a vector of numeric elements. Write R commands that create a vector y of character elements that assume the character strings "positive", "zero", or "negative" associated with the corresponding values of x. For example, the y vector associated with x = c(3, 5, 0, -7) is y = c("positive", "positive", "zero", "negative").

13.5 Let x be a vector that consists of numeric elements. Write a single R command to find the mean of the positive elements of x.

13.6 Let x be a vector that consists of numeric elements. Write a single R command that returns a vector containing the subscripts of the positive elements of x.

13.7 Write an R function named DoubleTriple with a single argument mx, which is a matrix that consists of integer-valued elements. This function should return a matrix with the same dimensions as mx, but with odd-valued elements in mx doubled and even-valued elements in mx tripled.

13.8 What is returned by the following R commands?

```
> A = matrix(1:15, nrow = 3)
> mean(A[1:2, 3:4] > 10)
```

Chapter 14

Coercion

The topic of coercion was first encountered in the context of automatic coercion in Chapter 11 when numeric values were automatically coerced to character strings. Subsequently, we have seen logical values coerced to 0's and 1's when certain functions, such as mean or sum, are applied to an object whose elements are logical values. This chapter could have been titled "explicit coercion" in order to signify that explicit steps can be taken to coerce the elements of an object. The two topics considered in this chapter are (a) the is and as family of functions, and (b) coercing elements.

14.1 The is and as families of functions

The is function is used to test whether the elements of an object are of a particular data type. The as function is used to explicitly coerce the elements of an object to be of a particular data type. The six data types ordered by the amount of information that they contain are:

- NULL

- logical

- integer

- numeric

- complex

- character

The numeric data type is also known as double. The is and as functions can be followed by a period, and then the question (for is) or coercion (for as) taking place. The first illustration asks whether 5 is numeric.

```
> is.numeric(5)        # is 5 numeric?
[1] TRUE
```

It is. Now for a trick question. Is 5 an integer?

```
> is.integer(5)        # is 5 an integer?
[1] FALSE
```

The answer is no. If you want 5 to be in the `integer` data type, it must be input as `5L` or be coerced by the `as.integer` function.

```
> as.integer(5)          # coerce 5 to be an integer
[1] 5
```

The previous three commands could have been executed using the `is` and `as` functions with the commands `is(5, "numeric")`, `is(5, "integer")`, and `as(5, "integer")`. The number 5 as an integer and the number 5 as a numeric look identical when displayed, but these two values are stored differently internally in R. Recall that elements stored as integers can be defined by appending an upper-case `L` as in

```
> is.integer(c(2L:7L))   # is this a vector of integers?
[1] TRUE
```

Next, check to see whether 5 is a character:

```
> is.character(5)        # is 5 character?
[1] FALSE
```

Nope. It can be forced to be a character with the `as.character` function:

```
> as.character(5)        # coerce 5 to be character
[1] "5"
```

The quotes around the 5 indicate that the numeric value 5 has been converted to a character. To check and see whether $5 + 12i$ is a complex number, use the `is.complex` function

```
> is.complex(5 + 12i)    # is 5 + 12i complex?
[1] TRUE
```

The data structures that have been introduced thus far—vectors, matrices, and arrays—are required to have elements of the same data type. Objects of this nature are known as "atomic." The `is.atomic` function tests to see whether an object is atomic.

```
> is.atomic(2:7)         # is this vector atomic?
[1] TRUE
```

Non-atomic data structures, namely lists and data frames, are introduced in the next two chapters.

14.2   Coercing elements

The `as` function is useful for coercing the elements of an object on your terms, as opposed to automatic coercion over which you have no control. As an illustration, consider finding $\sqrt{-1}$ with the R command

```
> sqrt(-1)               # square root of -1
[1] NaN
Warning message:
In sqrt(-1) : NaNs produced
```

R displays `NaN` (Not a Number) to indicate that the `sqrt` function will not accept negative arguments. The -1 can first be forced to be a complex number with the `as.complex` function before the square root is taken.

```
> sqrt(as.complex(-1))    # square root of -1 + 0i
[1] 0+1i
```

This returns *i* because $\sqrt{-1} = i$.

There is another set of functions named logical, integer, numeric, complex, and character, each with an integer argument, that creates a vector with elements of the associated data type. The default elements for each of the vectors created by these functions are FALSE for logical, 0 for integer, 0 for numeric, 0+0i for complex, and the empty character string "" for character. For example, to create a vector of length five that contains logical elements that all default to FALSE, type

```
> x = logical(5)         # establish x as a vector of 5 logical elements
> x                      # display x
[1] FALSE FALSE FALSE FALSE FALSE
```

The question of whether the vector x consists of logical elements can be tested with either the mode function or the is.logical function, for example,

```
> is.logical(x)          # are the elements of x logicals?
[1] TRUE
```

The elements of x, which are currently all FALSE, can be coerced to be numeric elements with the as.numeric function, which converts all FALSE values to 0:

```
> as.numeric(x)          # coerce x to be numeric
[1] 0 0 0 0 0
> x                      # display x
[1] FALSE FALSE FALSE FALSE FALSE
```

Finally, there is an is.na function that tests for whether an element assumes the value NA. The example below illustrates a call to is.na with an argument y, which is a vector of numeric values containing a single NA.

```
> y = c(1, 2, NA, 4, 5)  # a missing value (Not Available)
> y                      # display y
[1]  1  2 NA  4  5
> is.na(y)               # are there NAs in y?
[1] FALSE FALSE  TRUE FALSE FALSE
```

Subscripting can be used to extract the elements in y that do not contain NA:

```
> z = y[!is.na(y)]       # assign z to y with missing values removed
> z                      # display z
[1] 1 2 4 5
```

This concludes the discussion of coercion, more specifically explicit coercion. The table below summarizes the functions described in this chapter.

function	description
is	are the elements of an object of a particular data type?
as	coerce the elements of an object to be a particular data type

The `is` and `as` function names can be appended with a period, followed by, for example, `null`, `logical`, `integer`, `numeric`, `complex`, or `character`. In addition, the `is` function name can be appended with a period followed by `na` or `atomic` to test for missing values or whether the object is atomic.

The next chapter introduces a new data structure that extends your options beyond just vectors, matrices, and arrays. Lists are introduced as the first "non-atomic" data structure to allow mixed data types. For example, a list can contain `numeric`, `logical`, and `character` elements simultaneously.

Exercises

14.1 Write an R function named `Str2Num` which accepts a single argument which is a character vector whose elements are single digits. The function should convert this vector of characters to a numeric value. Test your function with the R command

```
> Str2Num(c("3", "6", "5"))
```

which should return

```
[1] 365
```

14.2 What is returned by the following R command?

```
> is.character(5 - 3i)
```

14.3 What is returned by the following R commands?

```
> x = 3 + 4i
> as.integer(x * Conj(x))
```

14.4 Write an R function named `benford` (after Benford's Law) that returns the leading digit of its single numeric argument. The leading digit of 365 is 3; the leading digit of 0.0243 is 2.

14.5 Guess the effect of automatic coercion in the following R commands.

```
> c(0, TRUE)
> c(2, FALSE)
> c(2L, 5)
> c(3L, 4.4)
> c(2.3, NA)
> c(3, "R")
> c(FALSE, 9L, 4.4, "S")
```

Chapter 15

Lists

Thus far, we have encountered three data structures: vectors, matrices, and arrays. An object is considered to be "atomic" if its elements are of a single data type. Vectors, matrices, and arrays, as they have been presented thus far, are atomic data structures for objects. This chapter introduces a new type of data structure known as a *list*, which is an ordered collection of objects known as "components." A list can be used to combine atomic objects with possibly different data types. Any of the data types considered thus far, namely logical, integer, numeric, complex, or character, can be used in forming a list. The topics considered in this chapter are (a) creating a list, (b) extracting components and elements of a list, and (c) functions that operate on lists.

15.1   Creating a list

The `list` function is used to create a list. The syntax is

$$\texttt{list(name1 = object1, name2 = object2, ...)}$$

where the names of the arguments name1, name2, etc. are optional. The names play the same role as they did in Chapter 11. Each of the objects that comprise the list is known as a *component*.

The first example of a list named list1 consists of seven components: the built-in constant pi, a vector containing the first three positive integers, the character string "A quick brown fox," the complex number $3 - 4i$, a three-element vector of the logical values T, F, and F, a one-element vector with the logical value TRUE, and a 2×2 matrix consisting of elements that are all equal to 7. Truly a diverse set of objects. The eclectic components of list1 are displayed by typing its name.

```
> list1 = list(pi, 1:3, "A quick brown fox", 3 - 4i, c(T, F, F), TRUE,
+             matrix(7, 2, 2))
> list1                   # display list1
[[1]]
[1] 3.141593

[[2]]
[1] 1 2 3

[[3]]
[1] "A quick brown fox"
```

```
[[4]]
[1] 3-4i

[[5]]
[1]  TRUE FALSE FALSE

[[6]]
[1] TRUE

[[7]]
     [,1] [,2]
[1,]   7    7
[2,]   7    7
```

When the list named list1 is displayed, each component begins with the heading [[1]], [[2]], etc. Each of the elements of each component has the usual labeling that is familiar from the previous chapters.

A second list named list2 with three named components (the first eight positive integers, the month abbreviations, and the complex number $3 + 4i$) is created with

```
> list2 = list(x = 1:8, y = month.abb, zcomplex = 3 + 4i)
> list2                 # display list2
$x
[1] 1 2 3 4 5 6 7 8

$y
 [1] "Jan" "Feb" "Mar" "Apr" "May" "Jun" "Jul" "Aug" "Sep" "Oct" "Nov" "Dec"

$zcomplex
[1] 3+4i
```

Since the three components have been named x, y, and zcomplex, R places the labels $x $y and $zcomplex before each component when list2 is displayed.

The two lists named list1 and list2 will be used for illustrations in the next two sections.

15.2 Extracting elements of a list

The designers of R had to concoct a way to access a component of a list. They decided to use double brackets to access a component. For example, to access the fifth component of the list named list1, type

```
> list1[[5]]            # display the fifth component
[1]  TRUE FALSE FALSE
```

To access the third element of the fifth component of list1, type

```
> list1[[5]][3]         # display the third element of the fifth component
[1] FALSE
```

The example involving `list1` defaulted the names of the components. This meant that the components and their associated elements could only be accessed by *number*, not by *name*. The next paragraph considers a list with named components.

The $ extractor operator can be used to extract a named component of a list. For example,

```
> list2$x              # display the component named x
[1] 1 2 3 4 5 6 7 8
```

extracts the component of `list2` named x. Likewise, obtaining the fourth element of the component named y in the list named `list2` can be done in two equivalent fashions, by using the name and number approach:

```
> list2$y[4]           # display the fourth element of the component named y
[1] "Apr"
> list2[[2]][4]        # display the fourth element of the second component
[1] "Apr"
```

A few keystrokes can be saved using the $ in that it only needs enough characters in the component name to identify it. Two examples of using the component operator to extract the component named `zcomplex` from the list named `list2` are

```
> list2$zcomplex       # display the component named zcomplex
[1] 3+4i
> list2$zcom           # display the component named zcomplex
[1] 3+4i
```

This partial matching is supported by the $ operator; it is not supported in all other settings. Two other equivalent ways of extracting this third component are

```
> list2[[3]]           # display the third component (number list components)
[1] 3+4i
> list2[["zcomplex"]]  # display the component named zcomplex
[1] 3+4i
```

So components and elements in a list (or any other data structure encountered thus far) can be accessed by a numeric subscript, a logical vector, or a character string denoting its name.

15.3   Functions that operate on lists

There are several functions that can be applied to lists. The first is the `names` function, which returns the names associated with a list as a vector of character strings.

```
> names(list2)         # an attribute of list2
[1] "x"         "y"         "zcomplex"
```

The `names` function is appropriate for vectors and lists. This function generalizes to the `rownames` and `colnames` functions for matrices and data frames (the data frame data structure is introduced in the next chapter). This further generalizes to the `dimnames` function for arrays. Not surprisingly, the `class` function returns the type of data structure as a list:

```
> class(list2)         # an attribute of list2
[1] "list"
```

The length function returns a count of the number of components in a list.

```
> length(list2)          # an attribute of list2
[1] 3
```

More generally, the attributes function can be used to list the attributes of an object.

```
> attributes(list2)      # attributes of list2
$names
[1] "x"          "y"          "zcomplex"
```

Since the list data structure allows for components of differing data types, the is.atomic function returns FALSE when list2 is passed as an argument.

```
> is.atomic(list2)       # is list2 atomic?
[1] FALSE
```

Many of the R functions that have been introduced previously can be applied to lists. For example, the two lists created in this chapter can be pasted together with c(list1, list2). Lists are recursive in the sense that the components of a list are allowed to be lists themselves.

The unlist function can be used to convert a list to a vector. Automatic coercion is used to force all of the elements of the vector to be of the same data type, which is a requirement for vectors because they are an atomic data structure.

```
> unlist(list2)          # convert list2 to a vector
     x1       x2       x3       x4       x5       x6       x7       x8
    "1"      "2"      "3"      "4"      "5"      "6"      "7"      "8"
     y1       y2       y3       y4       y5       y6       y7       y8
  "Jan"    "Feb"    "Mar"    "Apr"    "May"    "Jun"    "Jul"    "Aug"
     y9      y10      y11      y12 zcomplex
  "Sep"    "Oct"    "Nov"    "Dec"   "3+4i"
```

Notice how R handles the names associated with list2 in the conversion from a list to a vector. A consecutive integer is appended to the name that is inherited from the original list data structure.

This concludes the introduction to lists. The table below summarizes the operators and functions described in this chapter.

operator or function	description
list	create a list
$	extract a component from a list
attributes	display the attributes of an object
unlist	convert a list to a vector

In addition to the $ operator, double brackets, that is [[ ]], can be used to extract components from a list. The list as a data structure is analogous to the vector. The data types must be identical in the elements of a vector; the data types can differ in a list. In other words, vectors are atomic; lists are non-atomic. Both are one-dimensional data structures.

Lists are the first of the two non-atomic data structures in R. Lists lead naturally to the second type of non-atomic data structure, namely data frames, that are introduced in the next chapter. Data sets often fit naturally into the framework of a data frame.

Exercises

15.1 What is returned by the following R commands?

```
> my.list = list(x = 7:2, y = letters)
> my.list$y[4]
```

15.2 Write a single R command that assigns a list named x to the following three components: the character string "gnu"; a five-element vector containing the integers 3, 4, 5, 6, 7; and a 12-element vector containing the abbreviations of the names of the months. Write a second R command that extracts the fourth element of the third component.

15.3 All of the varieties of objects encountered thus far may have names attached to their elements. Type the following R commands into an R session.

```
> x = 1:3
> names(x) = c("first", "second", "third")
> x
> y = c(first = 1, second = 2, third = 3)
> y
> x == y
> z = c(first = 1, second = 2, 3)
> z
> z == x
> x == z
```

What do you conclude about attaching names to some elements but not to others?

Chapter 16

Data Frames

A distinctive characteristic of vectors, matrices, and arrays is that all of their elements are of the same data type, that is, these data structures are atomic. Many statistical experiments generate data sets with data values of differing types, for example, numeric for a patient's cholesterol level, character for a patient's gender, and logical to record the presence or absence of a particular disease for a patient. A data structure that can store data of differing modes is needed to accommodate data sets of this type. A *data frame*, which is the new data structure introduced in this chapter, carries the best features of a matrix and a list. The format of a data frame is similar to that of a matrix, but the columns of a data frame can have different modes.

A data frame is an ideal data structure for storing and manipulating statistical data. The rows in a data frame tend to be "observational units," such as people, cars, etc. The columns in a data frame tend to be values collected on the observational units such as eye color, miles per gallon, etc. An entry in a data frame is known as a "cell."

The three topics considered in this chapter are (a) creating a data frame, (b) functions that can be applied to a data frame, and (c) extracting elements of a data frame.

16.1   Creating a data frame

Data frames can be created with the data.frame function. The syntax for the data.frame function is

```
data.frame(name1 = col1, name2 = col2, ..., row.names = NULL, ...)
```

where the column names name1, name2, etc. are optional parts of the arguments. The data.frame function is illustrated below for creating a data frame that consists of five rows and four columns. The first column is a set of five capital letters; the second column contains the numbers $5, 6, 7, 8, 9$; the third column contains the complex numbers $2+6i, 3+5i, 4+4i, 5+3i, 6+2i$; the fourth column contains the logical values TRUE, FALSE, TRUE, FALSE, TRUE.

```
> char = LETTERS[18:22]                   # vector of 5 characters
> numb = 5:9                              # vector of 5 numeric values
> comp = complex(5, 2:6, 6:2)            # vector of 5 complex numbers
> bool = c(TRUE, FALSE, TRUE, FALSE, TRUE)  # vector of 5 logical values
> d = data.frame(char, numb, comp, bool)  # d is a data frame
> d                                       # display d
```

```
  char numb comp  bool
1   R    5 2+6i  TRUE
2   S    6 3+5i FALSE
3   T    7 4+4i  TRUE
4   U    8 5+3i FALSE
5   V    9 6+2i  TRUE
```

The data frame d that is displayed has column names, which are inherited as the names of the objects that formed the data frame. These column headings are known as the "header." Since the row.names argument in the call to data.frame was defaulted, there are no row names, and R simply uses consecutive integers to identify the rows when displaying d.

16.2   Functions that operate on data frames

R has a number of functions that can be applied to data frames. Some of these functions can also be applied to matrices. The nrow and ncol functions return the number of rows and the number of columns of a data frame, respectively.

```
> nrow(d)                           # number of rows
[1] 5
> ncol(d)                           # number of columns
[1] 4
```

The data frame d has five rows and four columns. The head function displays the first few rows of a data frame—which can be helpful in getting a compact view of the structure of a large data frame.

```
> head(d)                           # display header
  char numb comp  bool
1   R    5 2+6i  TRUE
2   S    6 3+5i FALSE
3   T    7 4+4i  TRUE
4   U    8 5+3i FALSE
5   V    9 6+2i  TRUE
```

Since this data frame is so small, the entire data frame gets displayed. Calling head(d, 3), for example, displays the first three rows of d. The head function can also be applied to vectors, matrices, and arrays. There is also a tail function that displays the last few rows of a data frame. The str function displays the structure of a data frame (or any other arbitrary R object).

```
> str(d)                            # display structure of d
'data.frame':   5 obs. of  4 variables:
 $ char: Factor w/ 5 levels "R","S","T","U",..: 1 2 3 4 5
 $ numb: int  5 6 7 8 9
 $ comp: cplx  2+6i 3+5i 4+4i ...
 $ bool: logi  TRUE FALSE TRUE FALSE TRUE
```

The response shows that d is a data frame consisting of five observations of four variables, which are named char, numb, comp, and bool. The first few values of the elements in each of the columns are displayed. The summary function gives a summary of the contents of a data frame (or any other arbitrary object).

```
> summary(d)                            # display summary of d
 char        numb        comp              bool
 R:1    Min.   :5    Length:5        Mode :logical
 S:1    1st Qu.:6    Class :complex  FALSE:2
 T:1    Median :7    Mode  :complex  TRUE :3
 U:1    Mean   :7                    NA's :0
 V:1    3rd Qu.:8
        Max.   :9
```

The summary function treats each column of d individually based on its mode as it displays its summary report. Since the elements in a data frame can be of varying type, the is.atomic function returns FALSE when d is passed as an argument.

```
> is.atomic(d)                          # is d atomic?
[1] FALSE
```

16.3   Extracting elements of a data frame

The elements that reside in the cells of a data frame can be accessed using subscripting in a similar fashion to matrices and lists. For example,

```
> d[1, 1]                               # upper-left cell
[1] R
Levels: R S T U V
```

extracts the upper-left cell, that is, the [1, 1] cell, of d. In addition to displaying the contents of the upper-left cell, R displays the various levels of variables in the first column. The second row of the data frame d can be extracted with

```
> d[2, ]                                # second row
  char numb comp  bool
2    S    6 3+5i FALSE
```

which displays the header, followed by the second row of d. Since the columns of the data frame d have column names, they can be referred to by number or by name. The five R commands below are five different ways of extracting the third column of d as a vector.

```
> d[[3]]                                # third column
[1] 2+6i 3+5i 4+4i 5+3i 6+2i
> d[["comp"]]                           # third column
[1] 2+6i 3+5i 4+4i 5+3i 6+2i
> d[ , 3]                               # third column
[1] 2+6i 3+5i 4+4i 5+3i 6+2i
> d[ , "comp"]                          # third column
[1] 2+6i 3+5i 4+4i 5+3i 6+2i
> d$comp                                # third column
[1] 2+6i 3+5i 4+4i 5+3i 6+2i
```

When a single subscript is passed to a data frame, it is assumed to be a column. The column (or columns) of interest are returned as a data frame, as illustrated in the two examples below.

```
> d[3]                                    # third column
  comp
1 2+6i
2 3+5i
3 4+4i
4 5+3i
5 6+2i
> d["comp"]                               # third column
  comp
1 2+6i
2 3+5i
3 4+4i
4 5+3i
5 6+2i
```

A portion of a data frame consisting of multiple columns can be accessed by using the c function within the braces used for the subscripts. So to extract the comp and bool columns of d use

```
> d[c("comp", "bool")]                    # third and fourth columns
  comp  bool
1 2+6i  TRUE
2 3+5i FALSE
3 4+4i  TRUE
4 5+3i FALSE
5 6+2i  TRUE
```

R does not mind mixing numbers and names when accessing elements of a data frame. For example, the element in the [5, 4] cell of d can be extracted with

```
> d[5, "bool"]                            # the [5, 4] cell
[1] TRUE
```

Likewise, the sum of the elements in the [3, 2] and [1, 4] cells of d is

```
> d[3, "numb"] + d[1, "bool"]             # sum of [3, 2] and [1, 4] cells
[1] 8
```

Automatic coercion was used to coerce the TRUE to 1 for the addition operation. The R command

```
> d$bool == TRUE                          # relational operator
[1]  TRUE FALSE  TRUE FALSE  TRUE
```

returns a logical vector associated with the bool column of d. In addition to having columns that might be of interest, it is also possible that there might be rows that are of interest. If this vector is used as a row subscript in d, the rows associated with the bool column being TRUE are extracted.

```
> d[d$bool == TRUE, ]                     # rows with TRUE in fourth column
  char numb comp bool
1    R    5 2+6i TRUE
3    T    7 4+4i TRUE
5    V    9 6+2i TRUE
```

The previous command was inefficient in that the == TRUE portion of the command was redundant. The proper way to extract the rows associated with the bool column being TRUE is

```
> d[d$bool, ]                          # rows with TRUE in fourth column
  char numb comp bool
1    R    5 2+6i TRUE
3    T    7 4+4i TRUE
5    V    9 6+2i TRUE
```

Automatic coercion is used when multiplying the third and fourth columns of d. The TRUE elements in the fourth column are coerced to 1; the FALSE elements in the fourth column are coerced to 0.

```
> d[ , 3] * d[ , 4]                    # automatic coercion
[1] 2+6i 0+0i 4+4i 0+0i 6+2i
```

In order to extract the elements of the third column of d associated with elements in the fourth column of d that are TRUE, use the R command

```
> d[d[ , 4], 3]                        # logical indexing
[1] 2+6i 4+4i 6+2i
```

Finally, as an illustration of a data frame that has row names as well as column names, a data frame named charity can be created in the following fashion.

```
> charity = data.frame(cash = 1:3, check = 2:4, credit = 3:5,
+           row.names = c("Harpo", "Chico", "Groucho"))
> charity                              # display charity
        cash check credit
Harpo      1     2      3
Chico      2     3      4
Groucho    3     4      5
```

Oftentimes it is useful to append a new column to a data frame. This can be done with the transform function, which can be applied to objects of all types. The first argument is the object to be transformed, in this case charity; the second argument is the new column to be added, in this case total.

```
> charity2 = transform(charity, total = cash + check + credit)
> charity2                             # display charity2
        cash check credit total
Harpo      1     2      3     6
Chico      2     3      4     9
Groucho    3     4      5    12
```

The subset function is often a more efficient and more intuitive way to extract particular parts of an object than using subscripts. The first argument is the object to subset, in this case charity2; the second argument is a logical condition indicating which rows to keep, in this case credit > 3; the third argument select is an expression that indicates which columns to keep, in this case the cash and total columns.

```
> subset(charity2, credit > 3, select = c(cash, total))
        cash total
Chico      2     9
Groucho    3    12
```

This produces the same result as the much-less-intuitive command

```
> charity2[2:3, c(1, 4)]
        cash total
Chico      2     9
Groucho    3    12
```

This concludes the brief introduction to the important topic of data frames. The table below summarizes the functions described in this chapter.

function	description
data.frame	create a data frame
head	first part of an object
tail	last part of an object
summary	summary of an object
transform	transform an object
subset	find a subset of an object

The elements of a data frame can be accessed by numeric subscripts, logical subscripts, or character string subscripts using single brackets or double brackets, or by using the $ operator.

We have now encountered five data structures in the R language: vectors, matrices, arrays, lists, and data frames. The table below classifies these data structures by the number of dimensions and the data types of the elements that comprise the object. The column headings in the table, "atomic" and "non-atomic," could have been replaced with "homogeneous" and "nonhomogeneous." Data frames, which were introduced in this chapter, are a non-atomic analog of matrices.

	atomic	non-atomic
one dimensional	vector	list
two dimensional	matrix	data frame
n dimensional	array	

You might have noticed that the R language took considerable time to download. This is because R is a very large language. One of the reasons that R is so big is the data sets that are built into the language. These built-in data sets, which are stored using one of the five data structures given in the table above, are investigated in the next chapter. The data sets are a reminder of the roots of R, which lie in the statistical analysis of data.

Exercises

16.1   What is returned by the following R commands? (Waking hours from wikipedia.)

```
> creatures = c("dog", "cat", "armadillo", "human")
> friendly = c(TRUE, TRUE, FALSE, TRUE)
> diet = c("cats", "mice", "termites", "Twinkies(tm)")
> waking.hours = c(13.9, 11.5, 5.9, 16.0)
> creature.data = data.frame(friendly, diet, waking.hours,
+                 row.names = creatures)
> creatures[creature.data$waking.hours < 12 & !creature.data$friendly]
```

16.2   Write a single R command that alphabetizes the rows of the data frame `creature.data` from Exercise 16.1 by creature name.

16.3   Use the R `subset` function to create a data frame consisting of just the creature name and diet associated with friendly creatures who are awake more than 12 hours a day from the data frame `creature.data` from Exercise 16.1.

16.4   Consider the data frame `creature.data` from Exercise 16.1.

    (a) Extract the waking hours for a dog using two different R commands.

    (b) Extract the waking hours for all creatures using two different R commands.

    (c) Create a data frame that consists only of the rows for dogs and armadillos using two different R commands.

    (d) Create a data frame that consists only of friendly creatures.

16.5   Consider a data frame named `a` with 4 rows and 3 columns populated with positive integers and -1, where -1 denotes a missing value. Write an R command that replaces each -1 with `NA`.

16.6   Create the objects `v`, `m`, `a`, `l`, and `d` as a vector, matrix, array, list, and data frame. Apply the functions `class`, `typeof`, and `mode` to each of the objects and summarize the results in a table.

16.7   Create a data frame named `w` that consists of the following three named columns:

    • `x`, the first four positive integers,

    • `y`, the abbreviations of the first four months,

    • `z`, the first names of the Beatles.

Remove the second column of `w` in the following two fashions:

    • set `w$y` to `NULL`, that is, `w$y = NULL`,

    • subset the columns to keep, that is `w[c("x", "z")]`.

Show that the first technique alters the data frame `w` but the second technique does not alter the data frame `w`.

Chapter 17

Built-In Data Sets

R has dozens of data sets that are built into the base language. This chapter introduces these data sets and performs some elementary operations on the associated data values. The topics discussed in this chapter are (a) the iris data set, (b) extracting elements of a data set, and (c) a taxonomy of some built-in data sets.

17.1   The iris data set

One of the built-in data sets in R is named iris. The iris data set contains five measurements (Sepal.Length, Sepal.Width, Petal.Length, Petal.Width, all in cm, and Species) on $n = 150$ flowers. The three species of flowers considered were 50 setosa, 50 versicolor, and 50 virginica. Typing iris at the R command prompt reveals that iris is a data frame (only the data values for the first three flowers and last three flowers are shown here for brevity):

```
> iris                          # built-in data set
     Sepal.Length Sepal.Width Petal.Length Petal.Width   Species
1             5.1         3.5          1.4         0.2    setosa
2             4.9         3.0          1.4         0.2    setosa
3             4.7         3.2          1.3         0.2    setosa
...
148           6.5         3.0          5.2         2.0 virginica
149           6.2         3.4          5.4         2.3 virginica
150           5.9         3.0          5.1         1.8 virginica
```

The mode, class, length, and dim functions operate on iris as they have previously.

```
> mode(iris)                 # mode of iris
[1] "list"
> class(iris)                # class of iris
[1] "data.frame"
> length(iris)               # length of iris
[1] 5
> dim(iris)                  # dimensions of iris
[1] 150    5
```

The head function displays the header and first few rows of the iris data frame.

```
> head(iris)                    # display first few rows of iris
  Sepal.Length Sepal.Width Petal.Length Petal.Width Species
1          5.1         3.5          1.4         0.2  setosa
2          4.9         3.0          1.4         0.2  setosa
3          4.7         3.2          1.3         0.2  setosa
4          4.6         3.1          1.5         0.2  setosa
5          5.0         3.6          1.4         0.2  setosa
6          5.4         3.9          1.7         0.4  setosa
```

The tail function displays the header and the last few rows of a data frame. The str function reveals the structure of the iris data frame.

```
> str(iris)                     # display structure of iris
'data.frame':   150 obs. of  5 variables:
 $ Sepal.Length: num  5.1 4.9 4.7 4.6 5 5.4 4.6 5 4.4 4.9 ...
 $ Sepal.Width : num  3.5 3 3.2 3.1 3.6 3.9 3.4 3.4 2.9 3.1 ...
 $ Petal.Length: num  1.4 1.4 1.3 1.5 1.4 1.7 1.4 1.5 1.4 1.5 ...
 $ Petal.Width : num  0.2 0.2 0.2 0.2 0.2 0.4 0.3 0.2 0.2 0.1 ...
 $ Species     : Factor w/ 3 levels "setosa","versicolor",..: 1 1 1 1 1 1 1 ...
```

The first four columns of the data frame contain numeric values; the fifth column contains a "factor" (see Section 11.6) that can assume one of three "levels" (namely, setosa, versicolor, and virginica). The summary function reveals summary information about the iris data frame.

```
> summary(iris)                 # display summary of iris
  Sepal.Length    Sepal.Width     Petal.Length    Petal.Width          Species
 Min.   :4.300   Min.   :2.000   Min.   :1.000   Min.   :0.100   setosa    :50
 1st Qu.:5.100   1st Qu.:2.800   1st Qu.:1.600   1st Qu.:0.300   versicolor:50
 Median :5.800   Median :3.000   Median :4.350   Median :1.300   virginica :50
 Mean   :5.843   Mean   :3.057   Mean   :3.758   Mean   :1.199
 3rd Qu.:6.400   3rd Qu.:3.300   3rd Qu.:5.100   3rd Qu.:1.800
 Max.   :7.900   Max.   :4.400   Max.   :6.900   Max.   :2.500
```

One might expect that the fourth column of iris, which is named Petal.Width, might be available by just typing its name

```
> Petal.Width                   # display Petal.Width
Error: object 'Petal.Width' not found
```

but this is clearly not the case. The attach function is designed to overcome this issue. By first attaching the iris data set using the attach function, R places the five columns of the data frame onto the search path. (The detach function undoes this operation.) The objects in the iris data frame can then be accessed directly—there is no longer a need to prefix the name of the data frame. So typing Petal.Width now reveals the widths of the petals (in cm) as a vector of 150 numeric elements.

```
> attach(iris)                  # attach the iris data set
> Petal.Width                   # display Petal.Width
  [1] 0.2 0.2 0.2 0.2 0.2 0.4 0.3 0.2 0.2 0.1 0.2 0.2 0.1 0.1 0.2 0.4 0.4 0.3
```

```
 [19] 0.3 0.3 0.2 0.4 0.2 0.5 0.2 0.2 0.4 0.2 0.2 0.2 0.2 0.4 0.1 0.2 0.2 0.2
 [37] 0.2 0.1 0.2 0.2 0.3 0.3 0.2 0.6 0.4 0.3 0.2 0.2 0.2 0.2 1.4 1.5 1.5 1.3
 [55] 1.5 1.3 1.6 1.0 1.3 1.4 1.0 1.5 1.0 1.4 1.3 1.4 1.5 1.0 1.5 1.1 1.8 1.3
 [73] 1.5 1.2 1.3 1.4 1.4 1.7 1.5 1.0 1.1 1.0 1.2 1.6 1.5 1.6 1.5 1.3 1.3 1.3
 [91] 1.2 1.4 1.2 1.0 1.3 1.2 1.3 1.3 1.1 1.3 2.5 1.9 2.1 1.8 2.2 2.1 1.7 1.8
[109] 1.8 2.5 2.0 1.9 2.1 2.0 2.4 2.3 1.8 2.2 2.3 1.5 2.3 2.0 2.0 1.8 2.1 1.8
[127] 1.8 1.8 2.1 1.6 1.9 2.0 2.2 1.5 1.4 2.3 2.4 1.8 1.8 2.1 2.4 2.3 1.9 2.3
[145] 2.5 2.3 1.9 2.0 2.3 1.8
```

Using `attach` in this fashion can introduce unintended errors. Setting `Petal.Width[3]` to 7.7, for example, alters the third element of the vector `Petal.Width`, but does not alter the corresponding value in the `iris` data frame. Finally, the `help` function can be applied to built-in data sets. So typing

```
> help(iris)              # further information on the iris data set
```

(lengthy output suppressed) reveals more information about the data values, the source of the data values, and some interesting examples associated with `iris`.

17.2   Extracting elements of a data set

There are many data sets beyond just `iris` that are built into the base package of R. Typing

```
> library(help = "datasets")          # list names of data sets
```

reveals their names and a short description. The output has been suppressed for brevity. One of these data sets is the data frame `state.x77`, which contains values of eight variables collected on the 50 United States. The eight variables collected on each state are: `Population`, the population estimate as of July 1, 1975; `Income`, the per capita income in 1974; `Illiteracy`, the illiteracy in 1970 as a percent of the population; `Life Exp`, the life expectancy in years from 1969–1971; `Murder`, the murder and non-negligent manslaughter rate per 100,000 residents in 1976; `HS Grad`, the percent of high-school graduates in 1970; `Frost`, the mean number of days with minimum temperature below freezing (1931–1960) in the state capital or a large city; and `Area`, the land area in square miles. This section provides some elementary examples of how the `state.x77` data set can be manipulated. As before, typing the name of the data set reveals its contents. Only the header, the first three rows, and the last three rows are shown for brevity.

```
> state.x77                      # built-in data set
               Population Income Illiteracy Life Exp Murder HS Grad Frost    Area
Alabama              3615   3624        2.1    69.05   15.1    41.3    20   50708
Alaska                365   6315        1.5    69.31   11.3    66.7   152  566432
Arizona              2212   4530        1.8    70.55    7.8    58.1    15  113417
...
West Virginia        1799   3617        1.4    69.48    6.7    41.6   100   24070
Wisconsin            4589   4468        0.7    72.48    3.0    54.5   149   54464
Wyoming               376   4566        0.6    70.29    6.9    62.9   173   97203
```

The eighth row of the `state.x77` data frame, which corresponds to the state of Delaware, can be extracted by

```
> state.x77[8, ]                        # row 8:  Delaware
Population   Income Illiteracy   Life Exp   Murder   HS Grad    Frost      Area
   579.00  4809.00      0.90      70.06     6.20     54.60    103.00   1982.00
```

The eighth column of the `state.x77` data frame, which corresponds to the area in square miles, can be extracted by

```
> state.x77[, 8]                        # column 8:   area in square miles
        Alabama         Alaska         Arizona        Arkansas      California
          50708         566432          113417           51945          156361
       Colorado    Connecticut        Delaware         Florida         Georgia
         103766           4862            1982           54090           58073
         Hawaii          Idaho        Illinois         Indiana            Iowa
           6425          82677           55748           36097           55941
         Kansas       Kentucky       Louisiana           Maine        Maryland
          81787          39650           44930           30920            9891
  Massachusetts       Michigan       Minnesota     Mississippi        Missouri
           7826          56817           79289           47296           68995
        Montana       Nebraska          Nevada   New Hampshire      New Jersey
         145587          76483          109889            9027            7521
     New Mexico       New York  North Carolina    North Dakota            Ohio
         121412          47831           48798           69273           40975
       Oklahoma         Oregon    Pennsylvania    Rhode Island  South Carolina
          68782          96184           44966            1049           30225
   South Dakota      Tennessee           Texas            Utah         Vermont
          75955          41328          262134           82096            9267
       Virginia     Washington   West Virginia       Wisconsin         Wyoming
          39780          66570           24070           54464           97203
```

The eighth column is given in the same order that it appeared in the data frame `state.x77`, ordered alphabetically by state name. If you would prefer to have the area in square miles ordered from the smallest state (Rhode Island) to the largest state (Alaska), use the `sort` function:

```
> sort(state.x77[, 8])                  # sort by area in square miles
   Rhode Island        Delaware     Connecticut          Hawaii      New Jersey
           1049            1982            4862            6425            7521
  Massachusetts   New Hampshire         Vermont        Maryland   West Virginia
           7826            9027            9267            9891           24070
 South Carolina           Maine         Indiana        Kentucky        Virginia
          30225           30920           36097           39650           39780
           Ohio       Tennessee       Louisiana    Pennsylvania     Mississippi
          40975           41328           44930           44966           47296
       New York  North Carolina         Alabama        Arkansas         Florida
          47831           48798           50708           51945           54090
      Wisconsin        Illinois            Iowa        Michigan         Georgia
          54464           55748           55941           56817           58073
     Washington        Oklahoma        Missouri    North Dakota    South Dakota
          66570           68782           68995           69273           75955
       Nebraska       Minnesota          Kansas            Utah           Idaho
          76483           79289           81787           82096           82677
```

Oregon	Wyoming	Colorado	Nevada	Arizona
96184	97203	103766	109889	113417
New Mexico	Montana	California	Texas	Alaska
121412	145587	156361	262134	566432

In order to shorten subsequent R commands, the illiteracy percentage and the number of days of frost are placed in vectors named `ill` and `frost` with the R commands

```
> ill = state.x77[ , 3]       # ill:  illiteracy (percent of pop.)
> frost = state.x77[ , 7]     # frost:  mean number days below 32
```

Next, the values in the vector `ill` are displayed, which includes the column labels.

```
> ill                              # display ill
```

Alabama	Alaska	Arizona	Arkansas	California
2.1	1.5	1.8	1.9	1.1
Colorado	Connecticut	Delaware	Florida	Georgia
0.7	1.1	0.9	1.3	2.0
Hawaii	Idaho	Illinois	Indiana	Iowa
1.9	0.6	0.9	0.7	0.5
Kansas	Kentucky	Louisiana	Maine	Maryland
0.6	1.6	2.8	0.7	0.9
Massachusetts	Michigan	Minnesota	Mississippi	Missouri
1.1	0.9	0.6	2.4	0.8
Montana	Nebraska	Nevada	New Hampshire	New Jersey
0.6	0.6	0.5	0.7	1.1
New Mexico	New York	North Carolina	North Dakota	Ohio
2.2	1.4	1.8	0.8	0.8
Oklahoma	Oregon	Pennsylvania	Rhode Island	South Carolina
1.1	0.6	1.0	1.3	2.3
South Dakota	Tennessee	Texas	Utah	Vermont
0.5	1.7	2.2	0.6	0.6
Virginia	Washington	West Virginia	Wisconsin	Wyoming
1.4	0.6	1.4	0.7	0.6

Let's say we are interested in illiteracy and frost, sorted by illiteracy. The first step is to define the ordering permutation vector named `xorder` using the `order` function.

```
> xorder = order(ill)              # ordering permutation based on ill
> xorder                           # display xorder
 [1] 15 28 41 12 16 23 26 27 37 44 45 47 50  6 14 19 29 49 25 34 35  8 13 20 22
[26] 38  5  7 21 30 36  9 39 32 46 48  2 17 42  3 33  4 11 10  1 31 43 40 24 18
```

The 15 that appears in the first element of the ordering permutation vector indicates that the 15th state alphabetically (Iowa) had the lowest illiteracy rate (0.5%) in the United States. Likewise, the 18 that appears in the last element of the ordering permutation vector indicates that the 18th state alphabetically (Louisiana) had the highest illiteracy rate (2.8%) in the United States. Next, define a matrix y using the `cbind` function that binds the two columns associated with `ill` and `frost`.

```
> y = cbind(ill[xorder], frost[xorder])   # ill and frost sorted by illiteracy
```

Now y is a 50×2 matrix of illiteracies and number of days of frost, sorted by illiteracy.

Next, write a one-line R function named is.max that returns a vector of logical values indicating the largest element(s) of a vector.

```
> is.max = function(x) x == max(x)      # is.max returns vector of logicals
```

Applying the is.max function to the ill vector to retrieve the state name with the highest illiteracy results in

```
> state.name[is.max(ill)]              # state name(s) with high illiteracy
[1] "Louisiana"
```

Applying the is.max function to the frost vector to retrieve the state abbreviation of the coldest state results in

```
> state.abb[is.max(frost)]             # abbreviation of coldest state
[1] "NV"
```

Most people would not guess that Nevada would have the highest number of days of frost. Next, to list all states, in alphabetical order, with illiteracy rates which are less than 1%, type

```
> ill[ill < 1]                          # states, illiteracies with ill < 1
      Colorado       Delaware          Idaho       Illinois        Indiana
           0.7            0.9            0.6            0.9            0.7
          Iowa         Kansas          Maine       Maryland       Michigan
           0.5            0.6            0.7            0.9            0.9
     Minnesota       Missouri        Montana       Nebraska         Nevada
           0.6            0.8            0.6            0.6            0.5
 New Hampshire   North Dakota           Ohio         Oregon   South Dakota
           0.7            0.8            0.8            0.6            0.5
          Utah        Vermont     Washington      Wisconsin        Wyoming
           0.6            0.6            0.6            0.7            0.6
```

Finally, to list ten coldest states, ordered by the number of days of frost, type

```
> sort(frost)[41:50]                    # ten chilliest states
       Montana      Minnesota          Maine       Colorado        Vermont
           155            160            161            166            168
  South Dakota        Wyoming  New Hampshire   North Dakota         Nevada
           172            173            174            186            188
```

17.3   A taxonomy of some built-in data sets

This final section provides a brief overview of several of the built-in data sets in the base R language, categorized by the type of data set. In all cases, the lengthy output is suppressed because many of the data sets are huge. The reader is encouraged to either type in the name of the data set at the R command prompt or to call the help function to obtain more information about the data set.

We begin with univariate data sets involving a data set of n observations $x_1, x_2, \ldots, x_n$ on a single value. Three representative univariate data sets are

```
> islands       # areas of the 48 landmasses exceeding 10,000 square miles
> precip        # average annual precipitation (inches) for 70 US cities
> rivers        # lengths (miles) of 141 major rivers in North America
```

Oftentimes data comes as (x, y) pairs, as is the case with the bivariate data sets given below.

```
> cars          # speed (mph) and stopping distance (ft) of 50 cars (1920s)
> women         # average heights and weights for 15 US women aged 30-39
> crimtab       # Gosset's heights and left middle finger measurements (cm)
> faithful      # eruption time and waiting time (min) for Old Faithful
> sleep         # effect of two drugs on sleep time relative to a control
> Formaldehyde  # carbohydrate (ml) versus optden (optical density)
```

The last data set on this list, Formaldehyde, shows a strong linear relationship between the data pairs, so a simple linear regression model can be used to describe the relationship between the two variables. More information concerning a simple linear regression model is given in Chapter 26.

Sometimes an experiment is conducted that has a single factor that might influence a response variable. The data set

```
> PlantGrowth    # plant weights classified by 3 levels of a single factor
```

is an example of such a single factor experiment. An example of a data set associated with an experiment that has been conducted with two factors is

```
> Puromycin      # reaction velocity classified by 2 factors (conc and state)
```

A data set associated with three factors is the same data set graphed using the barplot function in the preface to this book is

```
> VADeaths       # Virginia death rates classified by age, sex, and location
```

A data set that is collected over time is known as a *time series*. Many of the built-in data sets in R fall into this category. Examples include

```
> uspop         # US population 1790-1970
> discoveries   # number of "great" discoveries per year, 1860-1959
> AirPassengers # number of international airline passengers, 1949-1960
> JohnsonJohnson # Johnson & Johnson quarterly earnings, 1960-1980
> co2           # atmospheric concentrations of CO2 (ppm), 1959-1997
> presidents    # quarterly approval ratings of US presidents, 1945-1974
> sunspots      # monthly sunspot data, 1749-1983
```

Other examples of built-in times series data sets in R include LakeHuron, Nile, UKDriverDeaths, USAccDeaths, airmiles, and austres.
Another class of data set involves a response variable that is a count. Examples of data sets that consist of counts include

```
> InsectSprays  # n = 72 insect counts classified by type of spray
> warpbreaks    # number of yarn breaks for 2 types of wool and 3 tensions
> HairEyeColor  # hair color, eye color, and gender for statistics students
> UCBAdmissions # admission status classified by department and gender
> Titanic       # binary response (Survived) with 3 independent variables
```

The last of these data sets, `Titanic`, has a 0/1 response that is coded in the data set as `Survived = No` and `Survived = Yes`, which could potentially be a function of one or more of the independent variables: class (1st class, 2nd class, 3rd class, crew, which was a function of economic status), gender, and age.

Multivariate statistical models can be fitted to data that consists of observations on multiple variables. Some examples of such data sets built into R are

```
> randu          # consecutive nonoverlapping triples from the IBM's randu
> trees          # girth, height, and volume of n = 31 black cherry trees
> npk            # nitrogen, phosphate, and potassium levels for pea yield
> quakes         # five variables collected on n = 1000 earthquakes near Fiji
```

Other examples of multivariate data sets include `LifeCycleSavings`, `mtcars`, `stackloss`, and `swiss`.

Finally, some data sets look like a from–to matrix, such as

```
> eurodist           # distances between European cities
> occupationalStatus # occupational status of fathers and sons
```

This completes the discussion of data sets that are built into the R language. The table below summarizes the data sets and functions described in this chapter.

data set or function	description
`iris`, `state.x77`, `islands`, `precip`, `rivers`, `cars` `women`, `crimtab`, `faithful`, `sleep`, `Formaldehyde` `PlantGrowth`, `Puromycin`, `VADeaths`, `uspop`, `discoveries`, `AirPassengers`, `JohnsonJohnson`, `co2`, `presidents`, `sunspots`, `LakeHuron`, `Nile`, `UKDriverDeaths`, `USAccDeaths`, `airmiles`, `austres`, `InsectSprays`, `warpbreaks`, `HairEyeColor`, `UCBAdmissions`, `Titanic`, `randu`, `trees`, `npk`, `quakes`, `LifeCycleSavings`, `mtcars`, `swiss`, `stackloss`, `eurodist`, `occupationalStatus`	some built-in data sets
`attach`	attach objects to the search path
`detach`	detach objects from the search path

The next chapter considers input/output in R, which allows you to pull your own data set into the R language and to write output to a file.

Exercises

17.1 The built-in data frame `cars` contains two columns, `speed` and `dist`, which represent the speed in miles per hour and the stopping distance in feet. Write a single R command that calculates the mean stopping distance.

17.2 The built-in data frame `cars` contains two columns, `speed` and `dist`, which represent the speed in miles per hour and the stopping distance in feet. Write a single R command that displays a subset of this data frame associated with even-valued speeds.

17.3 The built-in data frame cars contains two columns, speed and dist, which represent the speed in miles per hour and the stopping distance in feet. Write a single R command that displays a subset of this data frame associated with cars whose stopping distance is less than twice their speed.

Chapter 18

Input / Output

So far, all of the interaction in an R session has stayed within that R session. This chapter concerns input and output, often abbreviated as I/O by computer scientists, in R. This topic is important because it allows you to interface between R, external data sets, and other programs. It is how R interacts with the world outside of R. The topics considered in this chapter are (a) input, and (b) output.

18.1   Input

One of the most versatile functions for reading data into R is the scan function. The syntax for the scan function is

```
scan(file = "", what = 0, n = -1, sep = "", skip = 0, ...)
```

All twenty of the arguments to scan are optional. The five arguments listed above are adequate for most applications.

- The file argument tells R the file from which the data values should be read. The default is to read data values from the keyboard.

- The what argument tells R the type of data to be read. The default value of 0 indicates that numeric data is to be read. All of the data types encountered thus far are supported by scan.

- The n argument tells R how many data values are to be read. The default value of -1 indicates that R should continue reading from the file until an end-of-file character is encountered.

- The sep argument tells R what character delimits the data values. The default of "" indicates that one or more spaces, to include tabs and end-of-line characters, should delimit the data values. Data files having comma separated values (csv) are also common.

- The skip argument tells R the number of lines to skip before beginning to read data values. This argument is useful when there are column headings, metadata, text describing the data set, etc. at the beginning of a file that should be ignored when reading the data set.

The simplest application of the scan function is to read data from the keyboard. Pressing return once gives a newline; pressing return twice terminates the input. R provides a prompt in the form of an index followed by a colon at the beginning of each line so that you will know how many values have been keyed in. An example of the use of the scan function to read the Florida population values that were given at the beginning of Chapter 4 is

```
> x = scan()                          # read data from keyboard into x
1: 529 753 968          1468 1897
6: 2771
7: 4952 6789 9746    12938
11:
Read 10 items
> x                                    # display x
 [1]    529    753    968  1468  1897  2771  4952  6789  9746 12938
```

In a similar fashion, the readline function is used to read a single line entered using the keyboard.

```
> y = readline()                       # read line of characters from keyboard
Now is the time for all good men to come to the aid of their country.
> y                                    # display y
[1] "Now is the time for all good men to come to the aid of their country."
```

The remaining illustrations in this chapter involve an external file. The entire pathname associated with a file can be included as an argument to one of these functions or a "working directory" can be established using the setwd (set working directory) function. We take the latter approach here, and set the working directory to the Desktop. Two similar approaches are required for the Apple and PC platforms. Assuming that my machine name is my initials, lml, the appropriate setwd function call on an Apple platform is

```
> setwd("/Users/lml/Desktop")         # set working dir on an Apple platform
```

This same call to setwd also works on a PC platform, with the assumption that the file resides on the C: drive. If the file of interest resides in another location, then the letter for that drive must precede the pathname. The getwd (get working directory) function can be used to determine the current working directory. The scan function will now be used to read the contents of a file into an object. For example, to read the data values in a file named file1, which resides in the current working directory, into the object x, type

```
> x = scan("file1")                    # read data from "file1" into x
```

But the scan function is not limited to populating just vectors. It can be used with the matrix function to populate a 3×4 matrix y with the contents of a file named file2, which resides in the current working directory, with the command

```
> y = matrix(scan("file2"), 3, 4)      # read data from "file2" into matrix y
```

If you are connected to the internet during your R session, scan also accepts a URL enclosed in quotation marks. This works in the same fashion as scanning the contents of a file.

The read.table function can be used to read a data frame into an object. The syntax for the read.table function is

```
            read.table(file, header = FALSE, sep = "", skip = 0, ...)
```

All twenty-three of the arguments to read.table are optional except for the filename. The four arguments listed above are adequate for most applications.

- The `file` argument tells R the file from which the data values should be read.

- The `header` argument tells R whether a header line that contains the names of the variables is present.

- The `sep` argument tells R what character delimits the data values.

- The `skip` argument tells R the number of lines to skip before beginning to read data values.

The `read.table` function can be used, for example, to populate the data frame z with the contents in `file3` with the command

```
> z = read.table("file3", header = TRUE)  # read "file3" into data frame z
```

The `header = TRUE` argument indicates that the first line of `file3` contains variable names. This concludes the brief survey of some functions for reading external data. The next section considers output, that is, saving calculations, objects, and sessions to an external file.

18.2 Output

R has the capability to save a calculation to an external file. Assume again that the `setwd` function has been called to set the current working directory. The `sink` function can be used to send R output to a file. The commands to calculate and save the mean U.S. high school graduation rate from the built-in data set named `state.x77` in a file named `file4`, for example, are

```
> sink("file4")              # begin saving calculations in file4
> mean(state.x77[ , 6])      # mean U.S. high school graduation rate
> sink()                     # stop saving calculations
```

The first call to the `sink` function begins the saving of calculations to the file named `file4`. When the command `mean(state.x77[ , 6])` is executed, the result is sent to `file4` rather than to the screen. The second call to the `sink` function ends the saving of calculations. In many other languages, the mean high school graduation rate would be stored in a secret format, which would require you to purchase another program in order to read the file. But this is not the case in R. The results of any calculations that are made between the calls to the `sink` function are stored as plain text, that is, as ASCII characters.

In addition to saving calculations to a file, R can also save objects to a file using the `dump` function and retrieve objects from a file using the `source` function. The R commands given next illustrate the use of the `dump` and `source` functions. The first command sets the vector a to the integer elements 3, 4, and 5. The second command writes the vector a to the file named `file5` in the current working directory. The contents of `file5` are in the ASCII (plain text) format and consist of a <- 3:5, which is an R command that is adequate to recreate the object a. The next R command sets b to a 2×3 matrix. The next command dumps both a and b into `file6`. Next, the objects a and b are removed with the `rm` function. Finally, the `source` function is used to execute the R commands contained in `file6`, which reinstate the objects a and b.

```
> a = 3:5                     # a is a vector
> dump("a", "file5")          # save object a to "file5"
> b = matrix(1:6, 2, 3)       # b is a matrix
> dump(c("a", "b"), "file6")  # save objects a and b to "file6"
> rm(a, b)                    # remove objects a and b
> source("file6")             # retrieve objects from "file6"
```

The source function is not limited to just executing a sequence of R commands associated with saved objects. Many experienced R users write their R commands in a separate file, then execute them with a call to the source function. The commands in the file constitute a computer program. Storing the commands in this fashion makes the code easy to modify and share with others. The typical R style for naming a file containing a computer program is with a meaningful filename appended with a .R extension.

The save function can also be used to save objects to a file. It uses a different file format than the dump function. The dump function saves R commands that can recreate the object in ASCII format; the save function saves the object in an internal format. The choice between the two might depend on the size of the object.

Occasions might arise in which it is helpful to save the objects from an entire R session. You might have an R session that created objects that are so magnificent that you want to save them for future access. The objects in a session can be saved with the save.image function and retrieved with the load function. In the example below, we again assume that the setwd command has been executed to set the current working directory. The call to save.image saves the objects in the session up to the point at which the save.image function is called. In a subsequent R session, the load function can be invoked to retrieve the objects that have been stored. The session is stored in file7 in a binary format.

```
> save.image("file7")          # save current objects to binary file "file7"
> load("file7")                # retrieve the current objects from "file7"
```

This concludes the discussion of input/output in R. The table below summarizes the functions described in this chapter.

function	description
scan	read data into R
readline	read a line from the keyboard into R
getwd	get the working directory
setwd	set the working directory
read.table	read a data frame into R
sink	write R output to a file
dump	write text representations of R objects to a file
source	read and execute R code from a file
save	write R objects to a file
save.image	write all R objects to a file
load	load objects saved previously into R

The remaining chapters in the book contain brief surveys of various topics. R contains a suite of functions that can be used to perform probability calculations, and those functions will be described in the next chapter.

Exercises

18.1   Use the help function to learn about the write.table function. Use the write.table function to write the built-in data set Formaldehyde (which is a data frame) to an external file named "file8".

18.2   Create a file (on your computer desktop or elsewhere) that contains the following two R commands:

```
SmallVector = c(1, 2, 6)
print(mean(SmallVector))
```

Then enter R and use the `source` function to execute the two commands.

18.3   Create a file (on your computer desktop or elsewhere) that contains the data values

1, 2, 18.

The data values should be separated by spaces. Then enter R and read these data values into a vector named x with the `scan` function. Print the average of the three values.

18.4   Create a file (on your computer desktop or elsewhere) that contains the data values

1, 2, 18.

The data values should be separated by commas. Then enter R and read these data values into a vector named x with the `read.csv` (read comma separated values) function. Print the average of the three values.

18.5   Enter R and set the object y to 4 with the R command y = 4. Use the R `dump` function to save y to a file (you choose the filename). Use the R `rm` function to remove the object named y with the command `rm(y)`. Type y to assure that the object no longer exists. Finally, use the `source` function to recover the object named y and print its value.

Chapter 19

Probability

There is a group of R functions that perform probability calculations that deserve a chapter of their own. R has a suite of well-organized functions that are able to calculate certain quantities associated with the probability distributions of random variables. The topics considered in this chapter are (a) random numbers, (b) the binomial distribution, (c) the Poisson distribution, (d) the uniform distribution, (e) the normal distribution, (f) other distributions, and (g) random sampling. Two of the distributions from this list are discrete distributions, namely the binomial and Poisson distributions, and two of the distributions from this list are continuous distributions, namely the uniform and normal distributions. A rudimentary familiarity with probability is helpful for reading this chapter.

19.1   Random numbers

A *random number* is synonymous with a number that is uniformly distributed between 0 and 1. When the R function runif (the first letter r is short for random and the final letters unif are short for uniform) is called with a single integer argument n, it generates n random numbers. To generate a vector of four random numbers, for example, type

```
> runif(4)              # four U(0, 1) random numbers
[1] 0.4217342 0.6876219 0.7168266 0.2083409
```

All four of the numbers generated lie between 0 and 1. Although these four values appear to be independent and random, they are, in fact, generated by a deterministic algorithm within R (more details on this algorithm are given in Chapter 25). If the runif function is called again, four different random numbers are generated.

```
> runif(4)              # four more U(0, 1) random numbers
[1] 0.44711476 0.09281929 0.33164046 0.08111221
```

Situations can arise in which it is helpful to get the same set of random numbers in a subsequent call to runif. The set.seed function sets the random number seed for the generation of random numbers; its argument is an integer. A call to set.seed with an argument of 6 (the integer argument 6 was chosen arbitrarily), followed by a call to runif(4) yields

```
> set.seed(6)           # set the random number stream to 6
> runif(4)              # four more U(0, 1) random numbers
[1] 0.6062683 0.9376420 0.2643521 0.3800939
```

Now if set.seed is again called with an argument of 6, the random number stream has been reset to the same position as before, which means that the same random numbers will be generated:

```
> set.seed(6)              # set the random number stream to 6
> runif(4)                 # the same four U(0, 1) random numbers
[1] 0.6062683 0.9376420 0.2643521 0.3800939
```

A random number by itself can be useful, but more useful still is when it is transformed to a *random variate* associated with a random variable coming from a particular probability distribution. A random variate is a realization of a random variable. Although random variates can be generated by hand, they are usually generated on a computer for efficiency. The next four sections illustrate how various aspects of a probability distribution can be calculated for the binomial, Poisson, uniform, and normal distributions.

19.2   Binomial distribution

The *binomial distribution* models the number of "successes" in n independent Bernoulli trials (each of which has probability of success p and probability of failure $1 - p$), where n is a fixed positive integer. The definition of success is determined by the modeler. It could be passing an exam, making a free throw, or even a negative event such as getting the flu. When n Bernoulli trials are conducted, each with an identical probability of success, p, the entire experiment is known as a *binomial random experiment*, which satisfies the following criteria.

- The random experiment consists of n identical Bernoulli trials, where n is fixed.

- There are two possible outcomes for each Bernoulli trial, typically known generically as "success" and "failure."

- The Bernoulli trials are mutually independent.

- The probability of success p on each Bernoulli trial is identical.

The probability mass function $f(x) = P(X = x)$ of a binomial random variable X with parameters n and p is

$$f(x) = \binom{n}{x} p^x (1 - p)^{n-x} \qquad x = 0, 1, 2, \ldots, n.$$

The syntax for four R functions that calculate various quantities associated with a binomial random variable X is given in the table below. The symbol $\sim$ is read "is distributed as."

function	returned value for $X \sim$ binomial(n, p)
dbinom(x, n, p)	calculates the probability mass function $f(x) = P(X = x)$
pbinom(x, n, p)	calculates the cumulative distribution function $F(x) = P(X \leq x)$
qbinom(u, n, p)	calculates the quantile (percentile) $F^{-1}(u)$, for $0 < u < 1$
rbinom(m, n, p)	generates m binomial(n, p) random variates

The first example calculates the probability mass function of a binomial random variable with parameters $n = 5$ and $p = 1/2$ for $x = 3$. The practical interpretation of the quantity calculated is that it is the probability of flipping exactly three heads ($x = 3$) in five tosses ($n = 5$) of a fair ($p = 1/2$) coin.

```
> dbinom(3, 5, 1 / 2)    # pmf at x = 3 for X ~ binomial(5, 1 / 2)
[1] 0.3125
```

This quantity could also have been calculated by hand with

$$f(3) = \binom{5}{3} \left(\frac{1}{2}\right)^3 \left(1 - \frac{1}{2}\right)^{5-3} = \frac{5!}{2!3!} \cdot \frac{1}{8} \cdot \frac{1}{4} = 10 \cdot \frac{1}{32} = \frac{5}{16} = 0.3125.$$

The second example calculates the cumulative distribution function of a binomial random variable with parameters $n = 5$ and $p = 1/2$ for $x = 3$. The practical interpretation of the quantity calculated is that it is the probability of flipping three or fewer heads ($x = 3$) in five tosses ($n = 5$) of a fair ($p = 1/2$) coin.

```
> pbinom(3, 5, 1 / 2)    # cdf at x = 3 for X ~ binomial(5, 1 / 2)
[1] 0.8125
```

This quantity could also have been calculated by hand with

$$
\begin{aligned}
F(3) &= P(X \leq 3) \\
&= P(X = 0) + P(X = 1) + P(X = 2) + P(X = 3) \\
&= \binom{5}{0}\left(\frac{1}{2}\right)^0\left(\frac{1}{2}\right)^5 + \binom{5}{1}\left(\frac{1}{2}\right)^1\left(\frac{1}{2}\right)^4 + \binom{5}{2}\left(\frac{1}{2}\right)^2\left(\frac{1}{2}\right)^3 + \binom{5}{3}\left(\frac{1}{2}\right)^3\left(\frac{1}{2}\right)^2 \\
&= \frac{1}{32} + \frac{5}{32} + \frac{10}{32} + \frac{10}{32} \\
&= \frac{26}{32} \\
&= \frac{13}{16} \\
&= 0.8125.
\end{aligned}
$$

The last example concerning the binomial distribution involves generating random variates. The rbinom function can be used to generate 12 random binomial variates with $n = 5$ and $p = 1/2$ with the R command

```
> rbinom(12, 5, 1 / 2)   # 12 random variates from X ~ binomial(5, 1 / 2)
 [1] 3 5 4 3 3 1 3 4 1 2 3 2
```

Each of the 12 random variates generated can be interpreted as a count of the random number of heads in five flips of a fair coin. These values must necessarily be integers that lie between 0 and 5 inclusive.

19.3   Poisson distribution

The Poisson distribution was introduced by French mathematician Simeon Poisson (1781–1840). There are two common ways to apply the Poisson distribution. First, the Poisson distribution can be used as an approximation to the binomial distribution, which is effective for large n and small p. Second, the Poisson distribution can be used to model the number of events that occur at random over a continuum of time or space in what is known as a *Poisson process*. Regardless of which perspective is taken, a discrete random variable X with probability mass function

$$f(x) = \frac{\lambda^x e^{-\lambda}}{x!} \qquad x = 0, 1, 2, \ldots$$

for $\lambda > 0$ is a Poisson(λ) random variable. The parameter λ is the rate of occurrence of events that occur over a fixed amount of time or space. The syntax for four R functions that calculate various quantities associated with a Poisson random variable X is given in the table below.

function	returned value for $X \sim \text{Poisson}(\lambda)$
dpois(x, lambda)	calculates the probability mass function $f(x) = P(X = x)$
ppois(x, lambda)	calculates the cumulative distribution function $F(x) = P(X \leq x)$
qpois(u, lambda)	calculates the quantile (percentile) $F^{-1}(u)$, for $0 < u < 1$
rpois(m, lambda)	generates m Poisson(λ) random variates

The first example of a probability calculation involving the Poisson distribution calls the function dpois with arguments $x = 2$ and $\lambda = 5$:

```
> dpois(2, 5)          # pmf at x = 2 for X ~ Poisson(5)
[1] 0.08422434
```

One practical interpretation of this result is that if an emergency room averages five patient arrivals per hour and patients arrive at random, then the probability of exactly two patients arriving in a given hour is 0.084. This result could have been calculated by hand with

$$f(2) = \frac{5^2 e^{-5}}{2!} = \frac{25 e^{-5}}{2} \cong 0.08422.$$

The second example of a probability calculation involving the Poisson distribution calls the function ppois, again with arguments $x = 2$ and $\lambda = 5$:

```
> ppois(2, 5)          # cdf at x = 2 for X ~ Poisson(5)
[1] 0.124652
```

Using the same emergency room interpretation, the probability of two or fewer patient arrivals in an hour is 0.1247. This result could have been calculated by hand with

$$F(2) = P(X \leq 2) = P(X = 0) + P(X = 1) + P(X = 2) = \frac{5^0 e^{-5}}{0!} + \frac{5^1 e^{-5}}{1!} + \frac{5^2 e^{-5}}{2!} \cong 0.1247.$$

The third example generates a dozen random variates from a Poisson(5) distribution and places them in the vector x.

```
> x = rpois(12, 5)     # set x to 12 random variates from Poisson(5)
> mean(x)              # mean of x
[1] 5.25
```

The mean of the 12 random variates, which is also random, is 5.25. Both the binomial and Poisson distributions are discrete distributions. The next two sections introduce two continuous distributions: the uniform and normal distributions.

19.4   Uniform distribution

A random variable has the uniform distribution if it is equally likely to occur anywhere between the constants a and b. The shorthand for a random variable X having the uniform distribution between a and b is $X \sim U(a, b)$. The probability density function for a $X \sim U(a, b)$ is

$$f(x) = \frac{1}{b-a} \qquad a < x < b.$$

(This differs from the discrete uniform distribution which, for example, is useful for modeling the outcomes associated with the roll of a single fair die.) Unlike the other three distributions presented in this chapter, the $U(a, b)$ distribution has a closed-form cumulative distribution function

$$F(x) = \int_a^x \frac{1}{b-a} dw = \frac{x-a}{b-a} \qquad a < x < b.$$

The syntax for four R functions that calculate various quantities associated with a $U(a, b)$ random variable X is given in the table below. The second and third arguments to these functions have defaults $a = 0$ and $b = 1$.

function	returned value for $X \sim U(a, b)$
dunif(x, a, b)	calculates the probability density function $f(x)$
punif(x, a, b)	calculates the cumulative distribution function $F(x) = P(X \leq x)$
qunif(u, a, b)	calculates the quantile (percentile) $F^{-1}(u)$, for $0 < u < 1$
runif(m, a, b)	generates m $U(0, 1)$ random variates

The first example calculates the value of the probability density function of $X \sim U(0, 10)$ at $x = 3$

```
> dunif(3, 0, 10)        # pdf at x = 3 for X ~ U(0, 10)
[1] 0.1
```

This value could have been calculated by hand as

$$f(3) = \frac{1}{10-0} = \frac{1}{10}.$$

The second example calculates the value of the cumulative distribution function of $X \sim U(0, 10)$ at $x = 3$

```
> punif(3, 0, 10)        # cdf at x = 3 for X ~ U(0, 10)
[1] 0.3
```

This value could have been calculated by hand as

$$F(3) = \frac{3-0}{10-0} = \frac{3}{10}.$$

The third example involves finding the 80th percentile of $X \sim U(0, 10)$.

```
> qunif(0.8, 0, 10)      # 80th percentile of X ~ U(0, 10)
[1] 8
```

This value could have been calculated by hand by solving $F(x) = 0.8$ for x, which is the 80th percentile of X. The fourth example generates a dozen random variates from the $U(0, 10)$ distribution.

```
> runif(12, 0, 10)        # 12 random variates from X ~ U(0, 10)
 [1] 2.7440154 4.3333807 5.2177349 1.2616914 9.5615189 7.6000278 1.3689571
 [8] 9.3086507 3.8618286 0.5922305 9.8635739 7.6690693
```

All of these values lie in the interval $(0, 10)$, as expected. Finally, the a and b parameters can be defaulted in `runif`, which results in 12 random numbers.

```
> runif(12)               # 12 random variates from X ~ U(0, 1)
 [1] 0.69803211 0.72332906 0.08002284 0.93868237 0.97804057 0.82670484
 [7] 0.11738552 0.42240890 0.57549463 0.98599541 0.12105363 0.33296557
```

19.5 Normal distribution

Many real-world phenomenon result in observations that fall into a bell-shaped probability distribution. Examples include

- heights of adult women,
- weights of newborn babies,
- crop yields,
- ball bearing diameters.

A continuous random variable X with probability density function

$$f(x) = \frac{1}{\sqrt{2\pi}\sigma} e^{-\frac{1}{2}\left(\frac{x-\mu}{\sigma}\right)^2} \qquad -\infty < x < \infty$$

is known as a normally distributed random variable with population mean μ and population variance σ^2. The shorthand for a random variable X having a normal distribution with population mean μ and population variance σ^2 is $X \sim N\left(\mu, \sigma^2\right)$. The normal distribution is also known as the Gaussian distribution.

The syntax for four R functions that calculate various quantities associated with a $N\left(\mu, \sigma^2\right)$ random variable is given in the table below. The second and third arguments to the functions have defaults $\mu = 0$ and $\sigma = 1$. This particular normal distribution is known as a *standard normal distribution*. Notice that the third argument in the `dnorm`, `pnorm`, `qnorm`, and `rnorm` is the population standard deviation σ rather than the population variance σ^2.

function	returned value for $X \sim N\left(\mu, \sigma^2\right)$
dnorm(x, mean, sd)	calculates the probability density function $f(x)$
pnorm(x, mean, sd)	calculates the cumulative distribution function $F(x) = P(X \leq x)$
qnorm(u, mean, sd)	calculates the quantile (percentile) $F^{-1}(u)$, for $0 < u < 1$
rnorm(m, mean, sd)	generates m $N\left(\mu, \sigma^2\right)$ random variates

The first example calculates the height of the probability density function of a standard normal random variable at $x = 1$.

```
> dnorm(1)                 # pdf at x = 1 for X ~ N(0, 1)
[1] 0.2419707
```

This quantity could have been calculated by hand with

$$f(1) = \frac{1}{\sqrt{2\pi}} e^{-1/2} \cong 0.2420.$$

The second example calculates the area under $f(x)$ to the left of -1.2 for a standard normal random variable.

```
> pnorm(-1.2)              # cdf at x = -1.2 for X ~ N(0, 1)
[1] 0.1150697
```

The 98th percentile of a standard normal random variable is

```
> qnorm(0.98)              # 98th percentile of X ~ N(0, 1)
[1] 2.053749
```

A dozen standard normal random variates can be generated with

```
> rnorm(12)                # 12 random variates from X ~ N(0, 1)
 [1] -0.03808156  2.35420426  1.39342626 -0.56033236 -0.67145938  0.49243855
 [7] -1.17939052 -1.05871745  1.13790261 -0.16026528  0.63049313  1.61695970
```

Finally, to generate a dozen random variates from the $N(68, 9)$ distribution, use

```
> rnorm(12, 68, 3)         # 12 random variates from X ~ N(68, 9)
 [1] 67.41950 63.17662 65.34451 66.70300 66.73513 67.48852 68.73743 65.76276
 [9] 67.17817 73.47374 68.04270 68.56413
```

These random variates could be interpreted as the adult heights of 12 individuals drawn from a normally distributed population with $\mu = 68$ inches and $\sigma = 3$ inches.

19.6   Other distributions

The four probability distributions considered thus far—the binomial, Poisson, uniform, and normal distributions—only scratch the surface of the probability distributions that are built into R.

By now you have probably recognized that the first letter of the name of the probability functions directs R to calculate the value of $f(x)$ with d, to calculate the value of $F(x)$ with p, to calculate the value of a quantile with q, or to generate random variates with r. These four letters are referred to as the "prefix" to the function name in the table below.

operation	prefix
probability mass/density function $f(x)$	d
cumulative distribution function $F(x) = P(X \leq x)$	p
quantile/percentile $F^{-1}(u)$	q
random variates	r

The letters that follow the prefix in the function name are referred to here as the "suffix" to the function name. So far, we have encountered the binomial distribution (binom), Poisson distribution (pois), uniform distribution (unif), and the normal distribution (norm). A list of the potential suffixes is given in the table that follows. This organized way of naming the functions associated with these probability distributions is an example of good language design. The suffixes given in the table are all built into the base package of R. It is possible that certain R packages might extend the number of distributions available (see Chapter 28).

distribution	suffix
beta	beta
binomial	binom
Cauchy	cauchy
chi-squared	chisq
exponential	exp
F	f
gamma	gamma
geometric	geom
hypergeometric	hyper
log-normal	lnorm
multinomial	multinom
negative binomial	nbinom
normal	norm
Poisson	pois
Student's t	t
uniform	unif
Weibull	weibull

There are relationships between probability distributions that should be taken into consideration when using these functions. For example, the Bernoulli distribution is a special case of the binomial distribution with $n = 1$. So a special function for the Bernoulli distribution is not necessary. Including the geometric distribution is also not necessary because it is a special case of the negative binomial distribution. Including the exponential distribution is also not necessary because it is a special case of the gamma distribution.

Beware also that some distributions have aliases. For example, the normal distribution is sometimes known as the Gaussian distribution and the negative binomial distribution is sometimes known as the Pascal distribution.

Finally, beware that some probability distributions have multiple parameterizations. As a simple example, the exponential distribution can be parameterized by its rate $\lambda > 0$ with the probability density function

$$f(x) = \lambda e^{-\lambda x} \qquad x > 0,$$

or it can be parameterized by its mean $\theta > 0$ with probability density function

$$f(x) = \frac{1}{\theta} e^{-x/\theta} \qquad x > 0.$$

The help function should be called to determine which parameterization was used by the designers of R.

19.7   Random sampling

Many applications in probability require the random sampling of balls from an urn, or perhaps a better analogy is the random sampling of tickets from a box. The sample function in R makes this type of random sampling straightforward to implement. The syntax for the sample function is

```
sample(x, size, replace = FALSE, prob = NULL)
```

The elements of the vector x are the items from which to sample. The size argument is a nonnegative integer containing the number of items to sample. The replace argument assumes a logical value and determines whether sampling should be performed with replacement (replace = TRUE) or without replacement (the default replace = FALSE). Finally, the prob argument is a vector of probabilities, which are weights associated with sampling each of the items in sample. The default value for prob is that each item is equally likely to be selected. If the replace argument is FALSE, then the algorithm adjusts the probability of choosing the next item to be proportional to the remaining weights. The first example of using the sample function involves taking a sample of size seven from the first seven positive integers. This is the same as generating a random permutation of the first seven integers.

```
> sample(7)            # random permutation of first 7 positive integers
[1] 4 5 7 1 6 2 3
```

The next example samples five integers from the first seven positive integers.

```
> sample(7, 5)            # 5 integers from the first 7 positive integers
[1] 6 1 4 5 7
```

The next example again samples five integers from the first seven positive integers, but this time sampling is performed with replacement. This allows an integer to be drawn more than once.

```
> sample(7, 5, replace = TRUE)      # same as previous but with replacement
[1] 1 3 1 7 4
```

The last example samples five integers from the first seven integers without replacement, but this time the probability of drawing 1 is $1/28$, the probability of drawing 2 is $2/28$, ... , the probability of drawing 7 is $7/28$. So the smaller integers are less likely to appear in the sample than the larger integers.

```
> sample(7, 5, prob = (1:7) / 28)  # larger integers more likely
[1] 4 5 7 3 6
```

The examples thus far have illustrated the sampling of integers from a vector. But it is also possible to sample real numbers, complex numbers, logical elements, and character strings. The example below generates the results of nine rolls of a fair die as character strings.

```
> x = c("one", "two", "three", "four", "five", "six")
> sample(x, 9, replace = TRUE)    # nine rolls of a fair die
[1] "five"  "three" "four" "six"   "one"   "three" "two"  "three" "six"
```

This concludes the discussion of the suite of probability functions that are built into R. The probability functions are particularly well organized in that their names consistently begin with one of the letters d (for density), p (for probability), q (for quantile), or r (for random variate). The remaining letters describe the distribution of interest, for example, `binom` (for binomial), `pois` (for Poisson), `unif` (for uniform), or `norm` (for normal). Left-hand tail probabilities are used consistently in R. In addition, the `sample` function is used to generate random samples and random permutations.

The next two chapters introduce R's graphics capability. The next chapter considers high-level functions that can be used to create generic plots. The chapter that follows considers custom graphics.

Exercises

19.1 The height of an adult male from Australia is normally distributed with population mean 70 inches and population standard deviation 3 inches. Write a single R command that calculates the probability that an adult male from Australia is over six feet tall.

19.2 Calculate $f(2) = P(X = 2)$, where X is a binomial random variable with parameters $n = 3$ and $p = 2/3$. Verify your answer by calling the appropriate R function.

19.3 Calculate $F(1) = P(X \leq 1)$, where X is a binomial random variable with parameters $n = 2$ and $p = 1/3$. Verify your answer by calling the appropriate R function.

19.4 Calculate the 5th percentile of X, where X is a binomial random variable with parameters $n = 3$ and $p = 1/2$. Verify your answer by calling the appropriate R function.

19.5 A fair die is rolled ten times. Write a single R command to calculate the probability that two or fewer sixes will occur in the ten rolls.

19.6 Use R to calculate the following quantities:

   (a) The probability that a binomial random variable with $n = 10$ and $p = 0.3$ equals 4.
   (b) The probability that a Poisson random variable with $\lambda = 7$ is less than or equal to 2.
   (c) The 90th percentile of a $U(30, 50)$ random variable.
   (d) The 99th percentile of a normal random variable with population mean $\mu = 68$ and population standard deviation $\sigma = 3$.
   (e) Fifteen realizations of a Poisson random variable with $\lambda = 8$.

19.7 Calculate $f(8)$, where $X \sim U(5, 9)$. Verify your answer by calling the appropriate R function.

19.8 Calculate $F(8) = P(X \leq 8)$, where $X \sim U(5, 9)$. Verify your answer by calling the appropriate R function.

19.9 What is returned by the following R command?

```
> qunif(0.7, 100, 200)
```

19.10 What is returned by the following R command?

```
> qnorm(pnorm(1.7))
```

19.11 Write a single R command that randomly permutes the rows of built-in data set named cars.

19.12 What value do you expect, on average, will be returned by the following R command?

```
> mean(runif(1000000))
```

19.13 What is returned by the following R command?

```
> qnorm(0.5, 23, 5)
```

19.14 What are the lowest and highest possible values returned by the following R command?

```
> prod(rbinom(2, 3, 0.4))
```

19.15 What are the lowest and highest possible values returned by the following R command?

```
> sum(runif(3, 2, 4))
```

19.16 Find the population mean (expected value) and the population variance of the binomial, Poisson, uniform, and normal distributions. This can be done mathematically or via an internet search. Write functions named `ebinom`, `vbinom`, `epois`, `vpois`, `eunif`, `vunif`, `enorm`, and `vnorm` that return the expected value and variance of the four distributions.

19.17 Write a single R command to calculate

$$\sum_{x=3}^{9} \frac{5^x e^{-5}}{x!}.$$

Chapter 20

High-Level Graphics

R is capable of producing publication-quality graphics. This chapter and the next chapter introduce some of the graphics capabilities in R. This chapter is titled "high-level graphics" because it considers graphics that are produced by R using graphical functions, with just a little tweaking of arguments from the user. The next chapter is titled "custom graphics" because it uses graphical functions that can be used to customize a graphic down to very fine detail. The topics introduced in this chapter are broken down by the type of data set encountered: (a) univariate data, (b) multivariate data, (c) categorical data, and (d) time-series data. This introduction to graphics just skims the surface of the functions that can be used to produce a graphic.

20.1   Univariate data

A univariate data value is a single numeric value, and n such data values comprise a univariate data set. The symbol n is generally used to denote the sample size. There are plenty of such univariate data sets built into R, such as islands, precip, and rivers. We create one here by extracting the second column of the state.x77 built-in data set.

```
> x = state.x77[ , 2]              # 50 average state incomes in 1977
> x                                # display x
       Alabama         Alaska         Arizona        Arkansas      California
          3624           6315            4530            3378            5114
      Colorado    Connecticut        Delaware         Florida         Georgia
          4884           5348            4809            4815            4091
        Hawaii          Idaho        Illinois         Indiana            Iowa
          4963           4119            5107            4458            4628
        Kansas       Kentucky       Louisiana           Maine        Maryland
          4669           3712            3545            3694            5299
 Massachusetts       Michigan       Minnesota     Mississippi        Missouri
          4755           4751            4675            3098            4254
       Montana       Nebraska          Nevada   New Hampshire      New Jersey
          4347           4508            5149            4281            5237
    New Mexico       New York  North Carolina    North Dakota            Ohio
          3601           4903            3875            5087            4561
      Oklahoma         Oregon    Pennsylvania    Rhode Island  South Carolina
```

3983	4660	4449	4558	3635
South Dakota	Tennessee	Texas	Utah	Vermont
4167	3821	4188	4022	3907
Virginia	Washington	West Virginia	Wisconsin	Wyoming
4701	4864	3617	4468	4566

This data set of $n = 50$ observations are the average annual per capita U.S. state incomes in 1977; the minimum is Mississippi with average income \$3098 and the maximum is Alaska with average income \$6315.

There are several graphical devices that statisticians use to perform a preliminary analysis of a univariate data set. One such device is known as the *histogram*, which gives an indication of the shape of the population probability density function. A histogram of the data is plotted in R with the hist function. Three different histograms of the average incomes are plotted with the R commands

```
> hist(x)                      # histogram
> hist(x, breaks = 4)          # histogram using 4 cells
> hist(x, probability = TRUE)  # histogram so it sums to 1
```

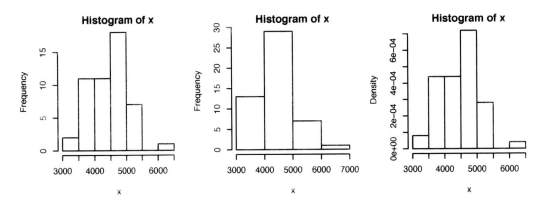

All three calls to hist result in a histogram appearing in a pop-up window. Leave the original pop-up window open to accommodate the results of the next graphic command. The three histograms are plotted together here to save space. In all three cases, the first argument to the hist function is x, the vector containing the 50 average incomes. The first call to hist results in a histogram that uses the default arguments. The horizontal axis corresponds to the elements of x and the vertical axis corresponds to a count of the number of observations in a particular cell. The hist function selects round numbers for the breakpoints for the cells, which in this case are 3000, 3500, ... , 6500. It also adds a main title and labels the two axes. If you decide that the first histogram is too bumpy (for example, there is no observation in the (5500, 6000] cell), then you can call the hist function and specify fewer cells using the breaks argument. The second call to hist requests just four cells. R will again choose some round values for the breakpoints, which are 3000, 4000, 5000, 6000, and 7000 on the second histogram. Finally, if you would like the area under your histogram to equal 1, then the probability argument should be used. The third histogram is useful in that a fitted probability distribution (for example, the fitted normal distribution) can be plotted on top of the histogram using the lines function, which will be introduced in the next chapter.

As a second example of a univariate data set, consider the depths of the $n = 1000$ earthquakes given in the built-in quakes data set. These depths are placed into the vector y with the R command

```
> y = quakes$depth             # 1000 earthquake depths
```

The depths range from 40 km to 680 km. Once again, three histograms of these depths are produced with

```
> hist(y)                      # histogram of 1000 earthquake depths
> hist(y, breaks = 7)          # histogram using 7 cells
> hist(y, seq(0, 700, by = 70))   # histogram using 10 cells
```

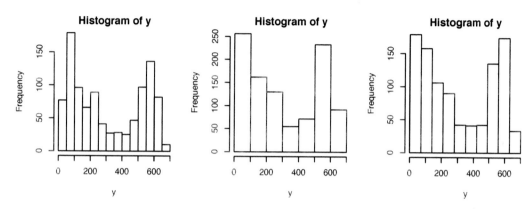

Each of the calls to hist uses the 1000 elements in y for data values. The first call to hist results in a histogram that uses the default arguments. Because the sample size is significantly larger (that is, $n = 1000$ versus $n = 50$), R uses more cells in the histogram with the default settings. The shape of this histogram is somewhat rare because there are two modes. Statisticians refer to such a parent population distribution as a *bimodal distribution*. One mode is around 100 km and the other mode is around 600 km. You can again reduce the number of cells by setting the breaks argument to the number of desired cells, as shown in the second histogram. Finally, if you specify the breaks argument (which is the second argument in the hist function) to be a vector, then the elements of the vector will be the breakpoints in the histogram. This is the approach used in the third histogram.

While histograms are helpful in assessing the shape of the population distribution, they have some weaknesses. The first weakness concerns the arbitrary grouping of observations into cells. Choosing too few cells can mask important features of the data set. Choosing too many cells can highlight the natural *random sampling variability* (that is, the chance fluctuations in the data associated with a finite sample size) rather than the shape of the parent probability distribution. Even if you choose the right number of cells, shifting the cells slightly to the left or the right can cause subtle or even dramatic differences in the shape of the histogram. The second weakness associated with histograms is that they are notoriously bad at comparing multiple populations; they do not stack well.

An alternative to the histogram, which is not as good at showing the shape of the population distribution but overcomes both weaknesses, is a plot of the *empirical cumulative distribution function*. The empirical cumulative distribution is a step function that takes an upward step of height $1/n$ at each data value. The values associated with the steps in the empirical cumulative distribution function can be seen with the ecdf function (the lengthy output is suppressed).

```
> ecdf(x)                      # empirical cumulative distn function
```

Three empirical cumulative distribution functions are plotted using the plot.ecdf function with

```
> plot.ecdf(x)                        # associated plot (income data)
> plot.ecdf(x, verticals = T, pch = "")   # add vertical lines and no dots
> plot.ecdf(y, verticals = T, pch = "")   # ecdf plot of 1000 earthquake depths
```

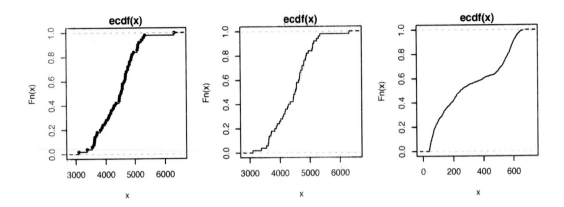

The first call to the `plot.ecdf` function plots the empirical cumulative distribution function of the $n = 50$ state incomes using the default arguments. The step function takes an upward step of $1/50$ at each numeric element in x. Since the points that are plotted at each step might be distracting, the second call to the `plot.ecdf` function adds a vertical line at each step with the `verticals` argument and suppresses the plotting of the points with the `pch` (plotting character) argument. Finally, the third call to the `plot.ecdf` function plots the empirical cumulative distribution function for the $n = 1000$ earthquake depth data values. The rapid increases in the empirical cumulative distribution function around 100 km and 600 km indicate the locations of the two modes of the probability distribution.

Another helpful tool for analyzing univariate data is the `qqnorm` function, which is a visual tool used to assess whether data is drawn from a normal population. This is a special case of a QQ (quantile–quantile) plot, which is used by statisticians to determine the plausibility of a data set being drawn from a particular distribution. Calls to the `qqnorm` function and the associated `qqline` function for the state income data values and the earthquake depth data values are

```
> qqnorm(x)              # qq plot for the state income data
> qqline(x, col = 2)     # col = 2 for red reference line
> qqnorm(y)              # qq plot for the earthquake depths
> qqline(y, col = "red") # red reference line
```

If the points associated with the data values fall in a line, this is visual evidence of a normal population distribution. For the state income values, all but the largest average annual income (attributed to Alaska) fall in a fairly linear pattern, so the normal distribution is plausible. For the earthquake depth data, the points do not follow a linear model. Notice that the value of the `col` (color) argument can be specified by the number 2, or the string `"red"` also produces the same colored line in the calls to `qqline`. Many colors can be referenced by number or name in this fashion.

A fourth function that can be useful for summarizing univariate data is known as a "box plot." A box plot gives a visual representation of a data set that includes the sample minimum, the sample 25th percentile, the sample median (which is the sample 50th percentile), the sample 75th percentile, and the sample maximum. In addition, a box plot can be used to identify data values that are deemed to be "outliers." The `boxplot` function generates a box plot. The first example generates a box plot for the state average income with

```
> boxplot(x)                       # box plot of the state income data
```

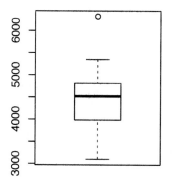

The box plot shows the minimum average income ($3098 for Mississippi), the 25th percentile at the bottom of the box, the sample median (the average of the two middle values, Nebraska at $4508 and Arizona at $4530) as a line in the middle of the box, the 75th percentile at the top of the box, and then the maximum is identified as an outlier by a circle ($6315 for Alaska). One significant advantage to box plots over histograms is that they can easily accommodate multiple data sets. Consider, for example, the counts of insects associated with the six insect sprays (A, B, C, D, E, and F) used in the built-in data set `InsectSprays`. The call to `boxplot` produces a box plot of the insect counts for the six types of sprays

```
> boxplot(count ~ spray, data = InsectSprays)  # classify count data by spray
```

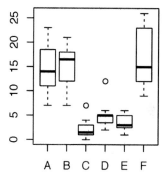

Based on this box plot, insect sprays C, D, and E appear to be superior to sprays A, B, and F. The sample sizes for each spray are small, however, so a formal statistical test should be conducted to

verify this conclusion. This ends the discussion of graphical tools that can be applied to univariate data. The natural extension is to consider graphical tools for multivariate data.

20.2 Multivariate data

A multivariate data set consists of data values that come in pairs, triples, etc. A simple example of a bivariate data set is the collection of the heights of n couples in which the x_i value corresponds to the husband's height and y_i corresponds to the wife's height, for $i = 1, 2, \ldots, n$. A scatterplot is an effective graphical tool for an initial assessment of a bivariate data set. Returning to the earthquake data set contained in the built-in data set `quakes`, a scatterplot of the longitude of the epicenter of the quake on the horizontal axis versus the latitude of the epicenter of the quake can be generated with the `plot` function:

```
> plot(quakes$long, quakes$lat)        # longitude vs. latitude of epicenters
```

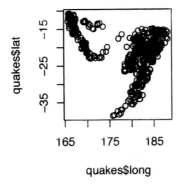

This plot reveals a pattern associated with the locations of the $n = 1000$ earthquakes. The axis labels default to the names of the two arguments to `plot`. It does not, however, incorporate the magnitude of the earthquake. The magnitudes of the earthquakes are stored in `quakes$mag`. The `symbols` function can be used to generate a scatterplot that also incorporates the magnitude of the earthquakes with

```
> symbols(quakes$long, quakes$lat, circles = 10 ^ quakes$mag)   # include mag.
```

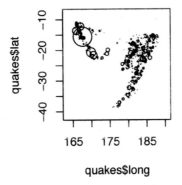

Even though there were more earthquakes that occurred in the eastern cluster, the western cluster contains the strongest earthquakes.

Data in three dimensions (trivariate data) is typically more difficult to visualize using graphics than bivariate data. Consider the built-in data set named `trees`, which consists of the `Girth` (the diameter, in inches, measured 4 ft., 6 in. above the ground), `Height` (in feet), and `Volume` (in cubic feet) of $n = 31$ felled black cherry trees. The `pairs` function draws two-dimensional scatterplots of all possible pairs of the data values:

```
> pairs(trees)                          # pairwise Girth, Height, & Volume
```

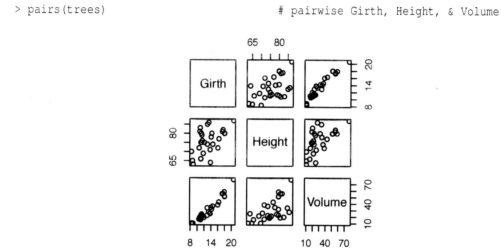

One observation that is immediately apparent from the scatterplots is that the two variables with the highest positive correlation are `Girth` and `Volume`. Since `Girth` is also an easier measure to obtain than the `Height` of a standing black cherry tree, it is considered the better predictor of the `Volume` of a standing black cherry tree.

A second way of viewing trivariate data (or, more generally multivariate data) is with the `stars` function. For the `trees` data set, a call to `stars` is

```
> stars(trees)                          # star plot for tree data
```

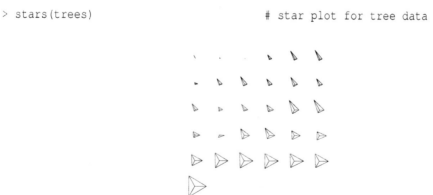

which produces a star for each of the $n = 31$ trees that contains the three variables (girth, height, and volume) by row. A slight variant of a star diagram uses the `draw.segments` argument to modify the look of each data point. For this data set, they look a bit more like a birds-eye view of the trees.

```
> stars(trees, draw.segments = TRUE)     # segment plot for tree data
```

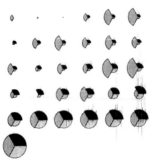

Sometimes bivariate data can come in the form of *counts*, rather than specific observed values. Such is the case of the built-in data set `crimtab`, which is a bivariate data set consisting of the middle finger lengths (in cm) and the heights (also in cm) of 3000 male criminals who were over 20 years old undergoing their sentences in prisons in England and Wales. The data is arranged into effectively a two-dimensional histogram with middle finger lengths as rows and heights as columns. Each element of `crimtab` is a count of the number of inmates falling into that particular cell. This data set was analyzed by William Sealy Gosset, who often went by the pseudonym "Student" at the request of his employer. He is credited with discovering the *t* distribution. There are three R graphical functions that could be helpful in visualizing this data set: `contour`, `image`, and `persp` (perspective).

```
> contour(crimtab)          # contour plot of criminal data
> image(crimtab)            # image plot of criminal data
> persp(crimtab)            # perspective plot of criminal data
```

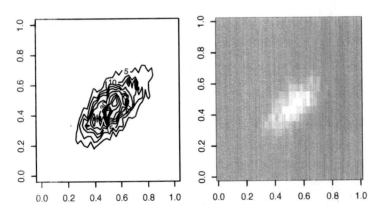
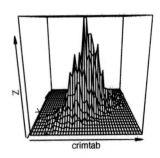

The graphs reveal the not-so-surprising conclusion: there is a positive correlation between the middle finger lengths and the heights. Taller guys have longer fingers.

This completes the brief survey of some of the graphical functions that can be applied to multivariate data sets. The next section considers categorical data.

20.3 Categorical data

A categorical data value can take on one of a limited number of potential values. A data set that consists of categorical data values is known as a *categorical data set*. Although statisticians generally prefer more sophisticated presentation tools for categorical data sets, one of the simplest graphics that can be generated is a *pie chart*, which can be created with the `pie` function.

```
> pie.sales = c(0.12, 0.30, 0.26, 0.16, 0.04, 0.12)
> names(pie.sales) = c("Blueberry", "Cherry", "Apple", "Boston Creme",
+                       "Other", "Vanilla Creme")
> pie.sales                          # proportion of pie sales
    Blueberry        Cherry         Apple  Boston Creme          Other
         0.12          0.30          0.26          0.16           0.04
Vanilla Creme
         0.12
> pie(pie.sales, col = c("blue", "red", "green", "wheat", "orange", "white"))
```

The `names` function appears on the left-hand side of the assignment operator. In this case it sets the names for `pie.sales`. As pointed out earlier, the `names` function both gets (retrieves) and sets (assigns) names.

The preferred mode of displaying categorical data is with a dot chart or a bar chart. The pie sales data can be displayed in a dot chart with the command

```
> dotchart(pie.sales, xlim = c(0, 0.3)) # force axis to include zero
```

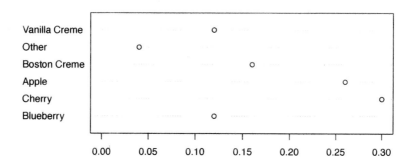

The `xlim` (*x* limit) argument forces the horizontal axis to run from 0 to 0.3. Similarly, a bar chart for the pie sales data can be graphed with the command

```
> barplot(pie.sales, col=c("blue", "red", "green", "wheat", "orange", "white"))
```

The `VADeaths` data set contains the annual death rates per 1000 persons in Virginia in 1940, broken down by age, gender, and urban/rural dwelling status. A bar chart for this more complicated data set can be generated with the R command

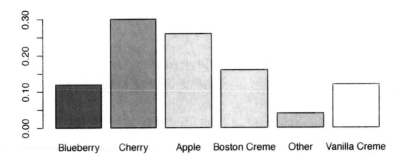

```
> barplot(VADeaths, beside = TRUE, legend = TRUE,
+          main = "Virginia Death Rates per 1000 in 1940")
```

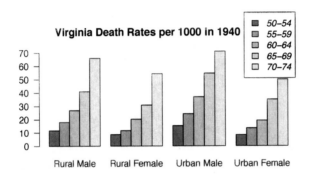

Lots of information has been packed into this graphic, which is generated with just a single R command. Death rates are consistently increasing with age; death rates are higher for men than for women; there might be a slight advantage for women who live in the city. All of these conclusions, however, would have to be verified using an appropriate statistical test.

This ends the discussion of graphics for categorical data. The last section concerns high-level graphics functions for time-series data.

20.4   Time-series data

Many data sets consist of observations that are collected over time. One of the primary graphical exploratory data analysis tools for a time series is simply a plot of the time-series values over time. The ts.plot function can be used to plot a time series. This is applied to the built-in data set named AirPassengers, which contains the monthly number of airline passengers (in thousands) between 1949 and 1960:

```
> ts.plot(AirPassengers)              # international airline passengers
```

The time-series plot reveals that there is a growth (perhaps nonlinear) in the number of passengers over time, a pronounced cyclic variation that appears to be seasonal, and an amplitude to the seasonal component that increases with time. A branch of statistics known as *time-series analysis* considers the development of probability models for complex time series such as this one. A second time series named presidents contains the quarterly U.S. presidential approval ratings from 1945 to 1974. This time series also contains several NA values in which such polls were not taken.

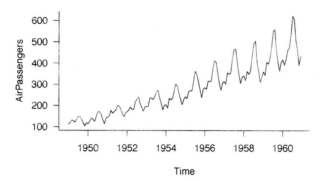

```
> ts.plot(presidents)                    # presidential approval ratings
```

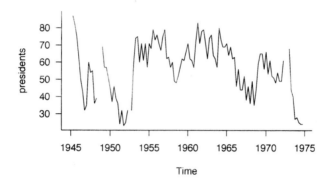

The points associated with the NA values are left as gaps in the time series plot.

This concludes the brief survey of some high-level graphical functions in R. The table below summarizes the functions introduced in this chapter.

function	description
hist	histogram
ecdf	empirical cumulative distribution function
plot.ecdf	plot empirical cumulative distribution function
qqnorm	draw normal quantile–quantile plot
qqline	add line to quantile–quantile plot
boxplot	box plot
plot	generic plotting function
symbols	draw symbols
pairs	matrix of scatterplots
stars	star plots
contour	contour plot
image	colored image plot
persp	perspective plot
pie	pie chart
barplot	bar chart
ts.plot	time-series plot

The graphical images generated in this chapter have been produced with high-level R functions that produce graphics that are adequate in most applications. In some cases, however, a graphic needs to be customized to suit a particular purpose. The next chapter considers methods for customizing these graphics.

Exercises

20.1 The built-in data frame `cars` contains two columns, `speed` and `dist`, which represent the speed in miles per hour and the stopping distance in feet. Write a single R command that graphs a scatterplot of speed on the horizontal axis and stopping distance on the vertical axis.

20.2 Suppose that x and y are vectors containing numerical elements. Write a single R command that generates side-by-side box plots.

20.3 Consider the R built-in data set called `warpbreaks`.

   (a) Draw two side-by-side box plots of the number of breaks broken out by the type of wool (A and B).

   (b) Draw three side-by-side box plots of the number of breaks broken out by the level of tension (L, M, and H, for low, medium and high).

20.4 Draw a QQ (quantile–quantile) plot for the built-in `islands` data set to assess the normality of the observations. Do you believe that the data set is well-modeled by a normal distribution?

Chapter 21

Custom Graphics

This chapter extends the introduction to graphics in the previous chapter to show how to customize graphics. Constructing a graph that displays quantitative information accurately and fairly in a manner that accounts for human visual perception brings a data set to life. Visualizing a data set via a graph is often the first view we get of a data set after the data is collected. It provides a first impression that often guides the next step, which might be using a statistical inference technique to draw a conclusion from the data. The topics considered here are (a) graphical issues that arise in constructing a graphic, and (b) examples of custom graphics.

21.1 Graphical issues

Do not let fancy fonts, color, shading, or highlighting dazzle your senses when it comes to graphics. The best work is often a rather simple plot that conveys only the appropriate information lurking in the data set. Make every bit of ink that you place on a graphic count. Use as little ink as possible to provide as much explanation as is necessary. Display the data succinctly and fairly, bringing the information contained in the data set to prominence in your graphic.

There are dozens of decisions that must be made when constructing a graph to display data. All decisions should be driven by human vision and perception considerations. A sampling of the related questions includes the following.

- *Aspect ratio.* Is there a reason (by virtue of the meaning of the scales) that the plotting area should be a square? If not, is a tall thin graph (portrait orientation) more appropriate, or is a short wide graph (landscape orientation) a better choice?

- *Axes.* Should axes be included? Does one of the variables naturally belong on the horizontal axis? Should axes be included on just the bottom and left sides of the plot, or should they be included on all four sides of the plot? Should the axes intersect or should there be a gap between them?

- *Scales.* Should the scales on the axes be linear? Should a logarithmic scale for an axis be used? Should a square root scale for an axis be used? Where should the scales begin and end? Is it helpful to have zero included on the scale? (This is not an option for a logarithmic scale.) Should a break be placed on a scale in order to include zero?

- *Axis labels.* Should the axis labels be in the same font style as the manuscript text? Should the axis labels be the same font size as the manuscript text? Should the labels be placed at the ends of the axes or in the center of the axes? Should the vertical axis label be displayed parallel to the axis or rotated clockwise 90° for easier reading?

- *Tick marks and tick labels.* Should the tick marks extend into the plotting area or out of the plotting area? How many tick marks should be included on each axis? Should all tick marks be the same size? How long should the tick marks be? Should all tick marks be labeled? Should the tick mark labels be in the same font style as the manuscript text? Should the tick mark labels be the same font size as the manuscript text? Should the tick mark labels for the vertical axis be displayed parallel to the axis or rotated clockwise 90° for easier reading?

- *Plotting region.* What symbol is appropriate for plotting a point? Is a legend necessary to describe the meaning of the plotted symbols? What should be done if two points fall on top of one another? Should points be connected with lines? Would placing text in the plotting area be helpful? Should reference lines be included in the plotting area? If so, should they be solid, dotted, or dashed? Should the elements placed in the plotting area be black, gray, or colored?

21.2 Examples

This chapter consists of a series of elementary examples that illustrate how a custom graphic is created in R. The first problem is to draw a graph of the probability mass function for the binomial distribution with $n = 5$ and $p = 2/5$. The first R command sets the vector x to the support of the binomial distribution, which is $x = 0, 1, 2, \ldots, 5$. The second R command uses the dbinom function to calculate the probability mass function for $X \sim \text{binomial}(5, 2/5)$. The third command plots points associated with the probability mass function with the plot function. Finally, the type argument is set to the string "h" to plot spikes for each of the mass values of X.

```
> x = 0:5                    # support of X
> y = dbinom(x, 5, 2 / 5)    # probability mass function
> plot(x, y)                 # plot of points
> plot(x, y, type = "h")     # histogram-like spikes
```

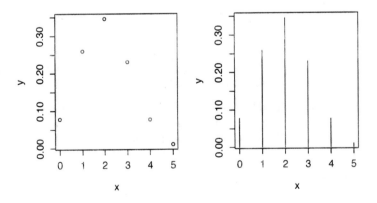

The two plots generated are displayed side-by-side here to save space. There are plenty of decisions that the R plot function makes as defaults: tick marks point outward, vertical labels are rotated counterclockwise 90° from horizontal, the axes touch, the vertical axis labels are typeset vertically, etc. The plot function requires that its first two arguments are vectors of the same length.

The second example uses the `plot` function to generate a graph of the probability density function of the standard normal distribution between -3 and 3. The viewer's eye will be tricked into thinking that this is a smooth function when in fact it is many tiny line segments connected at their endpoints. The first R command uses the `seq` function to set x to a vector beginning at -3, ending at 3, with an increment between elements of 0.01. Thus, x is a 601-element vector. The `dnorm` function is then used to set y to a second 601-element vector that contains the heights of the probability density function of the standard normal distribution for each element of x. Finally, the `plot` function is called with the `type` argument set to the letter `"l"` to connect the 601 points in x and y with lines.

```
> x = seq(-3, 3, by = 0.01)    # range of x
> y = dnorm(x)                 # probability density function
> plot(x, y, type = "l")       # plot of the probability density function
```

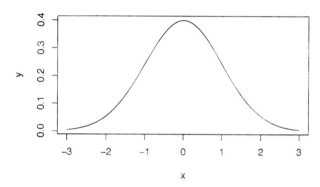

The next example plots two empirical cumulative distribution functions on a single set of axes using the `lines` function. Recall that the built-in `Puromycin` data set is a data frame with 23 rows and 3 columns that contain the instantaneous reaction rate (`rate`) in counts per minutes^2 versus substrate concentration (`conc`) in parts per million and a factor (`state`) with levels `treated` and `untreated` in an enzymatic reaction involving untreated cells or cells treated with Puromycin. We would like a plot of the empirical cumulative distribution functions of the reaction rates for the `treated` and `untreated` groups. The first two R commands place the reaction rates for the two groups into the vectors x and y. The third command uses the `plot.ecdf` function to create a graph of the empirical cumulative distribution function of the elements of x. The fourth command uses the `lines` function to add a graph of the empirical cumulative distribution function of the elements of y on the same axis that was created for x. The `xlim` (x-limit) argument is necessary on the two graphical commands to ensure that the same horizontal axis scales are used for the two empirical cumulative distribution functions.

```
> x = Puromycin$rate[Puromycin$state == "treated"]
> y = Puromycin$rate[Puromycin$state == "untreated"]
> plot.ecdf(x, verticals = TRUE, pch = "", xlim = c(40, 220))
> lines(ecdf(y), verticals = TRUE, pch = "", xlim = c(40, 220))
```

The next example of a customized plot is designed to show you how R lays out the plotting region with margins. Before executing this example, it is worthwhile typing

```
> help(par)
```

to read the help page on the graphical arguments.

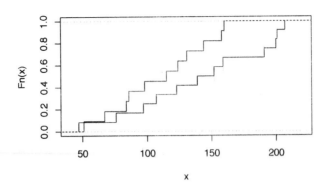

The first R command below calls the par function with the mar (margin) argument, which controls the sizes of the four margins, bottom, left, top, and right, in that order, measured in number of lines of text. This ordering of the margins is used by other R graphical functions. The second R command calls the plot function, which would ordinarily plot the points $(0, -10)$ and $(9, 20)$, but setting the type argument to the string "n" means that no points will be plotted. In addition, the y-axis will have no label because the ylab argument is set to an empty string. The text function is used to plot the string "plotting region" centered at the point $(6, 10)$. The points function is first called to plot the default style point at $(4, -10)$. Then points is called with the pch (plotting character) argument set to 3. It is called a third time to print four different characters (pch), in four different colors (col), in four different sizes (cex for character expand). The polygon function plots a shaded polygon with the points associated with the x-values given in the first argument and the y-values given in the second argument. The lines function plots a line by connecting the points associated with the x-values given in the first argument and the y-values given in the second argument, with the lwd (line width) argument specifying the thickness of the line and the lty (line type) argument specifying the type of line (1 for solid, 2 for dashed, 3 for dotted, etc.). The mtext (margin text) function places text in the margins. The srt (string rotate) argument in the text function allows for slanted text (the argument is in degrees). The font argument in the text function can be used for bold text (font = 2), italics text (font = 3), bold italix text (font = 4), and Greek text (font = 5). The adj (adjust) argument in the text function specifies whether the text should be left justified (adj = 0), centered (adj = 0.5, the default), or right justified (adj = 1). The adj argument can assume any value on the interval $[0, 1]$. The expression function can be used for plotting mathematical expressions like $\lambda_i/2^x$. The lines function plots the parabola $y = x^2 - 3$. Finally, the arrows function draws an arrow from $(6, 6)$ to a point on the parabola.

```
> par(mar = c(5, 8, 5, 8))
> plot(c(0, 9), c(-10, 20), type = "n", ylab = "")
> text(6, 10, "plotting region")
> points(4, -10)
> points(8, 16, pch = 3)
> points(6:9, 5:2, pch = c(".", "O", "W", "8"),
+        col = c("black", "red4", "navy", "gray2"),
+        cex = seq(1.0, 0.7, by = -0.1))
> polygon(c(0, 0, 1, 1), c(0, 2, 1, 0), col = "gold")
> lines(c(0, 4, 6, 8), c(-8, 2, 2, 0), lwd = 2, lty = 2)
> mtext(paste("margin", 1:4), side = 1:4, line = 4)
> mtext(paste("line", 0:7), side = 4, line = 0:7, at = 15)
> text(1.9, -5, "slanted text", srt = 42)
```

```
> text(2, 19, "bold font", font = 2)
> text(2, 17, "italics font", font = 3)
> text(2, 15, "bold & italics font", font = 4)
> text(2, 13, "abeG", font = 5)
> text(0, -10, "left/bottom justified", adj = c(0, 0))
> text(9, 20, "right/top justified", adj = c(1, 1))
> text(6, -5, expression(frac(lambda[i], 2 ^ x)), cex = 1.5)
> x = seq(0, 4, by = 0.1)
> y = x ^ 2 - 3
> lines(x, y)
> arrows(6, 6, x[33], y[33])
```

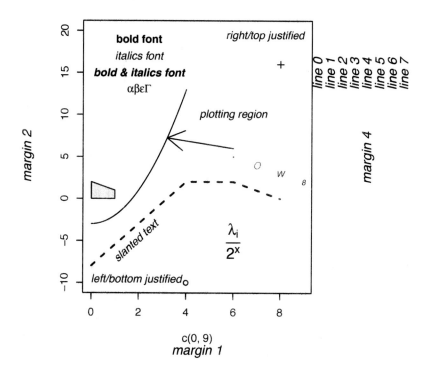

The `plot` function can also be used for plotting univariate data. The R command

```
> plot(precip)          # plot precipitation data
```

for example, plots the $n = 70$ average precipitation values contained in the built-in data set `precip` on the vertical axis and $1:70$ on the horizontal axis.

It is more often the case that the `plot` function is used to graph data pairs. Recall that the built-in `cars` data set contains two variables: `speed`, which is the speed of the vehicle in miles per hour, and `dist`, which is the stopping distance in feet. The $n = 50$ data pairs were collected in the 1920s,

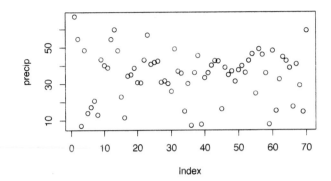

so the speeds are all under 30 miles per hour. The three calls to the plot function given below use the default for the type argument (just plot points), "l" for the type argument (connect the points with lines), and "b" for the type argument (both points and lines).

```
> plot(cars)                    # paired data
> plot(cars, type = "l")        # connect the points
> plot(cars, type = "b")        # both points and lines
```

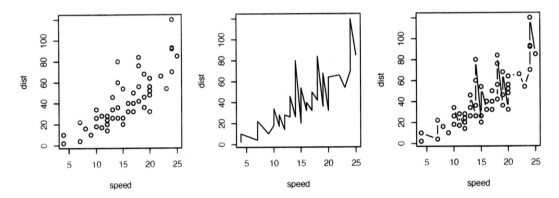

The plotting character can be altered using the pch (plotting character) argument. Using pch = 16, for example, gives a solid, rather than an empty circle as a plotting point. The scales for the axes can assume a logarithmic scale, often appropriate for values having a wide range, by using the log argument. Using log = "x" makes the horizontal scale logarithmic; using log = "y" makes the vertical scale logarithmic; using log = "xy" makes both scales logarithmic.

```
> plot(cars, type = "b", pch = 16)    # another plotting character
> plot(cars, log = "y")               # vertical axis logarithmic
> plot(cars, log = "xy")              # both axes logarithmic
```

R is capable of producing production-quality graphics. This next example illustrates all of the detail that I would put into a graph of $y = f(x) = x^2$ on $-2 < x < 3$ that I intend to fold into a document. The first step is to set the target directory for the graphic. Using the setwd (set working directory) function, which was introduced in Chapter 18, the working directory is set to the Desktop on a machine whose name is my initials lml.

```
> setwd("/Users/lml/Desktop")
```

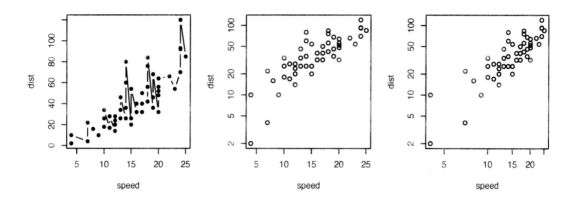

The second step is to determine a filename and format for the graphic. Using the `postscript` function below, a file named `filename.eps` is established as the target file in the working directory.

```
> postscript(file = "filename.eps", width = 4.4, height = 4.4, horizontal = F)
```

The third and final step is to create the graphic. Some features of the graphic are:

- the x and y vectors each consist of 501 elements,

- both *x* and *y* labels are suppressed via the `xlab` and `ylab` arguments in the call to `plot`,

- the line width for $y = x^2$ is 50% wider than the default via the `lwd` argument in the call to `plot`,

- the `xlim` and `ylim` arguments in the call to `plot` set the limits for the plotting region,

- the `axes = FALSE` argument in the call to `plot` suppresses the axes,

- the axes are generated in a custom fashion with the `axis` function,

- unlike previous plots, the axes do not touch,

- the `at` argument in the call to `axis` defines the positions of the tick marks and labels,

- the `las` argument in the call to `axis` rotates the labels on the vertical axis,

- the axis labels are placed at the end of the axes with the `text` function,

- the `xpd = TRUE` argument in the call to the `text` function is a "clipping parameter," which allows text to be displayed outside of the plot region,

- the `dev.off` (device off) function completes the plot, creating a postscript file.

```
> x = seq(-2, 3, by = 0.01)
> y = x ^ 2
> par(lty = 1, font = 3, mai = c(0.6, 0.6, 0.3, 0.3))
> plot(x, y,
+     type = "l",          # connect points with lines
+     lwd = 1.5,           # line width
+     xlab="",             # no x label
```

```
+     ylab="",              # no y label
+     xlim = c(-2, 3),      # limits on the horizontal axis
+     ylim = c(0, 9),       # limits on the vertical axis
+     axes = FALSE)         # no axes
> axis(side = 1, labels = TRUE, at = -2:3, font = 1)
> axis(side = 2, labels = TRUE, at = c(0, 4, 9), font = 1, las = 1)
> text(3.5, -0.3, "x", font = 1, xpd = TRUE)
> text(-2.2, 9.9, "y", font = 1, xpd = TRUE)
> dev.off()
```

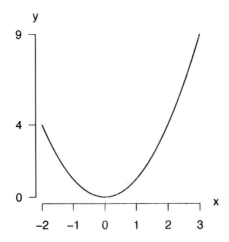

The lines function has been used previously to plot multiple functions on a single set of axes. The matplot function contains a similar capability. Consider the problem of plotting the sine and cosine functions on a single set of axes, that is, plot $y = \sin x$ and $y = \cos x$ on $0 \leq x \leq 2\pi$. The first R command given below sets the vector x to 100 equally-spaced values on $0 \leq x \leq 2\pi$ using the seq function. The second and third R commands set the vectors sine and cosine to the associated values of $y = \sin x$ and $y = \cos x$. The fourth command plots the two functions on the same set of axes in black (color number 1) using the matplot function. The cbind (column bind) function is used to combine the two functions being plotted into a matrix. By default, the matplot function plots the values in the first column of cbind(sine, cosine) in the solid line type (lty = 1). Likewise, the matplot function plots the values in the second column of cbind(sine, cosine) in the dotted line type (lty = 2).

```
> x = seq(0, 2 * pi, length = 100)
> sine = sin(x)
> cosine = cos(x)
> matplot(x, cbind(sine, cosine), col = c(1, 1), type = "l")
```

One way to produce multiple plots is to open additional graphics windows. The specifics on how to open additional graphics windows are platform dependent, and can be found by typing help(dev.new) and help(dev.control). Alternatively, multiple plots can be combined into a single graphics window using the mfrow or mfcol arguments in the par function. These plots are known in R as "multiple frame plots." Consider the problem of writing an R function named eda (for exploratory data analysis) that draws a boxplot, histogram, empirical cumulative distribution function, and a QQ plot for the normal distribution for a univariate data set.

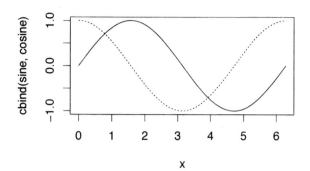

```
> eda = function(x) {          # eda: exploratory data analysis
+    par(mfrow = c(2, 2))      # a two row, two column display of graphics
+    boxplot(x)                # boxplot
+    hist(x)                   # histogram
+    plot.ecdf(x)              # empirical cumulative distribution function
+    qqnorm(x)                 # QQ plot for normality
+ }
```

Calling the eda function for the univariate data set precip results in a 2 × 2 set of plots.

```
> eda(precip)                  # precipitation data set
```

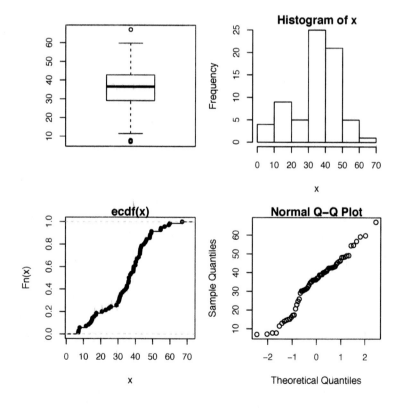

The eda function uses the mfrow argument in the call to par in order to create a 2 × 2 (two rows and two columns) array of plots, laid out in row-major fashion. The argument mfrow = c(nrow, ncol) gives an array of plots with nrow rows and ncol columns, which are filled by row. The argument mfcol = c(nrow, ncol) gives an array of plots with nrow rows and ncol columns, which are filled by column. Calling the eda function for the univariate data set rivers results in a 2 × 2 set of plots, which reveals a highly nonsymmetric data set.

```
> eda(rivers)              # lengths of rivers data set
```

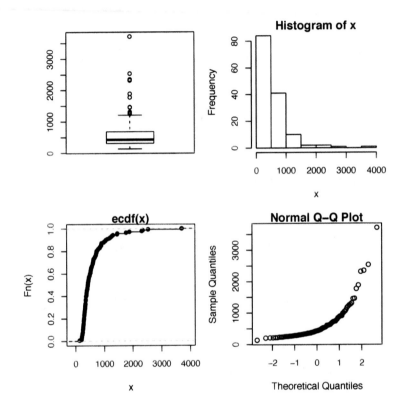

The next example shows how a simple graphic can be refined and improved by adding arguments that enhance the graphic. We return to the built-in Puromycin data set. Begin by creating a plot of conc as the independent variable versus rate as the dependent variable.

```
> plot(rate ~ conc, data = Puromycin)
```

Although this figure is helpful to establish a nonlinear relationship between conc and rate, the role of the third variable state is not yet apparent. So an enhanced call to the plot function uses the substr (substring) function to extract the first character of the strings "treated" and "untreated" so that a t and u are displayed on the plot.

```
> plot(rate ~ conc, data = Puromycin, pch = substr(state, 1, 1))
```

This figure reveals that the instantaneous reaction rate is typically higher for cells treated with Puromycin for equal levels of substrate concentration. Although this plot is probably adequate for

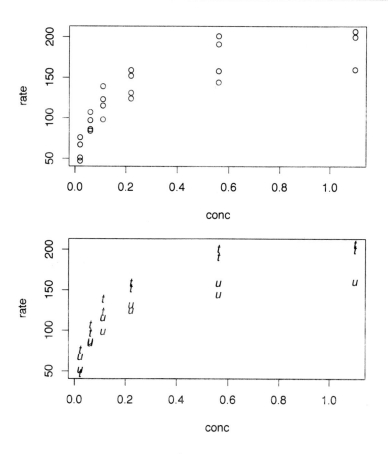

this particular data set, a larger data set or one that has many levels of a factor might need various plotting symbols and a legend. The R calls to the plot and legend functions use pch = 1 for the untreated observations and pch = 16 for the treated observations.

```
> plot(rate ~ conc, data = Puromycin, pch = 15 * (state == "treated") + 1)
> legend("bottomright", legend = c("Untreated", "Treated"), pch = c(1, 16))
```

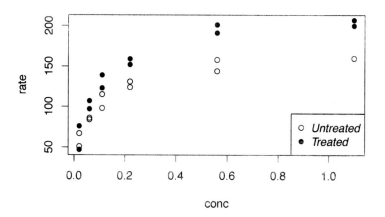

All of the custom plots considered in the chapter thus far have been two-dimensional plots. This final example illustrates the use of the `persp` function to plot a three dimensional relationship using what is known as a "wire mesh." More specifically, we would like to plot the function

$$f(x, y) = \frac{\sin\left(\sqrt{x^2 + y^2}\right)}{\sqrt{x^2 + y^2}}$$

on $-8 \leq x \leq 8$ and $-8 \leq y \leq 8$. The first two R commands below define the vectors x and y to have 100 equally-spaced elements between -8 and 8. The third R command defines the function $f(x, y)$. The fourth command uses the `outer` function to calculate the outer product of x and y using the function f. Finally, the `persp` function is called to create a perspective plot of the $100 \cdot 100 = 10,000$ points calculated in the previous command.

```
> x = seq(-8, 8, length = 100)
> y = x
> f = function(x, y) sin(sqrt(x ^ 2 + y ^ 2)) / (sqrt(x ^ 2 + y ^ 2))
> z = outer(x, y, f)
> persp(x, y, z)
```

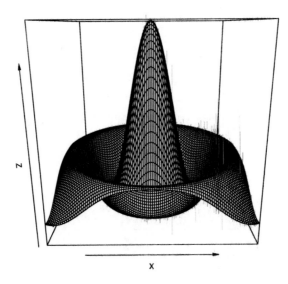

The result is a handsome sombrero-shaped graph. If you would like just the sombrero alone, then some additional arguments to `persp` are needed. If the arguments for the x-label, y-label, and z-label are set to the empty string, and the `axes` and `box` arguments are set to `FALSE`, then all that remains is the function $f(x, y)$.

```
> persp(x, y, z, xlab = "", ylab = "", zlab = "", axes = FALSE, box = FALSE)
```

Although this chapter has focused on the mechanics associated with custom graphics in R, designing an effective statistical graphic is somewhat of an art form. This chapter ends with four examples of effective statistical graphics, ignoring the mechanics required to create the graphic. Very

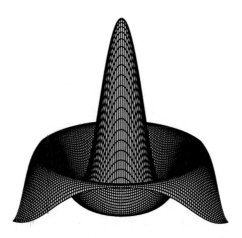

little information will be given in the text concerning the graphic. The hope is that the R graphic alone can tell most of the story.

The !Kung hunter-gatherers of Botswana and Nambia have long intervals between births, typically between 3 and 4 years, despite being a noncontracepting and nonabstinent population. Speculations linked the birth spacing to nutritional infertility, because the !Kung diet is sometimes low in calories, but no direct data had been collected to support this hypothesis. Harvard anthropologists Melvin Konner and Carol Worthman investigated the unusually long birth spacings. The figure below shows one daylight cycle of interaction between a mother and her 14-day old son.

The first thing that jumps out from the data (particularly to a Western mother) is the high frequency of nursing bouts. During the daytime hours when recordings were collected, there were 46 such bouts. This corresponds to a nursing bout every 15 minutes on average for this baby. There was a nursing bout every 13 minutes on average for all of the babies that the investigators observed. From blood samples and statistical graphics like the one given above, the researchers rejected the conclusion that the low-calorie diet alone produced the long birth spacings. Since nursing results in

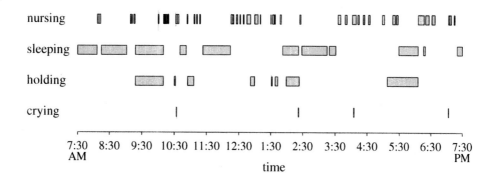

the release of the hormone prolactin, and prolactin has a half-life in the plasma of 10 to 30 minutes, they concluded that prolactin has an antigonadotrophic effect, which means that the mother will be less fertile if the prolactin level is high enough. It is only late into the second year of life, when the baby's separations from the mother are longer as the baby spends more time playing, that the mother once again becomes fertile.

The second example concerns demography, which is the statistical study of human populations. One aspect of human populations that can be summarized by two histograms is the age distribution for a particular sub-population. A *population pyramid* or *age structure diagram* consists of two histograms, one for males and one for females, rotated 90° and placed side-by-side. These diagrams are used to illustrate the longevity, birth rate, and probability distribution of the ages of the population by gender, race, etc. When two population pyramids are compared for the same sub-population at two different points in time, they reveal population dynamics due to various factors such as medical advances or immigration.

The figure below contains a population pyramid for France on January 1, 1960 using data from www.insee.fr. There are 100 ages plotted on the vertical axis, and corresponding male populations on the left and female populations on the right, in thousands, on the horizontal axis. The most pronounced features of this statistical graphic are the nearly-symmetric dents in the populations that achieve their lowest levels at ages 19 and 44. These dents cannot be attributed to random sampling variability because the sample size is so large. Using the birth year on the right-hand vertical scale, it can be concluded that the tragic effects of two world wars fought on French soil are the cause of the dents in the population pyramid. The durations of World War I (1914–1918) and World War II (1939–1945) coincide with the dents. There was a decreased birth rate during the wars, and a post-war baby boom after each war.

Both male and female births are affected equally by the decline and subsequent bump in the birthrate. Looking more closely at the elderly population at the top of the graphic also indicates that

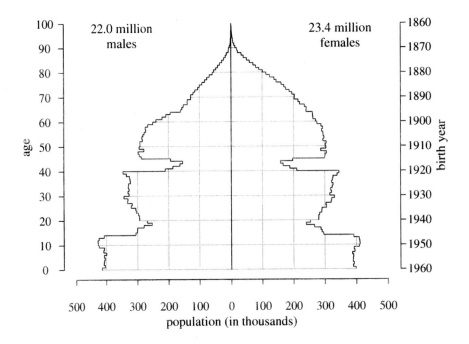

there are significantly more elderly women than men. This could be due to the increased longevity that women have over men, or there might be other factors at play. France's 1.7 million casualties in World War I and 600,000 casualties in World War II would also account for some of the difference between the male and female population sizes.

The third example comes from sports. *March Madness* occurs every spring when a 64-team, single-elimination tournament is used to determine the best college basketball team in the United States. One game, which is considered by some to be the greatest basketball game ever played, occurred in the East Regional final game of the men's tournament on March 28, 1992, between the Blue Devils of Duke and the Wildcats of Kentucky. Duke prevailed 104–103 in an overtime victory, winning on a last-second shot by Christian Laettner. The game featured perfect shooting for Laettner (10 for 10 from the field and 10 for 10 free throws for 31 points), five lead changes in the last 31.5 seconds, and both teams shooting 63% from the field in the second half and overtime. This game was the subject of a book by ESPN sportswriter Gene Wojciechowski titled *The Last Great Game*. The graphic below shows the scoring by the two teams over time.

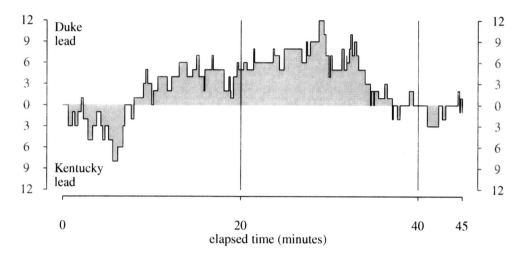

The Dow Jones Industrial Average (DJIA), also known as the Dow 30, was devised by Charles Dow and was initiated on May 26, 1896. The average bears Dow's name and that of statistician and business associate Edward Jones. The DJIA is the average stock price of 30 U.S.-based, publicly-traded companies, adjusted for stock splits and the swapping of companies in and out of the average so that it adequately reflects the composition of the domestic stock market. These adjustments are made by altering the average's denominator for historical continuity, which is now much less than 30.

The evolution of the DJIA is not a true reflection of the yield of the 30 stocks because two important factors are not incorporated into the average. First, the average does not factor in dividends that are paid by some of the 30 stocks. Second, the average does not factor in inflation, which erodes the true return that a stock investment provides. If dividends were factored in, the DJIA would be much higher than it is presently; if inflation were factored in, the DJIA would be much lower than it is presently. A plot of the average annual DJIA closing values during the 20th century as a time series is given in the graph that follows.

The DJIA had a sample mean closing value of 69.52 during 1901 and a sample mean closing value of 10731.15 during 2000. The linear scale that is used in this figure obscures most of the variability of the DJIA during the first half of the century. The graph can be made more meaningful

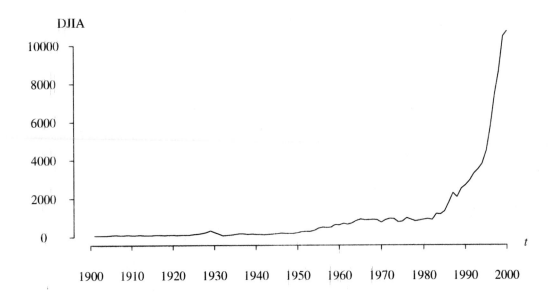

by using a logarithmic scale on the vertical axis, as shown next. In addition, labels have been added to help highlight events that might have influenced the DJIA.

The stock market crash in October of 1929 is much more pronounced in the second figure. The DJIA had peaked with a close of 381.20 on September 3, 1929. The market bottomed out on July 8, 1932, when it closed at 41.20, corresponding to a loss of almost 90%. Each of the two World Wars fought during the twentieth century was followed by a sustained bull market in the DJIA. The top marginal income tax rate was lowered from 70% to 28% in the early 1980s.

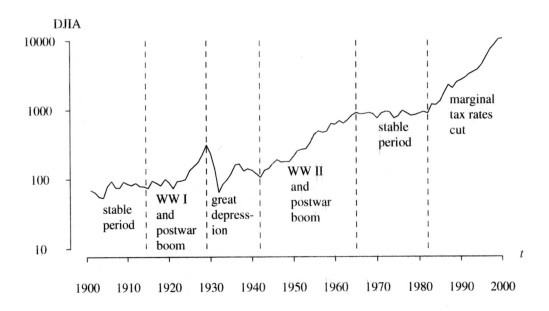

This concludes the discussion of creating custom graphics in R. The table below summarizes the functions introduced in this chapter.

function	description
lines	add connected line segments to a plot
par	get or set graphical parameters
text	add text to a plot
points	add points to a plot
polygon	add a polygon to a plot
mtext	add text to the margins of a plot
arrows	add arrows to a plot
postscript	start graphics device driver for postscript graphics
dev.off	shut down device
matplot	plot columns of matrices
legend	add legend to a plot

The next three chapters are an introduction to programming in R.

Exercises

21.1   Suppose that x and y are vectors containing numerical elements. Write R commands that generate a plot of the empirical cumulative distribution functions of the elements in the two vectors. The two empirical cumulative distribution functions should be plotted on a single set of axes, and the horizontal axis should include the entire range of both data sets.

21.2   Use R to plot the function $y = \cos x$ on $0 < x < 4\pi$.

21.3   Use R to plot the piecewise function

$$y = \begin{cases} x & 0 < x \le 1 \\ 2 & 1 < x \le 2 \\ 3 - x & 2 < x \le 3. \end{cases}$$

21.4   The built-in data set named AirPassengers consists of counts of the number of international airline passengers from 1949 to 1960. The built-in data set named sunspots consists of counts of the number of sunspots from 1749 to 1983. Both of these data sets give monthly observations. Using the R class function, these two data sets are classified as time series (abbreviated "ts"). Create two plots (in one R graphic) of the monthly AirPassengers time series on top and the monthly sunspots time series below for the common years 1949–1960. Use the help function on the R ts function to determine how to extract the appropriate values from the sunspots data set.

21.5   Plot the gamma function $\Gamma(x)$ using R function gamma for $-3 < x < 4$. Note that the gamma function is undefined for nonpositive integers. Use the limits $-6 \le \Gamma(x) \le 6$ for the vertical axis. Use dashed lines to indicate asymptotes.

21.6   Use the balance function from Chapter 8 to make a plot of the interest rate on the horizontal axis (ranging from 1% to 9%) versus the final balance on the vertical axis for an initial deposit of $1000 and a term of 20 years.

21.7   Write a function named uds (for univariate distribution summary) with arguments x (a vector of numeric data values) and plotit (a logical value). If plotit is TRUE, the function draws a histogram of the data values contained in x. If plotit is FALSE, the program calculates and prints the sample mean and sample standard deviation of the data values contained in x. The default value for plotit should be FALSE. Test your code with the following R commands.

```
> uds(precip)
> uds(precip, plotit = TRUE)
```

21.8   Use the ifelse function to plot the piecewise function

$$f(x) = \begin{cases} x^2 & x < 1 \\ x & x \geq 1. \end{cases}$$

on $-2 < x < 3$ using a single call to the plot function.

21.9   The curve function provides a mechanism for generating a graphic using a minimal number of keystrokes. View the help documentation page for the curve function and use it to

(a) plot $y = x^2$ between -2 and 3,

(b) plot $y = \sin x$ between $-\pi$ and π.

Chapter 22

Conditional Execution

In addition to the capabilities of R that have already been described, it can also serve as a programming language, as outlined in the next three chapters. This chapter introduces *conditional execution*; the next chapter introduces *looping*; the subsequent chapter introduces *recursion*. The topics considered in this chapter are (a) the if statement, and (b) applications of conditional execution.

An *algorithm* is a step-by-step procedure for performing a task, such as baking a cake. On a computer, algorithms are generally associated with calculations or data manipulation. The programming capabilities that will be introduced in this chapter and the next two chapters can be used to define an algorithm as a sequence of instructions for problem solving. Many programmers like to draw out the algorithm using a flow chart or d-chart prior to coding up the algorithm in a particular language. This important step of planning is encouraged, particularly for large or complicated algorithms. R supports "structured programming," which means that R commands can be indented in the code when contained within an if statement or a loop for clarity.

22.1 The if statement

This chapter introduces conditional execution, which can be thought of as an introduction to the if statement. The syntax for the if statement in its simplest form is

```
if (condition) command
```

The condition is a single logical value (a vector of length one whose element is logical) or if condition is numeric, then 0 is FALSE and non-zero is TRUE. The execution of the if statement in this simplest form is that if the condition is TRUE, then the command will be executed. If the condition is FALSE, then the command will not be executed. If the condition or the command is lengthy, it is acceptable to write the if statement involving a single command in the form

```
if (condition)
  command
```

These forms of the if statement work fine if there is just a single command to be executed. But if there are two or more commands to be executed, the syntax is

```
if (condition) {
  commands
}
```

It is good programming practice to left-align all of the R commands contained in the curly braces and to indent them two spaces (some programmers prefer four spaces, but whatever you choose, be consistent) as shown above for readability. This practice also emphasizes the logical structure of the program. The curly braces serve as delimiters to enclose the R commands that are to be executed if the condition is TRUE. R uses the + prompt as the R commands are entered from the keyboard, then returns to the > prompt after the closing curly brace has been entered.

It is oftentimes the case that there are also one or more commands that should be executed if the condition is FALSE. If there is just a single command to be executed when the condition is TRUE and another single command to be executed when the condition is FALSE, then the if statement can be written on a single line with the syntax

```
if (condition) command1 else command2
```

If the condition is TRUE, command1 will be executed; if the condition is FALSE, command2 will be executed. When there are two or more commands to execute when the condition is TRUE or FALSE, the curly braces are again used to enclose the commands:

```
if (condition) {
  commands1
}
else {
  commands2
}
```

It is good programming practice to left-align all of the R commands within each block of R commands and indent two spaces for readability. This particular style is fine when the R code has been stored in a file and is being executed with the source function. But if you are keying in the code line-by-line, R will assume that the if statement has concluded when it encounters the first closing curly brace. So when keying these commands into an R session, the syntax is

```
if (condition) {
  commands1
} else {
  commands2
}
```

We begin the illustration of the if statement with a simple illustration that prints the character string "x is negative" when x assumes a negative value.

```
> x = -3
> if (x < 0) print("x is negative")
[1] "x is negative"
```

The condition x < 0 evaluates to TRUE because x = -3, so the call to the print function gets executed.

As a second example, an if statement is used to replace x by its opposite if it is negative. The R commands to accomplish this are

```
> x = -3
> if (x < 0) x = -x
> x
[1] 3
```

Since x is negative, the R command x = -x gets executed, which means that x's value gets changed from -3 to 3.

Changing negative values to positive values is the role of the absolute value function. Even though there is an absolute value function named abs built into R that does a perfectly splendid job of taking the absolute value of the elements of an object, we can write our own personal absolute value function named my.abs. The function uses an if statement in much the same fashion as the previous examples.

```
> my.abs = function(x) {
+    if (x < 0) x = -x
+    return(x)
+ }
> my.abs(-3)
[1] 3
> my.abs(0)
[1] 0
> my.abs(3)
[1] 3
```

The my.abs function performs as we would hope when given -3, 0, and 3 as an argument. But what if we use a vector as an argument in my.abs? As will be seen below, the results are disastrous.

```
> my.abs(c(-5, 0, 5))
[1]  5  0 -5
Warning message:
In if (x < 0) x = -x :
  the condition has length > 1 and only the first element will be used
```

What happened? The warning message alerts us to the problem. The condition in the if statement must be a single logical element (which evaluates to TRUE or FALSE), but we pass x as a three-element vector. R uses just the first element of x and checks the condition -5 < 0, which evaluates to TRUE. So the assignment command x = -x gets executed, resulting in the entire vector getting negated, rather than just the negative elements.

So the next step is to modify the my.abs function so that it works properly for vectors, matrices, and arrays.

```
> my.abs = function(x) {
+    x[x < 0] = -x[x < 0]
+    return(x)
+ }
> my.abs(-3)
[1] 3
> my.abs(3)
[1] 3
> my.abs(c(-5, 0, 5))
[1] 5 0 5
```

The output of the three test cases seems to indicate that the function is working as intended. As long as the elements of the data structure passed are numeric, the my.abs function works fine. But now let's see what happens when we send it a string as an argument.

```
> my.abs("Hello")
Error in -x[x < 0] : invalid argument to unary operator
```

The error message indicates that R eventually tripped over the unary negation operator. What we would really prefer is an error message that indicates that our my.abs function only accepts an argument consisting of numeric elements. This is known as *defensive programming* or *error trapping*, and protects the function against inappropriate arguments, printing an appropriate error message for bad input. The next version of my.abs includes error trapping by calling the stop function.

```
> my.abs = function(x) {
+    if (mode(x) != "numeric") stop("non-numeric argument")
+    x[x < 0] = -x[x < 0]
+    return(x)
+ }
> my.abs("Hello")
Error in my.abs("Hello") : non-numeric argument
```

These incremental revisions of the my.abs function are typical of programming in R, or any other programming language. Often a simple function is tested, followed by revisions of that function that generalize, extend, or provide error trapping.

All of the uses of the if statement thus far have not included an else clause. The next example prints a string describing the sign of the object x, which is a vector of length one assumed to hold a numeric value.

```
> x = 3
> if (x >= 0) print("x is nonnegative") else print("x is negative")
[1] "x is nonnegative"
> x = -3
> if (x >= 0) print("x is nonnegative") else print("x is negative")
[1] "x is negative"
> x = 0
> if (x >= 0) print("x is nonnegative") else print("x is negative")
[1] "x is nonnegative"
```

This case allowed the entire if statement to be keyed into one line because there is just a single R command to be executed if the condition is TRUE and a single R command to be executed if the condition is FALSE.

22.2 Applications

Now consider an application of the if statement that is out of this world. Astronomers have determined that the time for the earth to orbit the sun is approximately 365.2422 days. A leap year adds February 29 to the calendar in order to adjust for the non-integer number of days, which means that the calendar will not go out of whack. A year is considered a leap year if it is divisible by four but not by 100, unless it is a year divisible by 400, which is a leap year. This results in the length of the average calendar year of

$$365 + \frac{1}{4} - \frac{1}{100} + \frac{1}{400} = 365.2425$$

days. Not quite right, but awfully close. A correction will not need to be made for several thousand years, and none of us will be around to deal with the issue. We would like to write a function named leapyear having a single argument year, which returns TRUE if year is a leap year and FALSE if it is not a leap year. The leapyear function below has a long condition that is required to determine if the argument year is a leap year, so the single commands, which are just calls to the return function, are placed on the lines following the if and else.

```
> leapyear = function(year) {
+    if (year %% 4 == 0 && year %% 100 != 0 || year %% 400 == 0)
+        return(TRUE)
+    else
+        return(FALSE)
+ }
> leapyear(1865)
[1] FALSE
> leapyear(1984)
[1] TRUE
> leapyear(2000)
[1] TRUE
> leapyear(2100)
[1] FALSE
```

The leapyear function seems to be working appropriately.

The next example considers the problem of writing a function named is.palin, which returns TRUE if its argument, a string, is a palindrome and FALSE otherwise. A palindrome is a character string that reads the same backward and forward. In addition, the function should contain error trapping to detect arguments that are not strings. The problem will be solved in two steps. The first step is to write a function named strRev that reverses the characters in a string. This can be done using the paste, rev (reverse), and substring functions.

```
> strRev = function(x) {
+    paste(rev(substring(x, 1:nchar(x), 1:nchar(x))), collapse = "")
+ }
```

The second step is to write the is.palin function, which uses an if statement to assure that the argument is of the character mode, then checks to see if the argument and its reverse are identical.

```
> is.palin = function(x) {
+    if (mode(x) != "character") stop("non-character input")
+    if (x == strRev(x)) return(TRUE) else return(FALSE)
+ }
> is.palin("abba")
[1] TRUE
> is.palin("Mr. Owl ate my metal worm.")
[1] FALSE
> is.palin("Palin")
[1] FALSE
```

The string "abba" is indeed a palindrome. The string concerning Mr. Owl is also a palindrome, but it is not detected by our is.palin function because it does not ignore case and strip out blanks and punctuation.

The final illustration of the if statement concerns writing a function named describe that prints a grammatically correct sentence that reports the number of elements in a vector. The R code for describe uses the cat function, which concatenates and prints objects. The cat function is oftentimes preferred to the more traditional print function because it allows objects of different data types (for example, character and numeric) as arguments. Notice that the cat function requires a \n at the end of the sentence in order to produce a carriage return.

```
> describe = function(x) {
+    n = length(x)
+    if (n == 1) cat("The vector has 1 element.\n")
+    else        cat("The vector has", n, "elements.\n")
+ }
> x = 17
> describe(x)
The vector has 1 element.
> x = 2:10
> describe(x)
The vector has 9 elements.
> describe(NULL)
The vector has 0 elements.
```

The three tests for the describe function indicate that it is working properly in these limited cases. There is an alternative way to write the describe function that requires one fewer line of R code. The condition can be embedded into the cat function.

```
> describe = function(x) {
+    n = length(x)
+    cat("The vector has", n, if (n == 1) "element.\n" else "elements.\n")
+ }
> x = 19
> describe(x)
The vector has 1 element.
> x = c(TRUE, FALSE, TRUE, FALSE)
> describe(x)
The vector has 4 elements.
```

The modified describe function works as expected in these two instances.

All of the examples considered thus far have required just a single if statement to perform the required operation. But if statements can be *nested*, that is, one if statement can be placed within another if statement. Let's say we want to write a function that prints the string "positive", "zero", or "negative" depending on the value of the numeric argument by nesting if statements.

```
> printType = function(x) {
+    if (x > 0) cat("positive\n")
+    else
+       if (x == 0) cat("zero\n")
+       else cat("negative\n")
+ }
> printType(-3)
negative
> printType(0)
zero
```

```
> printType(4)
positive
```

Notice how the indentation in the R commands in the `printType` function reflects the level of the nesting. In a complex programming application, the nesting can often go several levels deep.

This concludes the discussion of conditional execution using the `if` statement. The table below summarizes the functions introduced in this chapter.

function	description
if	if statement
stop	stop execution

The next chapter considers the important topic of iteration, which is also known as looping. Conditional execution and looping together provide the tools necessary to solve a wide variety of programming problems.

Exercises

22.1 Write a function named qe with arguments aa, bb, and cc that solves the quadratic equation

$$ax^2 + bx + c = 0$$

and returns the roots as a two-element vector of real or complex numbers. The arguments aa, bb, and cc are the coefficients of the quadratic equation. Test your qe function with the R commands given below.

```
> qe(1, 1, 1)
> qe(1, 2, 1)
> qe(1, 3, 1)
```

22.2 Write a function named HighFive with a single argument x, which is a vector of arbitrary length containing numeric values. HighFive should return a vector of the same length and elements as x, but increases the elements in the fifth, tenth, fifteenth, ..., positions by five.

22.3 The Catalan number, often denoted by C_n, can be defined in the following three fashions:

$$C_n = \frac{1}{n+1}\binom{2n}{n} = \frac{(2n)!}{(n+1)!n!} = \prod_{i=2}^{n}\frac{n+i}{i},$$

where n is a nonnegative integer. Note that zero factorial is defined to be one and the iterated product in the rightmost expression is one for $n = 0$ and $n = 1$. Assuming that n is a nonnegative integer, write three single R commands that calculate C_n by these three formulas.

22.4 Write a function named add.commas with a single argument x that holds a single numeric value that is a positive integer between 1 and 999,999,999, which prints the integer with commas inserted to separate the digits when appropriate for a more handsome display. Test your add.commas function with the R commands add.commas(1234) and add.commas(1234567), which should display 1,234 and 1,234,567, respectively.

22.5 A chessboard is an 8×8 matrix of positions. Two knights can attack one another if either (a) their row numbers differ by one and their column numbers differ by two, or (b) their column numbers differ by one and their row numbers differ by two. Write an R function named `attack.knights` with two arguments k1 and k2, which are each two-element vectors that represent the positions (row and column) of the two knights. Your program should return TRUE if the two knights can attack one another and FALSE otherwise. Test your function with the following R commands.

```
> attack.knights(c(4, 4), c(6, 5))
> attack.knights(c(1, 1), c(8, 8))
> attack.knights(c(4, 4), c(3, 6))
> attack.knights(c(8, 2), c(2, 8))
> attack.knights(c(8, 8), c(6, 7))
```

22.6 A chessboard is an 8×8 matrix of positions. Two queens can attack one another if they are (a) on the same row, (b) on the same column, or (c) on the same diagonal. Write an R function named `attack.queens` with two arguments q1 and q2, which are each two-element vectors that represent the positions (row and column) of the two queens. Your program should return TRUE if the two queens can attack one another and FALSE otherwise. Test your function with the following R commands.

```
> attack.queens(c(3, 8), c(2, 1))    # queens can't attack one another
> attack.queens(c(2, 5), c(3, 5))    # queens in same column
> attack.queens(c(7, 1), c(7, 3))    # queens in same row
> attack.queens(c(8, 2), c(2, 8))    # queens in same diagonal
> attack.queens(c(1, 2), c(7, 8))    # queens in same diagonal
```

22.7 Write R functions named `my.all` and `my.any`, each with a single argument x, which is a vector of logical values. Print an error message if anything other than a vector of logical values is passed to either function. The function `my.all` should return TRUE if all of the elements of the vector are TRUE and FALSE otherwise. The function `my.any` should return TRUE if any of the elements of the vector are TRUE and FALSE otherwise. Your R functions should be written without calling the built-in R functions named `all` and `any`. Test your `my.all` and `my.any` functions on the following four vectors.

```
> x = c(TRUE, TRUE, TRUE)
> y = c(TRUE, TRUE, FALSE)
> z = c(FALSE, FALSE, FALSE)
> v = c("Cat", "Dog", "Rhino")
```

22.8 Write a function named `my.cos` with two arguments. Your function will return the cosine of the first argument, which is named angle. The second argument is named degrees, which has a default value of FALSE. Test your function with the following R commands.

```
> my.cos(pi / 2)
> my.cos(90, degrees = TRUE)
```

22.9 Write a one-line function named `are.conjugates` with complex arguments z1 and z2 that returns TRUE if z1 and z2 are complex conjugates and FALSE otherwise.

Chapter 23

Iteration

This is the second chapter on programming in R. The previous chapter introduced conditional execution with the `if` statement. This chapter introduces *iteration*, which is often known as *looping*. A loop is generally used to execute R commands repeatedly, oftentimes with conditions that vary with each pass through the loop. The four topics introduced in this chapter are (a) the `while` loop, (b) the `for` loop, (c) the `repeat` loop, and (d) debugging.

23.1 The `while` loop

The first of the three loops introduced in this chapter is the `while` loop. The syntax for the `while` loop when there is a single R command to be executed in the loop can be written in a single line:

```
while (condition) command
```

As was the case with the `if` statement, the `condition` is a single logical value (a vector of length one whose element is `logical`) or if the `condition` is numeric, then 0 is `FALSE` and non-zero is `TRUE`. The `while` loop executes in the following fashion. The `condition` is evaluated. If the `condition` is `TRUE`, then the `command` is executed. The `condition` is then re-evaluated, and the `command` is again executed if it is `TRUE`. This process continues until the `condition` becomes `FALSE`, and at that point execution continues with the command that follows the loop. The `while` loop evaluates the condition at the "top of the loop," which means that the `command` is not executed if the `condition` is initially `FALSE`. The `while` loop is appropriately named because the `command` is executed repeatedly *while* the `condition` remains `TRUE`. If the `condition` or the `command` is lengthy, it is acceptable to input the `while` loop involving a single command in the form

```
while (condition)
    command
```

These forms of the `while` loop work fine if there is just a single command to be executed. But if there are two or more commands to be executed in the loop, the syntax is

```
while (condition) {
  commands
}
```

As it was with the if statement, it is good programming practice to left-align all of the R commands contained in the curly braces and to indent them two spaces for readability. The curly braces serve as delimiters to enclose the R commands that are to be executed as long as the condition remains TRUE. R uses the + prompt as the R commands in the while loop are entered from the keyboard, then returns to the > prompt after the closing curly brace has been entered.

The first programming exercise involving a while loop is to compute the first ten numbers in the Fibonacci sequence, which are

$$1, 1, 2, 3, 5, 8, 13, 21, 34, 55.$$

The first two numbers in this sequence are defined to be

$$x_1 = 1 \qquad \text{and} \qquad x_2 = 1,$$

and subsequent numbers in the sequence are found using the formula

$$x_i = x_{i-1} + x_{i-2}$$

for $i = 3, 4, \ldots$. In other words, each number in the sequence is simply the sum of the previous two numbers. The Fibonacci sequence appears in Pascal's triangle, models the population growth in an idealized population of rabbits, can be used to form a golden spiral, appears in numerous applications in number theory and computer science, and appears in biological applications involving trees, flowers, pine cones, artichokes, and pineapples. The first R command below establishes Fib as a vector of 10 numeric elements that are each initialized to zero. The second and third commands set the first two elements of Fib to 1. The fourth command initializes an index named i to 3. The fifth command begins a while loop. The condition i <= 10 evaluates to TRUE on the first pass through the while loop, so the two R commands delimited by the curly braces are executed. The first command in the while loop calculates the ith element of the Fib vector. The second command in the while loop increments i. After the closing curly brace, the prompt returns to > and the Fib vector is displayed by typing its name. The while loop is executed eight times as i ranges from 3 to 10. When i is incremented to 11, the condition i <= 10 evaluates to FALSE, and control is passed to the R command following the closing curly brace.

```
> Fib = numeric(10)
> Fib[1] = 1
> Fib[2] = 1
> i = 3
> while (i <= 10) {
+   Fib[i] = Fib[i - 1] + Fib[i - 2]
+   i = i + 1
+ }
> Fib
 [1]  1  1  2  3  5  8 13 21 34 55
```

As the size of a program grows, it is beneficial to write the R code in an external file, then execute the code either using a cut and paste operation, using the source function, or using an integrated development environment such as RStudio.

The second example of using the while loop in an algorithm concerns the calculation of the greatest common divisor (gcd) of two integers. The gcd of two positive integers a and b is the largest integer that divides both evenly. An algorithm for calculating the gcd of two positive integers was developed by Euclid, a Greek mathematician from Alexandria who lived under the reign of Ptolemy I (323–283 BC). Euclid is known for his textbook *Elements*. Euclid's gcd algorithm in its original and simplest form begins with the pair of positive integers a and b, then forms a new pair of integers consisting of the smaller integer and the larger integer minus the smaller integer. This process continues until the two integers are equal, and that integer is the gcd of the original pair a and b. Finding the gcd of $a = 42$ and $b = 15$, for example, uses the following sequence of pairs:

$$(42, 15) \quad \rightarrow \quad (27, 15) \quad \rightarrow \quad (12, 15) \quad \rightarrow \quad (12, 3) \quad \rightarrow \quad (9, 3) \quad \rightarrow \quad (6, 3) \quad \rightarrow \quad (3, 3).$$

So the gcd of 42 and 15 is 3. Euclid's gcd algorithm is implemented below in R using a `while` loop. First, we check to see if gcd is used for another object in R (it is not). Then we proceed to implement Euclid's algorithm as described above. The R command within the `while` loop will be executed as long as a and b are not equal. Within the `while` loop, the larger of the two integers in the current pair is replaced by the larger integer minus the smaller integer. The gcd function returns a, but could also have returned b because a and b are equal when the `while` loop terminates.

```
> exists("gcd")
[1] FALSE
> gcd = function(a, b) {
+    while (a != b) {
+      if (a > b) a = a - b else b = b - a
+    }
+    return(a)
+ }
> gcd(42, 15)
[1] 3
```

The gcd function correctly returns the greatest common divisor of 42 and 15 as 3. One could imagine that this algorithm would run rather slowly if a and b were huge integers. Versions of Euclid's gcd algorithm that use the modulo operator `%%` execute much more quickly.

23.2   The `for` loop

The next type of loop is known as the `for` loop, which iterates through the components of a list. In terms of capability, a `for` loop is a special case of a `while` loop. In most settings, a `for` loop is more compact than the associated `while` loop. Every `for` loop can be written as a `while` loop, but the converse is not necessarily true. If there is a single command in a `for` loop, the syntax is

for (name in list) command

The object named `name` assumes the various components in the list named `list` sequentially as the for loop is executed. If the name of the `list` or the `command` is lengthy, it is acceptable to input the `for` loop involving a single command in the following form.

for (name in list)
command

If there are two or more commands in the body of the `for` loop, then the commands in the loop should be left-aligned and indented two spaces for readability:

```
for (name in list) {
  commands
}
```

The first example of a `for` loop creates a list named `my.list` using the `list` function, whose first component is a `numeric` vector of length one, whose second component is a `complex` vector of length two, and whose third component is a string. The `for` loop that follows contains just a single R command that calls the `print` function to display the value contained in component `j` of the list `my.list` upon each pass through the loop.

```
> my.list = list(7, c(3 + 4i, 5 + 6i), "string")
> for (j in my.list) print(j)
[1] 7
[1] 3+4i 5+6i
[1] "string"
```

When a vector, rather than a list, is used in a `for` loop, the loop iterates through the elements in the vector sequentially. The next example prints the squares and cubes of the first 12 positive integers.

```
> for (i in 1:12) print(c(i, i ^ 2, i ^ 3))
[1] 1 1 1
[1] 2 4 8
[1]  3  9 27
[1]  4 16 64
[1]   5  25 125
[1]   6  36 216
[1]   7  49 343
[1]   8  64 512
[1]   9  81 729
[1]  10  100 1000
[1]  11  121 1331
[1]  12  144 1728
```

The next example uses the `seq` function to limit the focus to the squares and cubes of just the first few *even* integers, and uses `cat`, rather than `print`, to display the output.

```
> for (i in seq(2, 12, by = 2)) cat(c(i, i ^ 2, i ^ 3, "\n"))
2 4 8
4 16 64
6 36 216
8 64 512
10 100 1000
12 144 1728
```

A `for` loop can be used to calculate the first ten values in the Fibonacci sequence in much the same fashion as with the `while` loop.

```
> Fib = rep(1, 10)
> for (i in 3:10) Fib[i] = Fib[i - 1] + Fib[i - 2]
> Fib
 [1]  1  1  2  3  5  8 13 21 34 55
```

In this instance, the `for` loop saved on the number of lines of code over the `while` loop. By stream-lining the initialization to a single line and streamlining the loop to a single line, the code has been reduced from nine lines to just three lines.

We now discuss the famous sieve of Eratosthenes algorithm for finding prime numbers. Named after the Greek scientist Eratosthenes of Cyrene (276 BC–194 BC) who devised the algorithm, the sieve of Eratosthenes finds all prime numbers between 2 and some specified positive integer N. We begin with a conceptual description of the sieve. Assume that we want to know all of the prime numbers between 2 and N. One way to proceed is as follows. For illustration, assume that $N = 100$. First, write all the integers between 2 and 100 in order:

$$2 \quad 3 \quad 4 \quad 5 \quad 6 \quad 7 \quad 8 \quad 9 \quad 10 \quad 11 \quad 12 \quad 13 \quad 14 \quad 15 \quad \ldots \quad 100$$

The sieve works from left to right on these integers in the following fashion. An arrow initially points to 2. We know that 2 is prime, but all other even numbers (that is, multiples of 2) cannot be prime, so we cross out $4, 6, 8, \ldots, 100$ to indicate that they are not prime numbers.

$$\downarrow$$
$$2 \quad 3 \quad \cancel{4} \quad 5 \quad \cancel{6} \quad 7 \quad \cancel{8} \quad 9 \quad \cancel{10} \quad 11 \quad \cancel{12} \quad 13 \quad \cancel{14} \quad 15 \quad \ldots \quad \cancel{100}$$

The arrow now advances to the next integer that has not been crossed out, 3, which is prime. The multiples of 3, namely $6, 9, 12, \ldots, 99$, cannot be prime, so they are crossed out. (This will result in the even multiples of 3 being crossed out twice.)

$$\downarrow$$
$$2 \quad 3 \quad \cancel{4} \quad 5 \quad \cancel{6} \quad 7 \quad \cancel{8} \quad \cancel{9} \quad \cancel{10} \quad 11 \quad \cancel{12} \quad 13 \quad \cancel{14} \quad \cancel{15} \quad \ldots \quad \cancel{100}$$

The arrow now advances to 5, the next integer that has not been crossed out. We know that 5 is a prime number. The multiples of 5, namely $10, 15, 20, \ldots, 100$, cannot be prime, so they are crossed out.

$$\downarrow$$
$$2 \quad 3 \quad \cancel{4} \quad 5 \quad \cancel{6} \quad 7 \quad \cancel{8} \quad \cancel{9} \quad \cancel{10} \quad 11 \quad \cancel{12} \quad 13 \quad \cancel{14} \quad \cancel{15} \quad \ldots \quad \cancel{100}$$

Finally, the arrow is advanced to 7, and the integers $14, 21, 28, \ldots, 98$ are crossed out.

$$\downarrow$$
$$2 \quad 3 \quad \cancel{4} \quad 5 \quad \cancel{6} \quad 7 \quad \cancel{8} \quad \cancel{9} \quad \cancel{10} \quad 11 \quad \cancel{12} \quad 13 \quad \cancel{14} \quad \cancel{15} \quad \ldots \quad \cancel{100}$$

The sieve only needs to advance the arrow to $\sqrt{N} = \sqrt{100} = 10$ to cross out all of the composite (non-prime) integers between 2 and 100. The 25 prime numbers that remain are:

2, 3, 5, 7, 11, 13, 17, 19, 23, 29, 31, 37, 41, 43, 47, 53, 59, 61, 67, 71, 73, 79, 83, 89, 97.

To implement this algorithm in a function named `sieve` in R, we define a vector `prime` that consists of N logical elements. The first element, which corresponds to 1, is initialized to FALSE, and the remaining elements are initialized to TRUE. A `for` loop whose index n runs from 2 to $\sqrt{N}$ effectively serves the same purpose as the arrows in the explanation of the algorithm. When the `condition` on the `if` statement within the outside `for` loop is met (that is, the arrow is pointing at a prime number), then the elements of `prime` that are multiples of the prime number are set to FALSE by the inside `for` loop. Finally, the `which` function is used to return the prime numbers determined by the algorithm.

```
> exists("sieve")
[1] FALSE
> sieve = function(N) {
+   prime = c(FALSE, rep(TRUE, N - 1))
+   for (n in 2:sqrt(N))
+     if (prime[n]) for (s in 2:(N / n)) prime[s * n] = FALSE
+   return(which(prime))
+ }
> sieve(100)
 [1]  2  3  5  7 11 13 17 19 23 29 31 37 41 43 47 53 59 61 67 71 73 79 83 89 97
> sieve(1000)
```

```
  [1]   2   3   5   7  11  13  17  19  23  29  31  37  41  43  47  53  59  61
 [19]  67  71  73  79  83  89  97 101 103 107 109 113 127 131 137 139 149 151
 [37] 157 163 167 173 179 181 191 193 197 199 211 223 227 229 233 239 241 251
 [55] 257 263 269 271 277 281 283 293 307 311 313 317 331 337 347 349 353 359
 [73] 367 373 379 383 389 397 401 409 419 421 431 433 439 443 449 457 461 463
 [91] 467 479 487 491 499 503 509 521 523 541 547 557 563 569 571 577 587 593
[109] 599 601 607 613 617 619 631 641 643 647 653 659 661 673 677 683 691 701
[127] 709 719 727 733 739 743 751 757 761 769 773 787 797 809 811 821 823 827
[145] 829 839 853 857 859 863 877 881 883 887 907 911 919 929 937 941 947 953
[163] 967 971 977 983 991 997
```

When the sieve function is tested for $N = 100$ and $N = 1000$, it correctly identifies the appropriate prime numbers.

The final example of using a for loop involves a sorting algorithm. These algorithms are pervasive in computer science because sorting arises in many applications. The *bubble sort*, which will be described here, is a conceptually simple sorting algorithm that can be applied to short lists of items. There are more efficient algorithms for longer lists. Assume that we want to sort the elements of a vector into increasing order. A bubble sort of n elements requires $n - 1$ passes through the elements. The bubble sort is based on pairwise comparisons of adjacent elements. Consider a vector that consists of just four elements in the following order:

$$3 \qquad 7 \qquad 0 \qquad -5.$$

In the diagrams below, the four elements will be stacked on top of one another to depict the vector. Since there are four elements in the vector, one fewer than four, that is, three passes through the vector are required. The initial state of the vector is on the left in the diagram below. The bubble sort begins by comparing the first two elements (this is indicated by the arrows to the right of the vector) and deciding if they are in the correct order. Since the first element, 3, is less than the second element, 7, these adjacent elements are in the correct order, so no further action is required. Next, the second and third elements are compared. Since the second element, 7, is greater than the third element, 0, these adjacent elements are not in the correct order, so the two elements are swapped. The first pass ends by comparing the third element, which is now 7, with the fourth element, -5. Since these two elements are out of order, the two are swapped.

Notice that at the end of the first pass, it must be the case that the largest number is now in the last position in the vector. So the term "bubble" sort might not be the best name. Bubbles rise to the top of a carbonated beverage, but a bubble sort might be better named a "sinking" sort because the largest number sinks to the bottom of the vector on the first pass. The second pass through the vector does not need to check the last element because we know it is in the correct position. The second pass through the vector begins with the vector in the ending state from the first pass. As before, the first element, 3, is compared to the second element, 0. Since they are out of order, they are swapped. Next, the second element, 3, is compared with the third element, −5. They are also out of order, so they are swapped. This ends the second pass through the vector.

The two largest elements now assume the appropriate positions at the end of the second pass. The third and final pass begins with the vector in its ending state from the second pass. The third pass compares the first element, 0, with the second element, −5. Since they are out of order, they are swapped, which leaves the vector in sorted order. The bubble sort has worked its magic on the elements of the vector.

The next step is to implement the bubble sort algorithm in R. The bubblesort function below sorts the elements of a vector x into ascending order. The first line in the function uses the length function to determine the number of elements in the vector, which is stored in n. The outside for loop takes the index i from 1 to n - 1, which corresponds to the n - 1 passes through the vector. The inside for loop takes the index j from 1 to n - i, which corresponds to the positions associated with the comparisons of adjacent elements. The if statement within the inside for loop compares adjacent values in the vector. If the elements are ordered incorrectly, the three commands inside of the if statement are used to swap the adjacent elements.

```
> bubblesort = function(x) {
+    n = length(x)
+    for (i in 1:(n - 1)) {
+      for (j in 1:(n - i)) {
+        if (x[j + 1] < x[j]) {
+          tmp = x[j]
+          x[j] = x[j + 1]
+          x[j + 1] = tmp
+        }
+      }
+    }
+    return(x)
+ }
```

Dropping the parentheses around (n - 1) and (n - i) on the vectors in the for loop is a common programming error. The parentheses are necessary because the : operator has a higher priority than the - operator. The bubblesort function can be applied to the vector with the elements given above with

```
> bubblesort(c(3, 7, 0, -5))
[1] -5  0  3  7
```

There is no assumption in the bubblesort function that the elements being sorted are numeric. A vector of elements that are strings is also possible.

```
> bubblesort(c("dog", "cat", "gnu"))
[1] "cat" "dog" "gnu"
```

23.3   The repeat **loop**

The while and for loops will handle nearly all of the programming applications involving loops. The third and final loop in R is known as the repeat loop. The repeat loop can be used when the terminal condition does not naturally occur at the top of the loop. As indicated by its name, the repeat loop is used to repeatedly execute a set of R commands. The syntax for the repeat loop is

```
repeat {
  commands
}
```

As with the if statement, while loop, and for loop, some programmers prefer to place the opening curly brace on a line by itself, which is typically vertically aligned with the closing brace. Whatever you choose as a programming style, it should be used consistently throughout your R code. As before, the R commands within the repeat loop should be left-justified and indented a consistent number of spaces. Two spaces of indention have been consistently used in this text. One immediate distinction associated with a repeat loop is that there is no condition to end the loop. A repeat loop must be terminated with the break command that is placed somewhere inside of the repeat loop. A loop that provides no mechanism for escape has been appropriately named by computer scientists as an "endless loop." If your program gets caught in an endless loop, there is a STOP button at the top of the R graphical user interface that can be used to break the loop. The break command immediately exits the innermost active for, while, or repeat loop. The related next command forces the next iteration of loop to begin immediately; control returns immediately to the top of the loop.

The first example of a repeat loop tests the terminal condition at the bottom of the loop. The R code segment below begins by setting x to 1, then enters the repeat loop. Since x is printed, then incremented by 2 before checking for the terminal condition x > 10, this program effectively prints the first five positive odd integers.

```
> x = 1
> repeat {
+   print(x)
+   x = x + 2
+   if (x > 10) break
+ }
```

```
[1] 1
[1] 3
[1] 5
[1] 7
[1] 9
```

Testing the terminal condition at the bottom of the repeat loop differs from the while loop, which tests its terminal condition at the top of the loop. When the repeat loop is written in this fashion, one iteration of the loop will always be executed.

The second example of a repeat loop is an implementation of an algorithm for calculating the square root of a nonnegative real number. Although there is an R function named sqrt that is perfectly capable of finding square roots, we will implement what is known as the "Babylonian algorithm" to write our own my.sqrt function to calculate a square root. The Babylonian algorithm to find $\sqrt{x}$ begins with an initial guess for the square root given by r_0. The closer that r_0 is to the true value of the square root, the faster that the algorithm will execute. Next, the following iterative equation is applied

$$r_{i+1} = \frac{1}{2}\left(r_i + \frac{x}{r_i}\right)$$

for $i = 1, 2, \dots$. This equation is applied repeatedly until it converges to the square root. One way to determine whether the r_i values have converged to the square root is to iterate until subsequent r_i values are sufficiently close together.

The implementation of my.sqrt as an R function begins by setting eps (short for epsilon) to a small, positive constant. Next, the initial estimate for the square root is arbitrarily set as r.new = 1. The repeat loop stores the current estimate for the square root in r.old, implements the iterative step in the Babylonian algorithm, then checks for convergence with an if statement. When adjacent estimates of the square root are within eps of one another, the repeat loop is terminated with a break command, and the estimate of the square root is returned.

```
> my.sqrt = function(x) {
+    eps = 0.00000001
+    r.new = 1
+    repeat {
+       r.old = r.new
+       r.new = (r.old + x / r.old) / 2
+       if (abs(r.old - r.new) < eps) break
+    }
+    return(r.new)
+ }
```

When the my.sqrt function is called with an argument of 2, for example, the square root of 2 is correctly calculated to the prescribed accuracy.

```
> my.sqrt(2)
[1] 1.414214
```

The break and next commands can be used in any of the loops described in this chapter. The next command is illustrated in the R code that contains a for loop that follows. This code segment prints the squares of the positive elements of the vector x, which consists of numeric elements.

```
> x = c(-4, -2, -1, 4, 8, -3)
> for (i in 1:length(x)) {
+   if (x[i] < 0) next
+   print(x[i] ^ 2)
+ }
[1] 16
[1] 64
```

When a negative element in x is encountered, the next command forces the next iteration of the for loop to begin immediately; control returns immediately to the top of the for loop. This code will work fine as long as x contains one or more elements. But if x contains zero elements (that is, x is NULL), then the loop runs from 1 to 0, which is not what is desired. An alternative solution that uses the along argument in seq that solves this issue is

```
> x = c(-4, -2, -1, 4, 8, -3)
> for (i in seq(along = x)) {
+   if (x[i] < 0) next
+   print(x[i] ^ 2)
+ }
[1] 16
[1] 64
```

This concludes the introduction of the while, for, and repeat loops. This chapter ends by introducing some of the "debugging" tools that are a part of the R language.

23.4   Debugging and optimization

Programming errors are known as "bugs," which can oftentimes be difficult to locate and correct. Debugging is the process of identifying, locating, and correcting unexpected actions taken by your R code. R contains some debugging tools that can be used to locate and correct bugs.

R distinguishes between the level of severity of certain types of problems that can arise. Sample output from the stop, warning, and message functions is

```
> stop("OhNo")                    # execution ceases with stop
Error: OhNo
> warning("UhOh")                 # warning falls between stop and message
Warning message:
UhOh
> message("Oops")                 # display a message
Oops
```

The stop function is used for errors, often referred to as "fatal errors." Execution ceases when the stop function is called. Typing the name of an object that has not been defined is an easy way to generate a fatal error.

```
> Disco                           # Disco not defined
Error: object 'Disco' not found
```

The warning function does not terminate execution, but rather indicates that a problem *might* be present, as in

```
> sqrt(-1)                              # square root of -1
[1] NaN
Warning message:
In sqrt(-1) : NaNs produced
```

Finally, the message function can be used to display useful information. One of the keys to what is known as "defensive programming" is to write code that fails quickly and gracefully when an unexpected action occurs. To illustrate, let's say you want to write a function that accepts a single integer-valued numeric value as its single argument. If this function is passed a real-valued numeric value, for example, the function should detect this immediately with an if statement, then use the stop function to halt execution and print an appropriate error message. This should occur at the top of the function before other less-easily-recognized problems might arise.

Perhaps the simplest way to locate bugs is to temporarily place print commands within the code. For example, if the print(r.new) command is placed within the repeat loop (just before the if statement) in my.sqrt and called with argument 2, the sequential estimates of the $\sqrt{2}$ are displayed.

```
[1] 1
[1] 1.5
[1] 1.416667
[1] 1.414216
[1] 1.414214
```

A second debugging tool is the debug function. In order to turn on the debugging functionality for the my.sqrt function, for example, use

```
> debug(my.sqrt)
```

Once the debugging functionality has been set for the my.sqrt function, a call to my.sqrt function now results in the display

```
> my.sqrt(2)
debugging in: my.sqrt(2)
debug at #1: {
    eps = 1e-08
    r.new = 1
    repeat {
        r.old = r.new
        r.new = (r.old + x/r.old)/2
        if (abs(r.old - r.new) < eps)
            break
    }
    return(r.new)
}
Browse[2]>
```

Calling my.sqrt in this fashion with the debugging functionality set effectively freezes the execution of my.sqrt with argument 2 as it begins. The Browse[2]> prompt is requesting a command from the user. For example, the command n (for next) advances the code by one command. The command c (for continue) advances the code to the end of the current context, for example, to the bottom of the current loop or to the bottom of the current function. Typing the name of an object at the prompt gives the value of the object at that particular point in the execution. This can be used to slow the execution of a segment of code so that it can be examined as it is executing. This can be helpful when trying to determine the location of a bug. The command Q exits the debug function for my.sqrt and returns the prompt to the usual >.

The browser function is similar to the debug function. A call to the browser() function in a program or a function temporarily suspends execution, which gives you the ability to inspect the value of an object. A set of commands that are similar to those associated with the debug function can be executed while execution is suspended.

Certain programming disciplines are helpful in reducing the likelihood of bugs in an R program. First, choosing meaningful variable names with a consistent format is helpful for you, others, and the future you who might be modifying the program. Second, consistent indentation of R commands within an if statement or a loop helps to make the code more readable. Blank lines are an effective way to partition sections of code. Third, there is no substitute for taking the extra time to carefully develop the algorithm. To quote my colleague Steve Park, "plan a lot, program a little; plan a little, program a lot." Fourth, choose clarity over cleverness in your code, which results in code that is easier to modify. Finally, code should be documented with comments that include, at a minimum, the programmer's name, date, program name, and description of the purpose of the program.

Once all of the bugs have been removed from a function, there is oftentimes a last step of optimizing the code by vectorizing calculations. This will cause the program to run faster because vectorized calculations are executed much more efficiently in R than loops. Consider the problem of estimating the mean of the maximum of a $N(68, 9)$ random variable and a $N(70, 16)$ random variable by generating 100,000 such random maximums, and then averaging the maximums. This technique, known as Monte Carlo simulation, is the topic of Chapter 25. Three R programs will be written that estimate the required value. The first will be written in an inefficient manner, and the next two programs will improve on the first. The code below generates a single normal random variate from each of the populations, then appends additional normal random variates to a vector.

```
> nrep = 100000
> x = rnorm(1, 66, 3)
> y = rnorm(1, 70, 4)
> for (i in 2:nrep) {
+    x = c(x, rnorm(1, 66, 3))
+    y = c(y, rnorm(1, 70, 4))
+ }
> z = max(x[1], y[1])
> for (i in 2:nrep) z = c(z, max(x[i], y[i]))
> mean(z)
[1] 70.60203
```

Continually reallocating memory for the x, y, and z vectors as additional random variates are generated is inefficient. The memory reallocation takes about as long as setting up a new vector. The next solution to the problem also uses a for loop, but this time the vectors x and y are set up just once during an initialization step, and the pmax and mean functions are used to calculate the maximums and average.

```
> nrep = 100000
> x = numeric(nrep)
> y = numeric(nrep)
> for (i in 1:nrep) {
```

```
+    x[i] = rnorm(1, 66, 3)
+    y[i] = rnorm(1, 70, 4)
+ }
> mean(pmax(x, y))
[1] 70.60369
```

Finally, this can be sped up further by vectorizing the loop. The shorter and more efficient code below runs much more quickly because it does not use any loops at all.

```
> nrep = 100000
> x = rnorm(nrep, 66, 3)
> y = rnorm(nrep, 70, 4)
> mean(pmax(x, y))
[1] 70.60163
```

Executing this code is nearly instantaneous. The speed of the three algorithms can be compared by using the system.time function. If the first program is stored in a file named code1, for example, then

```
> system.time(source("code1"))
   user   system  elapsed
 49.418  10.672   60.095
```

gives the time to execute the code. The user and system values should be added in order to find the CPU time consumed. So the first program took about 60 seconds to execute. Running the system.time function for the other two programs, the CPU time for the second program was just under one second, and the CPU time for the last program was about 1/50 of a second. Clearly, this last step of vectorizing calculations can pay huge dividends.

The lapply (list apply) function provides another mechanism for avoiding loops, which speeds calculations. Consider the list named x that consists of three components.

```
> x = list(1:4, -4:-1, c(TRUE, FALSE, TRUE, TRUE))
> x
[[1]]
[1] 1 2 3 4

[[2]]
[1] -4 -3 -2 -1

[[3]]
[1]  TRUE FALSE  TRUE  TRUE
```

The first argument to the lapply function is the list to be acted upon by the function given in the second argument. So to find the sample mean of each column of the list x, type

```
> lapply(x, mean)
[[1]]
[1] 2.5

[[2]]
[1] -2.5
```

```
[[3]]
[1] 0.75
```

This concludes the discussion of iteration in R. The two key concepts for programming in R are now in place: conditional execution (the `if` statement) and iteration (`while`, `for`, and `repeat` loops). The table below summarizes the functions introduced in this chapter.

function	description
while	while loop
for	for loop
repeat	repeat loop
break	break out of innermost loop
next	advance loop index in innermost loop
stop	stop execution and print error message
warning	print warning message
message	print message
debug	debug a function
browser	pause execution and initiate browser
lapply	list apply

The next chapter, which is the final chapter on programming in R, introduces recursion.

Exercises

23.1   What is returned by the following R commands?

```
> i = 4
> for (j in seq(2, 8, by = 3)) i = i + j
> i
```

23.2   What is returned by the following R commands?

```
> primes = c(2, 3, 5, 7, 11)
> for (i in 1:length(primes)) if (primes[i] > i ^ 2) print(i)
```

23.3   What is returned by the following R commands?

```
> sumsq = 0
> primes = c(2, 3, 5, 7, 11)
> for (i in 1:3) sumsq = sumsq + primes[i] ^ 2
> sumsq
```

23.4   The following R code contains a `for` loop and executes slowly. You feel the need for speed. Give a single line of R code that vectorizes this computation and executes quickly.

```
> n = 1000000
> x = numeric(n)
> for (i in 1:n) x[i] = rpois(1, 3) + rpois(1, 5)
```

23.5 What is returned by the following R commands?

```
> x = seq(12, 22, by = 3)
> for (i in 1:length(x)) {
+    y = i
+    if ((x[i] %% 5) == 1) y = c(y, 3 * x[i])
+ }
> y
```

23.6 Write an R function named `Pascal` with a single argument n that prints the first *n* rows of Pascal's triangle in a symmetric tree-like pattern. (The 0th row is just the 1 that appears at the top of the triangle.) Use the `choose` function to generate the elements in each row of the triangle. You may assume that *n* is a positive integer between 1 and 15 inclusive. Test your function with a call to

```
> Pascal(5)
```

which should produce the output that follows.

```
          1
         1 1
        1 2 1
       1 3 3 1
      1 4 6 4 1
     1 5 10 10 5 1
```

23.7 Write an R function called `wild.goose.chase` that accepts a 4 × 4 matrix x containing numerical values that are two-digit numbers from 11 to 44. Begin the chase at the (1, 1) element of the matrix. The tens digit in each entry of the matrix determines the row number of the next move in the chase and the ones digit in each entry of the matrix determines the column number of the next move in the chase. The chase ends when the row number and the column number are the same as the element. This function should return the two-digit value found at the end of the chase. Test your code with the following R commands.

```
> r1 = c(13, 41, 14, 22)
> r2 = c(31, 24, 33, 23)
> r3 = c(23, 21, 41, 12)
> r4 = c(41, 32, 23, 44)
> m  = rbind(r1, r2, r3, r4)
> wild.goose.chase(m)
```

23.8 Write a function named `checkerboard` with two arguments named `color1` and `color2`, which are character strings containing the names of the two colors on the checkerboard. Your `checkerboard` function should draw a handsome graphic containing the checkerboard drawn with colors `color1` and `color2`. Test your code with the commands given below.

```
> checkerboard("red", "black")     # traditional checkerboard
> checkerboard("green", "gold")    # Go Tribe!
> checkerboard("black", "gold")    # Go Boilers!
```

23.9 What is returned by the following R commands?

```
> j = 0
> x = NULL
> while (j < 5) {
+    if (j %% 2 == 0) x = c(x, j)
+    j = j + 1
+ }
> x
```

23.10 Review the synthetic division algorithm. Write an R function named `syndiv` with arguments `num` (which is a vector containing the coefficients of the numerator) and `den` (which contains the single real root of the denominator). Your function should return a vector that contains the coefficients of the quotient followed by the remainder. Test your function with the R command

```
> syndiv(c(1, 0, 2, -4), 3)
```

which is used to divide $x^3 + 2x - 4$ by $x - 3$.

23.11 Modify the `sieve` function to print all of the *twin primes* between 1 and N. The new function should be named `twin.sieve`. Two adjacent prime numbers are twin primes if they differ by 2.

23.12 Multiply each integer from 1 to 1000 by every integer from 1 to 1000. All one million of these products will have a leading digit that ranges from 1 to 9. Write an R program that calculates the fractions of occurrence of the various leading digits, and displays the results in an appropriate graphic.

23.13 The prime number theorem states that

$$\lim_{n \to \infty} \frac{\pi(n) \ln(n)}{n} = 1,$$

where $\pi(n)$ is the *prime-counting function*, which gives a count of the number of prime numbers that are less than or equal to n for some positive integer n. It was first suggested by Carl Friedrich Gauss at the age of about 15 in 1792. Modify the `sieve` function to return a vector of length N containing the values of the prime-counting function (that is, the nth value in the vector returned by the new function contains a count of the number of primes that are less than or equal to n, for $n = 1, 2, \ldots, N$). Name the new function `count.sieve`. Use `count.sieve` to plot $\pi(n) \ln(n)/n$ for $n = 1, 2, \ldots, 1000000$ to assess the plausibility of the prime number theorem.

23.14 Write an R function named `sum.list` with a single argument x, which is a list consisting of atomic components, that returns the sum of all numeric elements in the list.

23.15 Write an R program that reads in a text file and prints all sentences that contain the words "that" or "which." Test your program on Abraham Lincoln's Gettysburg Address.

Chapter 24

Recursion

This is the third and final chapter concerning programming in R. The topic introduced here is *recursion*, which is a feature of most modern computer languages. Recursion is a method used to solve certain problems by repeatedly using the same approach but on a smaller, and oftentimes simpler version of the same problem, until some terminating base case is reached. A recursive function is one that can call itself. The three illustrations of recursive functions given in this chapter are (a) an elementary application based on the `factorial` function, (b) an intermediate application based on the binary search algorithm, and (c) an advanced application based on the Tower of Hanoi problem.

24.1   Calculating factorials

There is a `factorial` function built into R. When called with a nonnegative integer, it computes the factorial. To calculate $5! = 5 \cdot 4 \cdot 3 \cdot 2 \cdot 1$, for example, type

```
> factorial(5)
[1] 120
```

When the `factorial` function is called with a negative integer, it returns NaN, along with a warning message.

```
> factorial(-1)
[1] NaN
Warning message:
In gamma(x + 1) : NaNs produced
```

Based on the warning message, there is another function, namely the `gamma` function, that is called internally by the `factorial` function. When called with 3.7 as an argument, the `factorial` function returns a value that is between $3! = 6$ and $4! = 24$.

```
> factorial(3.7)
[1] 15.43141
```

The built-in `factorial` function also accepts a vector as an argument, and returns the associated vector of factorials.

```
> factorial(3:8)
[1]      6     24    120    720   5040  40320
```

The factorial function returns an error when it is called with an undefined object or a string.

```
> factorial(ack)
Error in factorial(ack) : object 'ack' not found
> factorial("ack!")
Error in x + 1 : non-numeric argument to binary operator
```

We now turn to writing our own factorial function named fact. We will develop a sequence of four fact functions, two that do not use recursion, and two that use recursion. First, check to see if there is an object named fact that is available for us to use as a function name.

```
> exists("fact")
[1] FALSE
```

So fact is available. The first non-recursive fact function uses a for loop to calculate the factorials.

```
> fact = function(x) {
+   i = 1
+   for (j in 2:x) i = i * j
+   return(i)
+ }
> fact(5)
[1] 120
```

A second non-recursive, more compact version of a factorial function, again named fact, for a positive integer argument x, can be written using the prod function. This version of fact will overwrite the first version.

```
> fact = function(x) prod(1:x)
> fact(5)
[1] 120
```

We now rewrite the fact function using recursion. R supports functions that can call themselves. So the next version of the fact function for a positive integer argument returns a 1 when the argument x is 1 (the base case), but calls itself, with argument x - 1, when x is greater than 1.

```
> fact = function(x) if (x == 1) 1 else x * fact(x - 1)
> fact(5)
[1] 120
```

When the recursive fact function is called with argument 5, the condition x == 1 is FALSE, so the command 5 * fact(4) is executed. When the call to fact(4) is executed, the condition x == 1 is again FALSE, so the command 4 * fact(3) is executed. This continues until fact is called with an argument of 1, when the condition x == 1 is TRUE, and a 1 is returned. This is the base case, because no further recursive calls are required nor made. Then in the immediately previous call to fact(2), the expression 2 * fact(1) evaluates to 2 * 1 (because fact(1) has just returned the value 1), so that fact(2) returns 2. Similarly, in the previous call to fact(3), the expression 3 * fact(2) evaluates to 3 * 2, so that fact(3) returns 6. This continues until the original call to fact, containing the expression 5 * fact(4), evaluates its expression to be 5 * 24, returning 120.

The next experiment with the recursive version of fact is to execute it on a vector. Using a vector of the integers between 3 and 8 results in

```
> fact(3:8)
[1]  6 12 20 30 42 56
Warning messages:
1: In if (x == 1) 1 else x * fact(x - 1) :
  the condition has length > 1 and only the first element will be used
2: In if (x == 1) 1 else x * fact(x - 1) :
  the condition has length > 1 and only the first element will be used
3: In if (x == 1) 1 else x * fact(x - 1) :
  the condition has length > 1 and only the first element will be used
```

This is a clear failure. When the fact function is called initially with x = 3:8 as an argument, the condition x == 1 is FALSE because $3 \neq 1$, but R gives a warning message because it only uses the first element of x. Since the condition is FALSE, 3:8 * fact(3:8 - 1) is returned from the first call to fact. The recursive call to fact recycles the 1, so fact is called a second time with the argument 2:7. The condition is again FALSE on the second call because $2 \neq 1$, so fact is called a third time with argument 1:6. This time the condition is TRUE, so 1 is returned. So when the three calls to return a value from the function are completed, 1 gets multiplied by 2:7, which gets multiplied by 3:8, giving us the *incorrect* result above.

There is a way to correct the recursive fact function so that it works properly for a vector of positive integers. The version of fact given below begins by setting the vector of logical elements named recurse to TRUE for every element of the argument x that is greater than 1. The second command sets all elements of x that equal 0 or 1 to 1. The third command begins with an if statement that determines whether there are any values in x that are greater than 1. If this condition evaluates to TRUE, a recursive call to fact is made for those elements of recurse that are TRUE.

```
> fact = function(x) {
+   recurse = (x > 1)
+   x[!recurse] = 1
+   if (any(recurse)) x[recurse] = x[recurse] * fact(x[recurse] - 1)
+   return(x)
+ }
> fact(5)
[1] 120
> fact(3:8)
[1]     6    24   120   720  5040 40320
```

This vectorized, recursive version of fact works fine for a single positive integer and for a vector of positive integers. No error checking has been performed; that capability could easily be added to this function.

Using recursion to calculate the factorial of an integer is useful in presenting the notion of recursion, but it is not very efficient in practice. Each time a recursive call is made, a new copy of the (recursive) function is called, requiring a new environment to be created with a fresh set of local objects. When a recursive call is made, execution of the calling function is temporarily suspended while the execution of the called function is executed. In this sense, multiple calls to a function within itself are "nested," which is a problem in the factorial function when it is called with a large argument. Calculating the factorial of a positive integer by recursion creates nested calls that can lead to memory problems because each call is placed on a stack in memory. So in practice, it is more efficient in terms of both memory and execution speed to use one of the non-recursive implementations to calculate a factorial. Using recursion to calculate factorials is conceptually appealing, but inefficient computationally.

24.2   Binary search algorithm

As an intermediate application of recursion, consider the *binary search* algorithm for locating a particular element in a vector. The setting is as follows. A vector x contains unique numeric elements that are sorted in ascending order. You want to find the index (subscript) of the element in x that matches a value which will be named `target`.

As a general notion of how binary search works, consider the use of a now-antiquated "telephone book" which contains an alphabetical listing of names and associated phone numbers. In order to find a particular name, one way to proceed is to start at the beginning of the telephone book and begin searching the names one-by-one. In the paragraphs that follow, this will be known as the "naive linear search algorithm." A second way to locate a particular name is to open the book to the middle, drop your finger, and if that is not the name you are looking for, you successively repeat the process on either the first half or the second half of the book—until either the name is found or determined to not be in the phone book. This is the essence of the binary search algorithm.

As a small numeric example of such a problem, let the ten unique, sorted values in x be

$$-83, -55, -16, -4, 0, 12, 23, 46, 68, 99.$$

Assume that the value of `target` is 68. One way to proceed is to move from left to right in the vector until we encounter 68. Once it is found, its index in x, which is 9 in this case because 68 resides in the ninth position in x, is returned.

The naive linear search algorithm given above works fine if the length of the vector is small. But what if the vector x is, say, 1000 elements long? In the worst case, this could take 1000 comparisons, which is time consuming. There must be a better way.

The binary search algorithm keeps track of a range of subscripts in the vector that are potential subscripts for the target value. The binary search begins with the entire length of array x as potential subscripts. The range of subscripts is narrowed by comparing the middle element of x to `target`, which serves to discard half of the range as potential matches. This process is repeated until the target value is discovered or until the algorithm concludes that the target value is not in the vector. The repeated halving of the range of subscripts being searched determines the location or the absence of the target value much more quickly, on average, than the naive linear search algorithm applied to a large vector. Recursion can again be used in this case because each recursive call to the binary search algorithm results in an embedded search involving half the number of suspects.

A binary search of a 1000-element vector can be concluded by testing ten or fewer elements. The search time, rather than being a linear function of the length of the vector to be searched as in the naive linear search algorithm, is now a function of the log base 2 of the length of the vector to be searched. This is a significant improvement for a large vector.

The R function `binarySearch` given next uses recursion in its implementation of a binary search. The function prints an error message if `target` is not in x or it returns the appropriate subscript if `target` is in x. The four arguments to the `binarySearch` function are

- the vector x containing the unique elements sorted in ascending order,
- the `target` value to find in the vector,
- the `low` subscript for the range of the binary search, and
- the `high` subscript for the range of the binary search.

The arguments to `binarySearch` are not checked to see that they are numeric or in sorted order. On the initial call to `binarySearch`, the argument `low` defaults to the subscript 1 and the argument high defaults to the subscript length(x), specifying the range for searching to be the entire vector. The if statement that begins the body of the function is the stopping condition. If low > high, then the binary search was unable to find the target value, and prints an appropriate error message using the stop function. If this condition is not met, then mid, a subscript between low and high is calculated. The condition in the next if statement checks to see if x[mid] == target. If so, then the appropriate subscript has been found and is returned. If not, then the focus of the search is halved, and the appropriate recursive call to binarySearch is made. The binarySearch function terminates when either (a) the value target is found in x, and the appropriate subscript is returned, or (b) a recursive call with low > high is made, which triggers the terminating error message.

```
> binarySearch = function(x, target, low = 1, high = length(x)) {
+   if (low > high) stop("The target is not in the vector")
+   else {
+     mid = low + floor((high - low) / 2)
+     if (x[mid] == target) return(mid)
+     if (x[mid] > target)
+       binarySearch(x, target, low, mid - 1)
+     else
+       binarySearch(x, target, mid + 1, high)
+   }
+ }
```

The binarySearch function is tested with the 12-element vector x that consists of the integer elements $-1, 0, 1, 2, \ldots, 10$. A search is made for target value 2.

```
> x = -1:10
> binarySearch(x, 2)
[1] 4
```

Since there is a 2 in the fourth position of x, the algorithm correctly returns the index 4. It is also important to experiment with various cases that do not contain the target value. The three tests below search for -3, 13, and 2.8, none of which are in the vector x. In each case, an error message indicates that the target value is not present.

```
> binarySearch(x, -3)
Error in binarySearch(x, target, low, mid - 1) :
  The target is not in the vector
> binarySearch(x, 13)
Error in binarySearch(x, target, mid + 1, high) :
  The target is not in the vector
> binarySearch(x, 2.8)
Error in binarySearch(x, target, low, mid - 1) :
  The target is not in the vector
```

At least for this limited set of test cases, the binary search algorithm appears to be working correctly. Now consider a vector of ten million elements. For simplicity, use the vector 1:10000000. We would like to find the subscript of the element containing 8,675,309.

```
> binarySearch(1:10000000, 8675309)
[1] 8675309
```

The naive linear search algorithm takes 8,675,309 comparisons, whereas the binary search took just 22 comparisons. In the worst case, that is, determining that a value is not in the vector, the naive linear search algorithm would take 10,000,000 comparisons, whereas binary search would take only $\log_2 10,000,000 = 24$ comparisons.

This concludes the discussion of the binary search algorithm and its associated implementation in R. Using recursion to calculate factorials in the previous section and to conduct a binary search in this section was not necessary. These same algorithms could have been conducted without recursion. The advanced application presented in the next section does not have an easy solution using loops, and in fact, is best solved using recursion.

24.3 Tower of Hanoi

The *Tower of Hanoi* is a puzzle consisting of three rods and n disks of different sizes (that is, diameters) that can slide onto any of the rods. The initial state of the puzzle has the n disks on one rod sorted in order by diameter, with the largest at the bottom and the smallest at the top. A side view of the puzzle (plotted in R!) in the initial state of $n = 4$ disks placed on rod 1 is shown below.

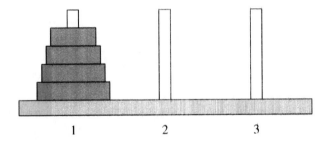

The goal of the puzzle is to move the entire stack of disks from the initial source rod s to a destination rod d, preferably in a minimum number of moves, following these rules:

- each move consists of taking the top disk from one of the stacks and placing it at the top of another stack,

- a larger disk may not be placed on top of a smaller disk.

The purpose of this programming exercise is to give a list of moves that solves the puzzle using a minimum number of moves.

To think of this problem in terms of recursion, consider the problem of moving n disks from source rod s to destination rod d via the following steps:

- move the top $n - 1$ disks from the source rod s to the other non-destination rod,

- move the bottom disk from the source rod s to the destination rod d,

- move the $n - 1$ disks from the non-destination rod to the destination rod d.

Moving the top $n - 1$ disks from one rod to another means that the $(n - 1)$-tower is moved in some manner, and may involve many individual moves.

Pseudo-code that is associated with a recursive function named toh (for Tower of Hanoi) with these steps for moving n disks from source rod s to destination rod d (indentation denotes nesting) is

```
toh(n, s, d)
  if (n == 1)
    output: move the top disk from rod s to rod d
  else
    toh(n - 1, s, 6 - s - d)
    output: move the top disk from rod s to rod d
    toh(n - 1, 6 - s - d, d)
```

If there is only one disk to be moved, then it is moved from rod s to rod d. Otherwise, toh is called to move the top n - 1 disks from the source rod s to the non-destination rod (which is the rod numbered 6 - s - d), then the bottom disk is moved from rod s to rod d, then toh is again called to move the top n - 1 disks from the non-destination rod to the destination rod d.

This pseudo-code is translated to the R function toh as

```
> toh = function(n, s, d) {
+   if (n == 1) {
+     cat("move the top disk from rod", s, "to rod", d, "\n")
+   }
+   else {
+     toh(n - 1, s, 6 - s - d)
+     cat("move the top disk from rod", s, "to rod", d, "\n")
+     toh(n - 1, 6 - s - d, d)
+   }
+ }
```

When this code is called with

```
> toh(4, 1, 3)
```

which corresponds to moving four disks initially on the source rod 1 to the destination rod 3, the minimal sequence of moves is displayed.

```
move the top disk from rod 1 to rod 2
move the top disk from rod 1 to rod 3
move the top disk from rod 2 to rod 3
move the top disk from rod 1 to rod 2
move the top disk from rod 3 to rod 1
move the top disk from rod 3 to rod 2
move the top disk from rod 1 to rod 2
move the top disk from rod 1 to rod 3
move the top disk from rod 2 to rod 3
move the top disk from rod 2 to rod 1
move the top disk from rod 3 to rod 1
move the top disk from rod 2 to rod 3
move the top disk from rod 1 to rod 2
move the top disk from rod 1 to rod 3
move the top disk from rod 2 to rod 3
```

This particular version of the problem corresponds to the one depicted in the figure at the beginning of this section. The solution took 15 moves. Notice that the initial goal is to somehow move the top three disks on rod 1 to another rod, a goal that is accomplished in the first seven moves. At this point the three smaller disks are on rod 2 and the largest disk is on rod 1. The pivotal eighth move consists of moving the largest disk from rod 1 (the source rod) to rod 3 (the destination rod). This is the only time that the largest disk is moved. The remaining seven moves are analogous to the first seven moves in that the three smaller disks are moved from rod 2 to rod 3.

The recursive solution is also helpful in determining the minimum number of moves to solve the puzzle. Let $f(n)$ be the minimum number of moves required to solve a Tower of Hanoi puzzle with n disks. It is trivial to see that $f(1) = 1$. Using rationale behind the algorithm, $f(n)$ can be written as

$$f(n) = 2f(n-1) + 1$$

because two problems involving $n-1$ disks must be solved, in addition to the one move from rod s to rod d. This means that

$$f(2) = 2f(1) + 1 = 3, \qquad f(3) = 2f(2) + 1 = 7, \qquad f(4) = 2f(3) + 1 = 15,$$

etc. The $n = 4$ case with $f(4) = 15$ is consistent with the 15-move solution given by the call to the toh function with an argument of 4. In general, the minimum number of moves to solve the puzzle with n disks is $f(n) = 2^n - 1$.

This concludes the discussion on recursion, and on programming in R in general. The next chapter uses R's programming capability to perform Monte Carlo simulation experiments.

Exercises

24.1   For a positive odd integer n, the *double factorial* is defined by

$$n!! = \prod_{i=1}^{(n+1)/2} (2i - 1).$$

For example, $5!! = 1 \cdot 3 \cdot 5 = 15$ and $7!! = 1 \cdot 3 \cdot 5 \cdot 7 = 105$.

   (a) Write a one-line R function named double.factorial that computes the double factorial of a single argument n (which can be assumed to be a positive odd integer) without using recursion.

   (b) Write a one-line R function named double.factorial2 that computes the double factorial of a single argument n (which can be assumed to be a positive odd integer) using recursion.

24.2   Write an R function named Fib with a single positive integer argument n that calculates the value of the nth number in the Fibonacci sequence using recursion.

Chapter 25

Simulation

The scientific method has traditionally been based on theory and experimentation. A third leg—computation—has emerged recently. At the center of the computational leg of science is simulation. This chapter introduces the topic of Monte Carlo simulation, which is often used in applications in which analytic solutions are mathematically intractable. The three topics introduced here are (a) random number generation, (b) generating Bernoulli trials, and (c) Monte Carlo simulation.

25.1   Random number generation

Most computer languages have a mechanism for generating random numbers. Recall from Chapter 19 that the R command

```
> runif(14)
 [1] 0.56093324 0.07543963 0.10238774 0.39954275 0.97144714 0.57721700
 [7] 0.81229148 0.12200562 0.02560291 0.81569883 0.79436896 0.94414166
[13] 0.53892063 0.90441844
```

generates 14 random numbers. The terms $U(0, 1)$ random variate and random number are synonymous. Random numbers are important because they typically serve as the source of randomness when conducting a Monte Carlo simulation. While it is possible to conduct Monte Carlo simulations without knowing how these random numbers are generated, the brief introduction to the first successful algorithm for generating random numbers given here can be helpful in knowing the potential and limitations of simulation. Although it has been enhanced over the years, rudiments of this algorithm are still in use today. The 14 random numbers given above are not truly random, but are rather generated by a deterministic algorithm. They appear to be random, but they are not. For this reason, they are often known as "pseudorandom numbers." This first section gives some background on how these random numbers are generated inside of R.

After initial attempts by leading scientists such as Nicholas Metropolis and John von Neumann to develop an algorithm for generating random numbers, American mathematician Derrick Lehmer developed an algorithm known as a *linear congruential generator*. A conceptual model of this generator uses the following steps:

- Choose a large positive integer m.

- Fill a (conceptual) urn with the elements $\{1, 2, \ldots, m-1\}$.

• Each time a random number u is required, select an integer x at random from the urn and set $u = x/m$.

This conceptual generator produces a series of integers that are scaled so that the associated random numbers fall between 0 and 1 exclusive of the endpoints. (The smallest random number is $1/m$ and the largest is $(m-1)/m$). Each draw simulates a realization of a $U(0, 1)$ random variable. It is preferable that the values $u = 0$ and $u = 1$ *not* be included as possible values of u for developing random variate generation algorithms that convert the random numbers to random variates. Because the possible values of u are $1/m, 2/m, \ldots, 1 - 1/m$, it is critical that m be very large so that the possible values of u are densely distributed between 0 and 1. Ideally, we would like to make the draws of the integers from the conceptual urn with replacement, but Lehmer's algorithm makes the draws without replacement. Fortunately, for large values values of m, and relatively short simulation runs, this distinction is not critical.

A special case of a linear congruential generator that is commonly used to generate random numbers in practice is a (take a deep breath) prime modulus multiplicative linear congruential generator, or just PMMLCG for short. The recursive formula for a PMMLCG is

$$x_i = (ax_{i-1}) \bmod m \qquad\qquad i = 1, 2, \ldots$$

for a carefully selected positive integer a known as the "multiplier," a larger positive integer m known as the "modulus," and a random number seed x_0. The modulo function is given by mod. The modulus m is typically large and prime; for example, the Park–Miller minimal standard (named after Steve Park and Keith Miller) uses $a = 16,807$ and $m = 2^{31} - 1 = 2,147,483,647$. The associated random numbers are $u_i = x_i/m$.

To illustrate a tiny version of such a random number generator, let $a = 5$, $m = 7$, and $x_0 = 3$. The associated PMMLCG is

$$x_i = (5x_{i-1}) \bmod 7$$

and the sequence of integers $x_0, x_1, \ldots$ is

$$3, 1, 5, 4, 6, 2, 3, \ldots \; .$$

Notice that all of the positive integers between 1 and $m - 1 = 6$ appear once and only once in the first six elements of this series. Once the seed $x_0 = 3$ reappears in the sequence, the sequence will repeat itself indefinitely with the integers appearing in the same order. This particular choice of $a = 5$ and $m = 7$ makes this PMMLCG known as a "full period generator," because the period of the generator is $m - 1$. Not all combinations of a and m correspond to a full period generator, so a lot of effort goes into choosing a and m to deliver a full period and good statistical properties (for example, the appearance of independence). The sequence of integers produced is one way of drawing six balls, numbered 1 through 6, without replacement from an urn. The associated sequence of random numbers $u_0, u_1, \ldots$ is

$$\frac{3}{7}, \frac{1}{7}, \frac{5}{7}, \frac{4}{7}, \frac{6}{7}, \frac{2}{7}, \frac{3}{7}, \ldots \; .$$

Now consider a slightly larger example with multiplier $a = 7$, modulus $m = 61$, and seed $x_0 = 3$. Like the previous tiny random number generator, this generator also has a full period. We will write R code to generate the first 14 pseudorandom numbers from the generator

$$x_i = (7x_{i-1}) \bmod 61.$$

The vector x will hold the first 14 integers; its first element is initialized to the seed 3.

```
> x = numeric(14)
> x[1] = 3
> for (i in 2:14) x[i] = (7 * x[i - 1]) %% 61
> u = x / 61
> x
 [1]  3 21 25 53  5 35  1  7 49 38 22 32 41 43
> u
 [1] 0.04918033 0.34426230 0.40983607 0.86885246 0.08196721 0.57377049
 [7] 0.01639344 0.11475410 0.80327869 0.62295082 0.36065574 0.52459016
[13] 0.67213115 0.70491803
```

This is again a full-period generator. One difference between these 14 random numbers and those produced by the built-in function `runif` is that these are much less dense on the interval $(0, 1)$. There are gaps of size $1/61$ between each of the potential random numbers.

In 1968, George Marsaglia wrote a paper with the clever title "Random Numbers Fall Mainly in the Plane" in which he pointed out a serious flaw with linear congruential generators. Even though the generator appropriately fills in the values $1/m, 2/m, \ldots, 1 - 1/m$ in one dimension, when adjacent pairs (or triplets, etc. in higher dimensions) are plotted, they tend to fall in lines or planes. The R code below creates a plot of the first 60 overlapping pairs from the generator with multiplier $a = 7$, modulus $m = 61$, and seed $x_0 = 3$. That is, the points (u_0, u_1), (u_1, u_2), (u_2, u_3), ... are plotted.

```
> x = numeric(60)
> x[1] = 3
> for (i in 2:60) x[i] = (7 * x[i - 1]) %% 61
> u = x / 61
> plot(0, 0, type = "n", xlim = c(0, 1), ylim = c(0, 1))
> for (i in 2:60) points(u[i - 1], u[i], pch = 16)
> points(u[60], u[1], pch = 16)
```

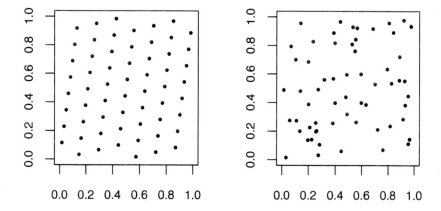

The clear pattern that emerges is that the entire unit square on the left-hand plot is not as densely populated as we would like it to be. Instead, these pairs fall into lines. Compare this to 60 points in the right-hand plot that are generated by `runif` via the code below.

```
> u = runif(60)
> plot(0, 0, type = "n", xlim = c(0, 1), ylim = c(0, 1))
> for (i in 2:60) points(u[i - 1], u[i], pch = 16)
> points(u[60], u[1], pch = 16)
```

The right-hand plot shows that the adjacent random numbers assume a less regular pattern than with the generator with $a = 7$ and $m = 61$. This is behaving in the manner that true adjacent pairs of random numbers should. However, all random numbers have the problem cited by Marsaglia. If all possible adjacent pairs from `runif` were plotted as tiny points and you had a very powerful magnifying glass, you would see that even the values generated by `runif` do indeed fall in lines. This results in degraded statistical properties, although this can be somewhat mitigated by good choices of a and m.

25.2   Generating Bernoulli trials

One of the most fundamental discrete distributions in probability theory is the Bernoulli distribution. A Bernoulli random variable X can assume just two values: 1 with probability p, and 0 with probability $1 - p$, where $0 < p < 1$. A single observation of a Bernoulli random variable is often known as a "Bernoulli trial." Tradition dictates that the two possible outcomes of a Bernoulli trial are generically referred to as "success" $(X = 1)$ and "failure" $(X = 0)$. Any random experiment that has two outcomes can be modeled as a Bernoulli trial. Examples include

- whether a registered voter supported a particular candidate,

- whether a coin came up heads when flipped,

- whether a child caught the flu last winter,

- whether a guest found the service at the hotel satisfactory,

- whether a high jumper cleared the bar,

- whether a cancer patient survived five years after diagnosis.

In all cases, there is a single trial and two outcomes. Choosing which outcome constitutes a success and which outcome constitutes a failure is a decision made by the modeler. So the probability mass function for a Bernoulli random variable is

$$f(x) = \begin{cases} 1 - p & x = 0 \\ p & x = 1 \end{cases}$$

for $0 < p < 1$. The Bernoulli distribution has a single parameter p that allows the distribution to be applied to a variety of situations that might arise. The probability mass function can also be written in a single line as

$$f(x) = p^x(1 - p)^{1-x} \qquad x = 0, 1$$

for $0 < p < 1$. This form highlights the fact that the Bernoulli distribution is a special case of the binomial distribution with $n = 1$.

There are two ways to generate Bernoulli trials in R. The first is to generate random numbers via the `runif` function, then compare these random numbers with p. For example, realizations of 14 mutually independent Bernoulli trials can be placed into the vector x with the R command

```
> x = runif(14) < 0.3
> x
 [1] FALSE FALSE FALSE FALSE FALSE  TRUE  TRUE FALSE FALSE FALSE FALSE FALSE
[13]  TRUE FALSE
```

In this case "success" corresponds to TRUE and "failure" corresponds to FALSE. If this command is executed repeatedly, about 30% of the elements will be TRUE and 70% will be FALSE. The as.numeric function can be used to coerce the logical values to 0's and 1's.

```
> x = as.numeric(x)
> x
 [1] 0 0 0 0 0 1 1 0 0 0 0 0 1 0
```

The results of the Bernoulli trials can be summed, for example, using the sum function.

```
> sum(x)
[1] 3
```

This value, which is the sum of 14 mutually independent Bernoulli random variables, has the binomial(14, 0.3) distribution. A binomial(14, 0.3) random variate can be generated more directly with the rbinom function.

```
> rbinom(1, 14, 0.3)
[1] 4
```

If 17 binomial(14, 0.3) random variates are required, the first argument can be used to specify the number of random variates desired.

```
> rbinom(17, 14, 0.3)
 [1] 3 3 5 1 7 6 6 3 2 1 6 3 2 5 4 6 1
```

25.3   Monte Carlo simulation

Monte Carlo simulation experiments use repeated random sampling to estimate numerical quantities. The experiment of interest is typically repeated a multitude of times on a computer in order to accurately estimate a target value of interest. The name Monte Carlo reflects the process of conducting gambling games repeatedly in order to estimate the probability of winning a particular game. Monte Carlo experimentation is appropriate when a closed-form expression is not available for a target quantity of interest. It can also be used to support an analytic solution to a probability problem. This section contains seven examples of using Monte Carlo simulation experiments to estimate quantities in probability problems.

Example 1. Three men and two women sit in a row of chairs in a random order. Use Monte Carlo simulation to estimate the probability that men and women alternate.

Central to Monte Carlo simulation is the notion of replication. The R code to approximate this probability essentially conducts this seating experiment repeatedly, say, 100,000 times. It counts the number of times that the men are sitting in the middle and extreme chairs, then prints the fraction of times that this event occurs.

The first R command sets the object nrep (short for number of replications) to 100,000. Then the object count, which will count the number of times that men and women alternate, is initialized to zero. A for loop runs the index i (which is not used in the simulation) from 1 to nrep, effectively conducting the experiment 100,000 times. The two commands in the for loop conduct the experiment. Men and women alternating in the chairs is equivalent to the order MWMWM. The first command, x = sample(c("M", "W", "M", "W", "M")), places a random permutation of the characters into the vector x. The order that the characters are placed in the vector that is used as an argument to sample is arbitrary. The event of interest, which is men sitting in positions 1, 3, and 5, is equivalent to all of the elements of x in odd positions containing the character "M". This is captured with the condition all(x[c(1, 3, 5)] == "M") in the if statement. The object count is incremented every time the men are seated in chairs 1, 3, and 5. Once the for loop has been completed, the fraction of times that the positions of the men and women alternate is printed using the print command.

```
> nrep = 100000
> count = 0
> for (i in 1:nrep) {
+    x = sample(c("M", "W", "M", "W", "M"))
+    if (all(x[c(1, 3, 5)] == "M")) count = count + 1
+ }
> print(count / nrep)
```

It is unwise to conduct a Monte Carlo simulation experiment a single time. The random numbers can conspire against you and provide a misleading result. It can be helpful to set the random number stream prior to conducting a series of Monte Carlo experiments. This way, if an unusual result occurs, it can be recreated subsequently. After a call to set.seed(4) to initiate the random number stream (the 4 is arbitrary), five runs of the Monte Carlo code given above result in the following five estimates of the probability that men and women alternate:

0.10074   0.10033   0.10150   0.09954   0.10000.

It is not clear how these five runs should be summarized. Since all five of these results round to 0.10, this is perhaps the safest way to report the result. Since the estimate given by the third simulation run is 0.102, rounded to three digits, it is probably not safe to report 0.100 as the estimate of the probability that men and women alternate positions. So we settle on just two digits of accuracy. If this is not adequate, nrep can be increased or more runs can be made.

The analytic solution to this problem uses combinatorics. There are $5! = 120$ different equally-likely arrangements of the five people in the chairs. Of these arrangements, there are just $3 \cdot 2 \cdot 2 \cdot 1 \cdot 1 = 12$ associated with alternating men and women by the multiplication rule, so the probability that men and women alternate is exactly

$$\frac{3 \cdot 2 \cdot 2 \cdot 1 \cdot 1}{5 \cdot 4 \cdot 3 \cdot 2 \cdot 1} = \frac{12}{120} = \frac{1}{10}.$$

So does the Monte Carlo simulation *prove* that the analytic solution is correct? It does not. It only *supports* the analytic solution in that the results hover about the analytic solution. The spectacular fifth simulation run, which resulted in exactly 10,000 of the 100,000 simulation experiments having men and women alternating, is rare.

Example 2. Use Monte Carlo simulation to estimate the probability of rolling a total of ten in a roll of three fair dice.

Given a fair die and lots of time, we could perform the Monte Carlo experiment by hand. Instead, we run a Monte Carlo simulation experiment in R to estimate the probability. We begin by once again initially setting the number of replications of the experiment nrep to 100,000 and initializing count, which will count the number of times that we get a total of ten, to zero. The first R command in the for loop simulates the rolls of three fair dice. The sample function sets the vector x to three elements corresponding to the outcomes of the three rolls. The second R command in the for loop increments count when the sum of the outcomes of the three dice equals ten. Finally, the fraction of times that a total of 10 arises is printed.

```
> nrep = 100000
> count = 0
> for (i in 1:nrep) {
+    x = sample(1:6, 3, replace = TRUE)
+    if (sum(x) == 10) count = count + 1
+ }
> print(count / nrep)
```

After a call to set.seed(4), five runs of this simulation yield the following results:

0.12666   0.12458   0.12465   0.12522   0.12654.

Based on these results, we are quite confident that the exact probability of obtaining a total of 10 is between 0.12 and 0.13. The analytic result could be found by enumerating the possible rolls, for example $(6, 2, 2)$, resulting in a total of 10 out of the $6^3 = 216$ possible rolls of three die. (The analytic solution is $27/216 = 1/8 = 0.125$.)

Example 3. Urn 1 contains three white balls and two black balls. Urn 2 contains one white ball and three black balls. The initial state of the two urns is shown below. A ball is selected at random from Urn 1 and transferred to Urn 2. Next, a ball is selected at random from Urn 2 and transferred to Urn 1. Finally, a ball is selected at random from Urn 1. Use Monte Carlo simulation to estimate the probability that the ball selected on this third draw is black.

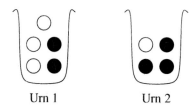

Urn 1   Urn 2

This problem contains more moving parts than the previous two. We once again begin by initializing nrep to 100,000 and count to 0 as in the previous two examples. Within the for loop, the vector urn1 establishes the initial state of Urn 1, where 0 denotes a white ball and 1 denotes a black ball. Likewise for urn2. The x = sample(5, 1) command sets x to the index of the first ball sampled. This ball is transferred to Urn 2 with the command urn2 = c(urn2, urn1[x]). There are now five balls in Urn 2. The y = sample(5, 1) command sets y to the index of the second ball sampled. This ball is transferred to Urn 1 with the command urn1[x] = urn2[y]. Finally, a third ball is drawn from Urn 1, and, if it is black, count is incremented. After the for loop terminates, the fraction of times that the third ball drawn is black is printed.

```
> nrep = 100000
> count = 0
```

```
> for (i in 1:nrep) {
+   urn1 = c(0, 0, 0, 1, 1)
+   urn2 = c(0, 1, 1, 1)
+   x = sample(5, 1)
+   urn2 = c(urn2, urn1[x])
+   y = sample(5, 1)
+   urn1[x] = urn2[y]
+   if (sample(urn1, 1) == 1) count = count + 1
+ }
> print(count / nrep)
```

After a call to set.seed(4) to initialize the random number stream, five runs of the simulation yield the following estimates:

$$0.45718 \qquad 0.45573 \qquad 0.45757 \qquad 0.45556 \qquad 0.45420.$$

Based on these results, we are reasonably sure that the probability that the ball selected on the third draw is black lies between 0.45 and 0.46. The analytic solution to this problem relies on conditional probability and is exactly $57/125 = 0.456$. Two of the simulation experiments have results that fall above the analytic solution, and three have results that fall below the analytic solution, so this Monte Carlo simulation supports the analytic solution.

Example 4. Use Monte Carlo simulation to estimate the 90th percentile of the distance between two points chosen at random in the interior of a unit square.

The tools required to solve this problem analytically are significant, although the problem poses no difficulty for Monte Carlo simulation. The two points in the unit square (x_1, y_1) and (x_2, y_2) are generated using four random variates that are uniformly distributed between 0 and 1. The distance between the two points,

$$\sqrt{(x_1 - x_2)^2 + (y_1 - y_2)^2},$$

can range from 0 (when the points are identical) to $\sqrt{2}$ (when the points are at opposite corners of the square). Three realizations of line segments between random points in the unit square are shown below.

  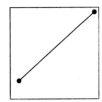

The R code to conduct the Monte Carlo simulations can be conducted without using loops, so we can increase the number of replications, nrep, to one million. The next four R commands set x1, x2, y1, and y2 to vectors of one million random numbers via the runif function. This establishes one million pairs of points (x_1, y_1) and (x_2, y_2). The next command uses the distance formula to calculate one million random distances. Finally, the distances are sorted, and the 900,000th sorted distance is printed.

```
> nrep = 1000000
> x1 = runif(nrep)
> x2 = runif(nrep)
> y1 = runif(nrep)
> y2 = runif(nrep)
> d  = sqrt((x1 - x2) ^ 2 + (y1 - y2) ^ 2)
> sort(d)[0.9 * nrep]
```

After a call to set.seed(4) to set the random number stream, five replications of runs of this code yield

| 0.85909 | 0.85880 | 0.85834 | 0.85858 | 0.85887. |

The Monte Carlo estimate for the 90th percentile of the length of the line between the two points is approximately 0.859, although there is uncertainty about the third significant digit.

Example 5. Xavier and Yolanda agree to meet at the sun dial at 2:00 PM. Neither, however, is particularly punctual, and their actual arrival times to the sun dial are independent and uniformly distributed between 2:00 PM and 3:00 PM. Assuming that each will wait 15 minutes for the other, use Monte Carlo simulation to estimate the probability that they will actually meet.

This is another simulation that can be conducted without loops. The number of replications is initially set to one million. Using minutes as the time scale, the vectors x and y are each set to one million $U(0, 60)$ random variables, which represent the number of minutes after 2:00 PM that Xavier and Yolanda arrive to the sun dial. Finally, the command sum(abs(x - y) < 15) / nrep calculates the fraction of times that the associated elements in x and y are within 15 of one another.

```
> nrep = 1000000
> x = runif(nrep, 0, 60)
> y = runif(nrep, 0, 60)
> sum(abs(x - y) < 15) / nrep
```

After a call to set.seed(4) to set the random number stream, five runs of this code result in

| 0.43780 | 0.43772 | 0.43768 | 0.43776 | 0.43734. |

We can conclude that the probability that Xavier and Yolanda meet seems to be between 0.437 and 0.438. This is consistent with analytic work to solve this problem, which involves computing a double integral over a joint probability density function, yielding an analytic solution of $7/16 = 0.4375$. Once again, the Monte Carlo solution supports the analytic solution.

Example 6. Let the continuous random variables A, B, and C be mutually independent $U(0, 1)$ random variables. Use Monte Carlo simulation to estimate the probability that the random quadratic equation $Ax^2 + Bx + C = 0$ has real roots.

The two distinct roots of the quadratic equation are both real if the discriminant $B^2 - 4AC$ is positive. This can once again be simulated without loops. The number of replications is set to one million. The vectors named A, B, and C are each filled with one million random numbers using the runif function. Even though the R command sum(B ^ 2 - 4 * A * C > 0) / nrep could be used to calculate the fraction of the quadratic functions containing a positive discriminant, we instead use the mean function, which performs the same task but uses fewer keystrokes.

```
> nrep = 1000000
> A = runif(nrep)
> B = runif(nrep)
> C = runif(nrep)
> mean(B ^ 2 - 4 * A * C > 0)
```

After a call to set.seed(4) to initialize the random number stream, five runs of this R code yield

$$0.25456 \qquad 0.25412 \qquad 0.25387 \qquad 0.25451 \qquad 0.25416.$$

The estimated probability that the quadratic will have real roots is 0.254, with some lingering doubt about the final digit. This is consistent with the analytic solution, which involves computing two triple integrals over a trivariate probability density function, resulting in a probability of 0.2544 to four digits of accuracy. Once again, the analytic solution is supported by the Monte Carlo simulation experiment.

Example 7. Reckless rectilinear Russell is taking a rectilinear walk from point H (home) to point W (work) along the grid lines shown in the grid in the figure. Assuming all of the paths of length 21 from point H to point W (that is, he doesn't go out of his way and each square on the grid is 1×1) are equally likely, use Monte Carlo simulation to estimate the probability that he will go past the mailbox at point M.

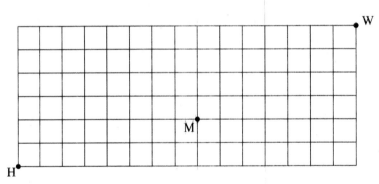

Russell's 21-move trek from point H to point W consists of 6 northward moves and 15 eastward moves. He passes the mailbox at point M if and only if his first 10 moves include exactly 2 northward moves and exactly 8 eastward moves. In order to formulate a Monte Carlo solution to this problem, we designate a northward move by 1 and an eastward move by 0. Since the Monte Carlo solution will require loops, we use only 100,000 replications. The first two R commands initialize nrep and count to the number of replications and the count of the number of times the mailbox is passed, respectively. The third command sets the vector named moves to 21 elements consisting of 6 ones (for the northward moves) and 15 zeros (for the eastward moves). Within the for loop, x = sample(moves) sets the 21-element vector x to a random permutation of the elements in the moves vector. This defines a path from point H to point W. If Russell has made exactly 2 northward moves in his first 10 moves, then he has gone past the mailbox at point M, and count is incremented. Finally, the fraction of the 100,000 replications in which he goes past the mailbox is printed.

```
> nrep = 100000
> count = 0
> moves = c(rep(1, 6), rep(0, 15))
```

```
> for (i in 1:nrep) {
+    x = sample(moves)
+    if (cumsum(x)[10] == 2) count = count + 1
+ }
> print(count / nrep)
```

After a call to set.seed(4) to initialize the random number stream, five runs of this code yield

$$0.27458 \qquad 0.27332 \qquad 0.27135 \qquad 0.27345 \qquad 0.27305.$$

We can conclude that we have a high degree of confidence that the probability that Russell will pass the mailbox at point **M** is 0.27.

The analytic solution in this case involves combinations and the multiplication rule. There are a total of

$$\binom{21}{15} = 54,264$$

equally-likely paths from point **H** to point **W**. Combinations are used here because Russell has 15 positions that he can select his eastward moves out of $15 + 6 = 21$ possible positions that those eastward moves can be made. Using the multiplication rule, the probability of passing by the mailbox at point **M** is

$$\frac{\binom{10}{8}\binom{11}{7}}{\binom{21}{15}} = \frac{45 \cdot 330}{54,264} = \frac{14,850}{54,264} = \frac{2475}{9044} \cong 0.2737.$$

The Monte Carlo simulation results support the analytic solution because the simulated values hover about the analytic solution.

Execution speed is important in Monte Carlo simulation because we would like as many replications of a simulation as possible in order to achieve as much precision as possible. Examples 1, 2, 3, and 7 all used loops to conduct the simulation experiments; loops tend to be slow in R. The replicate function can be used to avoid loops and shorten the code. The first argument to replicate is the number of replications to be conducted. The second argument to replicate is the function to be replicated.

As an illustration, return to Example 2, where the interest is in estimating the probability of rolling a total of ten with a roll of three fair dice. The first R command below defines a function named roll, which returns the sum of the rolls of three fair dice. The second R command uses the replicate function to replicate 100,000 instances of roll, which are placed in the vector y. At this point, the elements of y are random integers that range from 3 (rolling three ones) to 18 (rolling three sixes). Finally, the mean function is applied to the vector of Boolean values y == 10, which yields the fraction of the experiments that result in a total of 10 being tossed.

```
> roll = function() sum(sample(6, 3, replace = TRUE))
> y = replicate(100000, roll())
> mean(y == 10)
```

After a call to set.seed(4) to initialize the random number stream, this code returns exactly the same values as given previously. Although three lines of code were used for clarity, the following single R command is equivalent.

```
> mean(replicate(100000, sum(sample(6, 3, replace = TRUE)) == 10))
```

As a second example of using the `replicate` function, consider Example 7 in which we estimated the probability that Russell would pass the mailbox at point M. The first command in the R code below sets the vector `moves` to 21 elements, 6 of which are 1's (representing the northward moves) and 15 of which are 0's (representing the eastward moves). The `replicate` function is used in the next command to replicate 100,000 experiments of Russell's trek from home to work. Whenever the cumulative sum of a random sample of moves has its 10th element equal to 2 (that is, he has made exactly 2 northward moves in his first 10 moves), the value in the vector is set to `TRUE`. Finally, taking the sample mean of this vector of Boolean values with the `mean` function gives the fraction of times that Russell passed by the mailbox.

```
> moves = c(rep(1, 6), rep(0, 15))
> mean(replicate(100000, cumsum(sample(moves))[10] == 2))
```

Although this could have been written as a single line of code, this way is more efficient because the `c` and `rep` functions in the first line get called just once, rather than 100,000 times.

This ends the discussion of Monte Carlo simulation in R. Although simulation is a powerful computational tool, each problem requires a custom programming approach. Even though many of the examples given in this chapter have simple analytic solutions, it is not difficult to give a slight twist to the problem that makes it mathematically intractable. Monte Carlo simulation is a valuable tool for supporting analytic solutions or for estimating numerical quantities in mathematically intractable problems. With R's programming ability, it is also capable of conducting a *discrete-event simulation* in which time plays a significant factor, which means that the maintenance of an event calendar is necessary. The new function introduced in this chapter is the `replicate` function, which replicates calls to a function.

The next chapter introduces the important topic of statistics, which is one of the roots of R.

Exercises

25.1   Consider the relationship
$$x_i = (66x_{i-1}) \bmod 401$$
for $i = 1, 2, \ldots$, where mod is the modulo function and $x_0 = 12$. Write R commands that set the first ten elements of the vector x to $x_0, x_1, x_2, \ldots, x_9$.

25.2   Use Monte Carlo simulation to estimate the probability that all six faces appear exactly once in six tosses of a fair die.

25.3   A waiting line consists of 40 men and 10 women arranged in a random order. Use Monte Carlo simulation to estimate the probability that no two women in line are adjacent to one another.

25.4   You roll a fair die five times. Write R code that conducts a Monte Carlo simulation experiment with 500,000 replications that estimates the probability that you will see a string of three or more consecutive ones.

25.5   Xavier and Olivia are playing tic-tac-toe. They choose their moves randomly among the remaining positions. Xavier always goes first. Use Monte Carlo simulation to estimate the probability that Xavier wins, the probability that Olivia wins, and the probability that the game is a draw. Use enough replications to achieve two digits of accuracy.

25.6 Marylou's class has 34 students. Find the probability that there are exactly two birthday matches, with each birthday match consisting of exactly two students. Ignore leap years and assume that all 365 birthdays are equally likely. Support your analytic solution by conducting a Monte Carlo simulation in R.

25.7 Let A, B, and C be the results of three rolls of a fair die.

    (a) Write an R program that computes the exact probability that the roots of the random quadratic equation $Ax^2 + Bx + C = 0$ are real. (A single root with multiplicity two, for example the root $x = -1$ associated with $A = 1$, $B = 2$, and $C = 1$, counts as real roots.)

    (b) Support your analytic solution with a Monte Carlo simulation.

25.8 The cubic equation

$$ax^3 + bx^2 + cx + d = 0$$

with $a \neq 0$ having discriminant

$$\Delta = 18abcd - 4b^3d + b^2c^2 - 4ac^3 - 27a^2d^2$$

has three distinct real roots if $\Delta > 0$, has one real root with multiplicity one and another real root with multiplicity two if $\Delta = 0$, and has one real root with multiplicity one and two complex conjugate roots when $\Delta < 0$. If the coefficients a, b, c, and d are mutually independent $U(0, 3)$ random variables, use Monte Carlo simulation to estimate the probability that all of the roots are real to three digits.

25.9 Let $X_1, X_2, \ldots, X_{10}$ be mutually independent and identically distributed $U(0, 1)$ random variables. Write a Monte Carlo simulation in R that estimates the 90th percentile of the product $Z = X_1 X_2 \ldots X_{10}$.

25.10 Write a sentence that describes the quantity that is being estimated in the R Monte Carlo simulation code given below.

```
> nrep = 100000
> count = 0
> for (i in 1:nrep) {
+    x = sample(6, 5, replace = TRUE)
+    if (min(x) >= 2) count = count + 1
+ }
> print(count / nrep)
```

Chapter 26

Statistics

This chapter contains a brief introduction to statistical inference methods in R. Statistics involves the collection, presentation, and interpretation of data. Graphical tools such as

- the histogram generated by the `hist` function,
- the empirical cumulative distribution function generated by the `ecdf` function, and
- QQ plots generated by the `qqplot` function,

were introduced in Chapters 20 and 21 as techniques for visually summarizing data. Built-in functions such as

- `mean` for calculating the sample mean,
- `sd` for calculating the sample standard deviation, and
- `median` for calculating the sample median,

provide numerical summaries of a data set.

Using R to perform statistical inference is one of the hallmark aspects of the language. Since there are entire books written on using R for inferential statistics, this chapter serves only to briefly introduce three selected topics: (a) constructing a confidence interval, (b) conducting a goodness-of-fit test, and (c) fitting a statistical model to data. Some familiarity with statistics is helpful for reading this chapter.

26.1 Confidence intervals

One topic that often arises in the analysis of a univariate data set is the process of determining a confidence interval for an unknown parameter of interest. One such confidence interval will be illustrated here.

Assume that the data values $x_1, x_2, \ldots, x_n$ are a random sample of size n drawn from a normal population with unknown population mean μ and unknown population variance σ^2. The interest is in a point and interval estimator (also known as a confidence interval) for μ, which will reflect the precision afforded by the data values. The point estimator for μ is the sample mean $\bar{x}$, which is given by

$$\bar{x} = \frac{1}{n} \sum_{i=1}^{n} x_i.$$

This estimator is calculated in R with the `mean` function, and is derived mathematically by using the method of moments or maximum likelihood (for a normal population, both techniques give the same estimator). But the point estimator alone does not give any sense of the precision of the point estimator. *Confidence intervals* are used by statisticians to compute an interval that gives an indication of the precision of the point estimator. A well-known formula for an exact two-sided $(1 - \alpha)100\%$ confidence interval for μ when sampling is from a normal population with unknown population standard deviation σ is

$$\bar{x} - t_{\alpha/2, n-1} \frac{s}{\sqrt{n}} < \mu < \bar{x} + t_{\alpha/2, n-1} \frac{s}{\sqrt{n}},$$

where s is the sample standard deviation defined by

$$s = \sqrt{\frac{1}{n-1} \sum_{i=1}^{n} (x_i - \bar{x})^2}$$

and $t_{\alpha/2, n-1}$ is the $1 - \alpha/2$ fractile of the t distribution with $n - 1$ degrees of freedom. Common choices for the parameter α are 0.01, 0.05, and 0.1, which correspond to 99%, 95%, and 90% confidence intervals, respectively.

This confidence interval will be applied to the built-in `precip` data set, which consists of the annual rainfall (in inches) for $n = 70$ cities in the United States. The first step is to determine whether our assumptions concerning normality of the population distribution are justified. A histogram of the 70 averages can be plotted with

```
> hist(precip)                    # visual check for normality
```

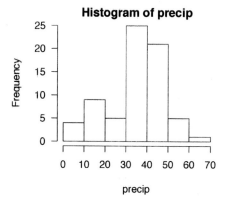

Although this is not a perfectly bell-shaped histogram, the discrepancies might possibly be attributed to random sampling variability, so we will proceed as if the assumption concerning sampling from a normal population is justified. Since this is only a visual assessment of the shape of the population distribution, a formal statistical *goodness-of-fit* test should be conducted. The point estimator for the population mean μ, which in this setting is the population mean rainfall amount for the entire United States, is calculated in R with the command

```
> mean(precip)                    # point estimator for mu
[1] 34.88571
```

A confidence interval will give us some sense of the precision of this point estimator. The code below calculates the lower and upper bounds of an exact two-sided 95% confidence interval for μ.

```
> n    = length(precip)           # n is the sample size
> xbar = mean(precip)             # sample mean
> sdev = sd(precip)               # sample standard deviation
> alph = 0.05                     # alpha = 0.05 for 95% confidence interval
> crit = qt(1 - alph / 2, n - 1)  # quantile for the t distribution
> half = crit * sdev / sqrt(n)    # interval halfwidth
> xbar + c(-1, 1) * half          # 95% confidence interval
[1] 31.61748 38.15395
```

So reporting the point and interval estimators to the appropriate number of significant digits based on the data values, the estimated mean annual rainfall in the United States is $\bar{x} = 34.9$ inches and an exact two-sided 95% confidence interval for μ is

$$31.6 < \mu < 38.2.$$

Assuming that the locations of the cities in the data set are selected at random, we are 95% confident that the population mean annual rainfall for the United States μ falls between 31.6 and 38.2 inches.

Since the calculation of this confidence interval arises so often in statistics, R provides a function named t.test that calculates the point estimator, the confidence interval, and performs the associated hypothesis test. These three calculations are performed for the precip data set with the single command

```
> t.test(precip)                  # fewer keystrokes

    One Sample t-test

data:  precip
t = 21.2944, df = 69, p-value < 2.2e-16
alternative hypothesis: true mean is not equal to 0
95 percent confidence interval:
 31.61748 38.15395
sample estimates:
mean of x
 34.88571
```

The first line of the output from the call to t.test that follows the heading gives the name of the data set: precip. The second line gives the test statistic associated with the default null hypothesis $H_0 : \mu = 0$, the degrees of freedom for the test statistic under the null hypothesis, and the p-value for the test of significance. The third line gives a verbal description of the default alternative hypothesis $H_1 : \mu \neq 0$. The next two lines give the lower and upper bounds of the 95% confidence interval for μ, which match the results calculated earlier. The final three lines give the point estimator $\bar{x}$. The values in this display can be extracted using the $ extractor, which was first used in Chapter 15 when lists were introduced. For example, the 95% confidence interval and p-value for the hypothesis test can be extracted with the commands

```
> t.test(precip)$conf.int         # extract confidence interval
[1] 31.61748 38.15395
attr(,"conf.level")
[1] 0.95
> t.test(precip)$p.value          # extract p-value
[1] 4.76966e-32
```

Although the t.test function is capable of conducting one of the most common hypothesis tests in statistics (and also computing the associated confidence interval), there are dozens of other statistical tests that are coded into the base version of R. The table that follows lists a sampling of a few of these tests in no particular order. The t.test function is appropriate when the mean value is of interest, but some of the other tests concern variances, proportions, correlations, medians, etc. The best way to find more information on the arguments for these tests, as well as some examples of how they can be invoked, is to use the help function with the name of the particular test as the argument.

function	description
t.test	one-sample, two-sample, and paired data t-test concerning means
var.test	two-sample F-test concerning variances
prop.test	test concerning proportions
cor.test	tests for correlation between paired samples
wilcox.test	Wilcoxon rank sum and signed rank tests
kruskal.test	Kruskal–Wallis rank sum test
friedman.test	Friedman rank sum test
quade.test	Quade test with unreplicated blocked data
chisq.test	Pearson's chi-squared tests
ks.test	one-sample and two-sample Kolmogorov–Smirnov test
shapiro.test	Shapiro–Wilk test of normality
mcnemar.test	McNemar's chi-squared test for count data
fisher.test	Fisher's exact test for count data
aov	fit an analysis of variance model

26.2   Goodness-of-fit tests

This section combines the graphical capabilities of R with the use of one of the statistical functions to assess the goodness of fit for a particular data set. More specifically, we want to determine whether the exponential distribution is a good statistical model for the built-in rivers data set.

We begin by displaying the rivers data set, which contains the lengths of $n = 141$ "major" rivers (in miles) in North America. The longest river in North America is the combination of the Missouri and Mississippi rivers with a length of 3710 miles.

```
> rivers                                         # lengths of rivers
  [1]  735  320  325  392  524  450 1459  135  465  600  330  336  280  315
 [15]  870  906  202  329  290 1000  600  505 1450  840 1243  890  350  407
 [29]  286  280  525  720  390  250  327  230  265  850  210  630  260  230
 [43]  360  730  600  306  390  420  291  710  340  217  281  352  259  250
 [57]  470  680  570  350  300  560  900  625  332 2348 1171 3710 2315 2533
 [71]  780  280  410  460  260  255  431  350  760  618  338  981 1306  500
 [85]  696  605  250  411 1054  735  233  435  490  310  460  383  375 1270
 [99]  545  445 1885  380  300  380  377  425  276  210  800  420  350  360
[113]  538 1100 1205  314  237  610  360  540 1038  424  310  300  444  301
[127]  268  620  215  652  900  525  246  360  529  500  720  270  430  671
[141] 1770
```

One way to compare an empirical and fitted distribution is to plot the empirical cumulative distribution function associated with this data set, along with the fitted exponential distribution. The plot.ecdf function plots the empirical cumulative distribution function. The exponential distribution is fitted with the maximum likelihood estimator, which is the reciprocal of the sample mean. This maximum likelihood estimator is placed in the object mle. In order to plot the fitted distribution on the same set of axes as the empirical cumulative distribution function, begin by setting the object x to 500 points along the horizontal axis using the seq function. The pexp function calculates the associated cumulative distribution function values of the fitted distribution, which are placed in the vector y. Finally, the lines function is used to plot the fitted cumulative distribution function.

```
> plot.ecdf(rivers, verticals = T, pch = "")    # plot empirical cdf
> mle = 1 / mean(rivers)                         # maximum likelihood estimator
> x = seq(0, max(rivers), length = 500)          # x-axis for plot of fitted cdf
> y = pexp(x, mle)                               # y-axis for plot of fitted cdf
> lines(x, y)                                    # plot fitted cdf
```

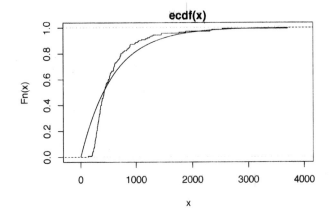

The step function associated with the empirical cumulative distribution function contains upward steps of height $1/141$ at each unique data value. When there are d tied data values, the step function increases by $d/141$. The smooth fitted distribution does not appear to do a particularly good job of approximating the empirical cumulative distribution function. But this visual assessment is subject to subjectivity! A formal statistical test is more appropriate. One of the classical statistical tests for goodness of fit is known as the Kolmogorov–Smirnov (often abbreviated with KS) test. The null hypothesis for this test is that the data values are drawn from a hypothesized or fitted distribution, in this case the exponential distribution. This test can be conducted with the ks.test function. For the exponential fitted distribution using the maximum likelihood estimator, the test is conducted with the R command

```
> ks.test(rivers, "pexp", mle)                   # kolmogorov-smirnov test

    One-sample Kolmogorov-Smirnov test

data:  rivers
D = 0.2848, p-value = 2.331e-10
alternative hypothesis: two-sided
```

```
Warning message:
In ks.test(rivers, "pexp", mle) :
  ties should not be present for the Kolmogorov-Smirnov test
```

Following the heading, the first line confirms that the data is in the object named `rivers`. The second line computes the test statistic $D_{141} = 0.2848$, which is the largest vertical distance between the fitted and the empirical cumulative distribution functions. This largest vertical distance occurs just to the left of the second sorted data value: 202 miles. Larger values of this test statistic imply a poorer fit. This line also contains the p-value, which is tiny in this case, indicating that H_0 should be rejected; the exponential distribution is not a good fit for the lengths of rivers. The third line states that the two-sided alternative hypothesis was used in computing the p-value for the test. There is also a warning message indicating that tied values in the data set (at 210, 230, 250, ... , 900 miles, almost certainly due to rounding the lengths of the rivers to the nearest 10 miles) decrease the statistical validity of the Kolmogorov–Smirnov goodness-of-fit test.

One reason that the exponential distribution fails to fit the lengths of the rivers comes from the help page for the `rivers` data set. The page indicates that only "major" rivers have been included, which means that smaller rivers have been excluded. This is reflected in the fact that the empirical cumulative distribution function remains at zero up to the smallest river length, 135 miles, which results in the large value for the test statistic. If shorter rivers were included in the data set, the exponential distribution might have provided a better fit.

26.3 Model fitting

R has functions that can be used to fit statistical models. One of the most basic models is known as *simple linear regression*. This model is appropriate for describing a linear relationship between a single independent variable x and a single dependent variable y. Recall that the built-in data set `Formaldehyde` contains just $n = 6$ data pairs (x_i, y_i), $i = 1, 2, \ldots, 6$.

```
> Formaldehyde                           # n = 6 observations
  carb optden
1  0.1  0.086
2  0.3  0.269
3  0.5  0.446
4  0.6  0.538
5  0.7  0.626
6  0.9  0.782
```

Assuming that `carb` is the independent variable and `optden` is the dependent variable, a scatterplot of the data values can be generated with

```
> plot(Formaldehyde)                      # linear relationship
```

At least on this range of the independent variable `carb`, a linear relationship between the independent and dependent variables appears to be appropriate. The R function `lm` (for linear model) is used to fit a linear model to a data set. The fitted linear model can be assigned to the object `fit` with the R command

```
> fit = lm(optden ~ carb, data = Formaldehyde) # simple linear regression
```

The `lm` function in R uses the *least squares criteria* to fit a regression line to the data pairs. A summary of the fitted linear model can be displayed with the `summary` function.

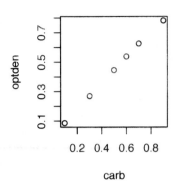

```
> summary(fit)                                  # summary of fit

Call:
lm(formula = optden ~ carb, data = Formaldehyde)

Residuals:
        1         2         3         4         5         6
-0.006714  0.001029  0.002771  0.007143  0.007514 -0.011743

Coefficients:
            Estimate Std. Error t value Pr(>|t|)
(Intercept) 0.005086   0.007834   0.649    0.552
carb        0.876286   0.013535  64.744 3.41e-07 ***
---
Signif. codes:  0 *** 0.001 ** 0.01 * 0.05 . 0.1   1

Residual standard error: 0.008649 on 4 degrees of freedom
Multiple R-squared:  0.999, Adjusted R-squared:  0.9988
F-statistic:  4192 on 1 and 4 DF,  p-value: 3.409e-07
```

R uses blank lines to separate portions of the summary. The first portion echos the call to lm, indicating that the data set is Formaldehyde, and optden, the dependent variable, is being modeled as a function of carb, the independent variable, via formula = optden ~ carb. Next, the summary function gives the values of the residuals, which are the signed vertical distances between each data value and the associated value on the regression line. The next portion gives the intercept, 0.005086, and the slope, 0.876286, of the regression line. This table also includes the standard error of these two statistics, the t statistic for the hypothesis test to determine whether the quantity differs statistically from zero, and the associated p-value. The large p-value, 0.552, for the intercept means that there is no statistical evidence that the intercept of the regression line, 0.005086, significantly differs from 0. The small p-value, $3.41 \cdot 10^{-7}$, for the slope means that there is overwhelming statistical evidence that the slope of the regression line, 0.876286, significantly differs from 0. The final portion contains additional calculated values that are helpful in determining the adequacy of the simple linear regression model.

The object fit that has been created by the lm function is a list. This can be determined by

```
> mode(fit)                                     # determine the mode of fit
[1] "list"
```

As with any list, various components of `fit` can be extracted. Three ways of picking off the intercept and slope of the regression line are

```
> summary(fit)$coefficients[ , 1]           # regression estimators
(Intercept)          carb
0.005085714 0.876285714
> coef(fit)                                   # regression estimators
(Intercept)          carb
0.005085714 0.876285714
> slr = fit$coefficients                      # regression estimators
```

The last of these commands places the intercept and slope in a two-element vector named `slr`. The regression line can be added to the plot with the `abline` function:

```
> abline(slr)                                 # plot regression line
```

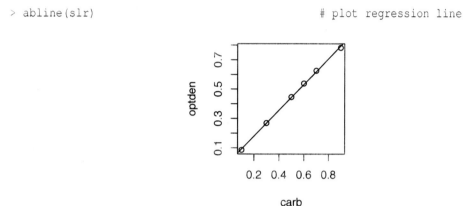

The first and last data points fall slightly below the regression line, but all in all, the simple linear regression model is a very good fit to this particular data set. It is good statistical practice to investigate the behavior of the residuals. The two commands below extract and plot the six residuals.

```
> resid = fit$residuals                       # extract residuals
> plot(resid)                                 # scatterplot of residuals
```

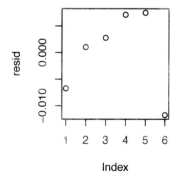

The first and last residuals are negative (because the associated data pairs fall below the regression line) and the other four residuals are positive. Even though a histogram of the residuals does not make sense for such a small data set, we provide one here for completeness.

```
> hist(resid)                               # residual histogram not useful
```

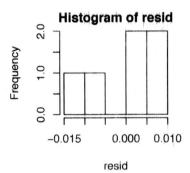

There is some advantage, in terms of the tractability of statistical inference concerning the regression line, of having normally distributed residuals. One visual method of determining whether the residuals are normally distributed is a QQ plot using the qqnorm function

```
> qqnorm(resid)                             # QQ normal plot of residuals
```

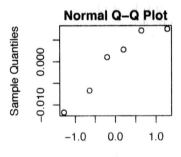

This plot should be viewed after viewing a dozen or so plots that result from invocations of the command qqnorm(rnorm(6)). This exercise helps the eye gauge how much random sampling variability associated with a sample of size $n = 6$ causes the points on the QQ plot to deviate from linearity.

Statistical models, in this case a simple linear regression model, are often formulated for the purpose of predicting, or forecasting, a future value. Let's say we would like to predict the optical density when the carbohydrate level is 1.1. This calculation can be performed with the predict function, which takes the fitted model as its first argument and a data frame containing the value (or values) of the independent variable associated with the prediction as its second argument. Assuming that the fitted linear model is appropriate outside of the range of the collected data values for the independent variable, typing

```
> newcarb = data.frame(carb = 1.1)          # new carb value is 1.1
> predict(fit, newcarb)                     # predict optden for carb = 1.1
      1
0.969
```

reveals that the predicted optical density associated with carb = 1.1 is 0.969. Standard errors can also be calculated by predict if a confidence interval, for example, is required.

The estimated variance–covariance matrix associated with the intercept and slope can be calculated with the vcov function:

```
> vcov(fit)                              # var-cov matrix fitted model
            (Intercept)          carb
(Intercept)  6.136653e-05 -0.0000946449
carb        -9.464490e-05  0.0001831837
```

The square roots of the diagonal elements of this matrix can be calculated with the sqrt and diag functions:

```
> sqrt(diag(vcov(fit)))                  # stderr regression estimators
(Intercept)        carb
0.007833679 0.013534536
```

These are the same numbers that appeared in the standard error column of the summary for the fitted regression model. These values can also be extracted from the summary with the command

```
> summary(fit)$coefficients[ , 2]        # stderr regression estimators
(Intercept)        carb
0.007833679 0.013534536
```

The simple linear regression model discussed so far assumes that the independent and dependent variables are treated differently. The independent variable is assumed to be observed without error; the dependent variable is viewed as a random response at a particular setting of the independent variable. Sometimes the two variables are each treated as random quantities, and the interest is in the correlation between the two random variables. We continue to analyze the Formaldehyde data set. The attach function is used to make the objects named carb and optden accessible.

```
> attach(Formaldehyde)                   # attach Formaldehyde data set
> carb                                   # display carbohydrate (ml)
[1] 0.1 0.3 0.5 0.6 0.7 0.9
> optden                                 # display optical density
[1] 0.086 0.269 0.446 0.538 0.626 0.782
```

The cor function calculates the sample correlation, $r = 0.9995232$, between the pairs of data values in carb and optden:

```
> cor(carb, optden)                      # Pearson's correlation
[1] 0.9995232
```

The nearly-perfect linear relationship with a positive slope between carb and optden results in a sample correlation that is very close to positive one. All sample correlations must lie between -1 and 1, inclusive.

The cor.test function can be used to calculate point estimators, calculate confidence intervals, and conduct hypothesis tests for paired data values. Calling cor.test for the data pairs in carb and optden yields

```
> cor.test(carb, optden)                 # test for correlation
```

```
Pearson's product-moment correlation
```

```
data:  carb and optden
t = 64.7444, df = 4, p-value = 3.409e-07
alternative hypothesis: true correlation is not equal to 0
95 percent confidence interval:
 0.9954259 0.9999504
sample estimates:
      cor
0.9995232
```

The heading indicates that the name of the particular test being carried out here is the Pearson's product-moment correlation test. The first line after the heading confirms that the data values are contained in the vectors `carb` and `optden`. The next line gives the value of the test statistic, the number of degrees of freedom (in this case $n - 2$), and the p-value associated with the hypothesis test $H_0 : \rho = 0$ versus the two tailed alternative $H_1 : \rho \neq 0$, where ρ is the population correlation. In this case the p-value is very small, indicating that H_0 should be rejected. There is overwhelming statistical evidence that the correlation between `carb` and `optden` differs from 0. The next line states the alternative hypothesis. The next two lines give a 95% confidence interval for ρ and the last three lines give the sample correlation between `carb` and `optden`.

There are other statistical tests that can be used to test the statistical significance of the correlation. These are invoked with the `method` argument. The Spearman's rho and Kendall's tau methods are invoked with the R commands

```
> cor.test(carb, optden, method = "spearman")   # Spearman's rho
> cor.test(carb, optden, method = "kendall")    # Kendall's tau
```

The lengthy output has been suppressed. Not surprisingly, both of these methods also conclude that the population correlation is significantly different from 0. This ends the analysis of the `Formaldehyde` data set.

Occasions arise in which it is appropriate to force a regression line to pass through the origin. For example, an experiment is conducted in which the number of employees working an eight-hour day is paired with the number of widgets that they are able to assemble. Four data pairs are given in the table below.

number of employees	1	2	3	4
number of widgets	12	19	32	40

Treat the number of employees as the independent variable x (because it can be observed without error) and the number of widgets assembled as the dependent variable y (because it is a random response that will vary for one particular setting of the independent variable). It is reasonable in this setting to force the regression line to pass through the origin because no employees will certainly assemble no widgets. Writing the `formula` in `lm` as `y ~ x - 1` forces the regression line to pass through the origin. The `plot` and `abline` functions plot the data pairs and the regression line.

```
> x = 1:4                                  # number of employees
> y = c(12, 19, 32, 40)                    # number of widgets
> fit = lm(y ~ x - 1)                      # regression through the origin
> plot(x, y, xlim = c(0, 4), ylim = c(0, 40))  # scatterplot of data pairs
```

```
> slr = c(0, coef(fit))                        # store intercept and slope
> abline(slr)                                  # plot regression line
```

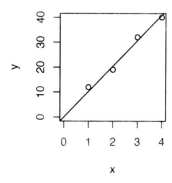

R is capable of fitting non-linear models to data. First consider the fitting of a polynomial model. More specifically, consider fitting a quadratic equation to the United States's national debt, in trillions of dollars, between 1975 and 2010 via least squares. The R code for fitting and plotting the linear and quadratic regression models to the debt data is

```
> year = seq(1975, 2010, by = 5)
> debt = c(0.53, 0.91, 1.82, 3.23, 4.97, 5.67, 7.93, 13.56)
> plot(year, debt)                             # scatterplot of data pairs
> abline(lm(debt ~ year)$coef)                 # simple linear regression line
> fit = lm(debt ~ year + I(year ^ 2))          # quadratic fit
> x = seq(1975, 2010, by = 0.1)                # x-values
> y = coef(fit)[1] + coef(fit)[2] * x + coef(fit)[3] * x ^ 2
> lines(x, y)                                  # plot quadratic fit
```

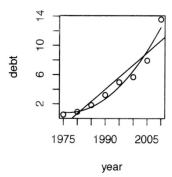

This shows that the quadratic fit is clearly superior to the linear fit. But a lingering doubt remains about the fit, in that both savings and debt tend to grow exponentially. So now instead fit the non-linear model

$$y = ae^{bx}$$

to the data set, where x is the year and y is the debt. Some algebra is necessary before fitting this model. First, taking the natural logarithms of both sides of this equation gives

$$\ln y = \ln a + bx.$$

This model is now in a linear form, so we regress x versus $\ln y$. The intercept of the fitted model is $\ln a$ and the slope of the fitted model is b. The R code below follows a similar pattern to the earlier examples, but this time the formula used in `lm` is `log(debt) ~ year`.

```
> year = seq(1975, 2010, by = 5)
> debt = c(0.53, 0.91, 1.82, 3.23, 4.97, 5.67, 7.93, 13.56)
> plot(year, debt)                          # scatterplot of data pairs
> fit = lm(log(debt) ~ year)                # fit exponential model
> a = exp(coef(fit)[1])                      # fitted a value
> b = coef(fit)[2]                           # fitted b value
> x = seq(1975, 2010, by = 0.1)             # x-values
> y = a * exp(b * x)                         # y-values for plotting
> lines(x, y)                                # plot exponential fit
```

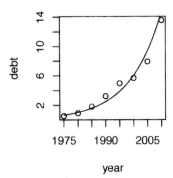

It is difficult to determine whether the quadratic or exponential model is more appropriate for forecasting the future of the national debt in the United States. It is possible that future growth might be somewhere in between these two models.

In order to provide a uniform approach for implementing certain statistical models (for example, regression or analysis of variance), R uses a formula interface that has the general form

```
response variable ~ function of explanatory variable(s)
```

This defines a statistical model. Although the tilde character ~ means "is distributed as" in probability, it is interpreted here as "is modeled as." The default function is a linear function of the explanatory variables. Equivalently, using "independent variable(s)" for the explanatory variable(s) and "dependent variable" for the response variable, the statistical model can be written as

```
dependent variable ~ function of independent variable(s)
```

On the right-hand side of the model formula, R uses arithmetic operators such as +, -, *, /, and : in a different manner than in numeric calculations. The table gives some illustrations with independent variables x and z and dependent variable y. Notice that oftentimes there are multiple ways of defining the same model.

Consider a multiple linear regression model with three independent variables X_1, X_2, and X_3 that are used to predict a dependent variable (response variable) Y. The standard model of this type that includes all two-way and three-way interaction terms can be written as

$$Y = \beta_1 X_1 + \beta_2 X_2 + \beta_3 X_3 + \beta_{12} X_1 X_2 + \beta_{13} X_1 X_3 + \beta_{23} X_2 X_3 + \beta_{123} X_1 X_2 X_3 + \varepsilon,$$

symbol	meaning	example	interpretation
+	include	y ~ x + z	model y as a function of x and z
:	interaction	y ~ x + z + x:z	include interaction of x and z
*	include with interaction	y ~ x * z	include x, z and their interaction
^	include with interaction	y ~ (x + z) ^ 2	include up to two-way interactions
−	exclude	y ~ x − z	include x but exclude z
|	condition	y ~ x | z	include x conditional on z
/	nest	y ~ x / z	include z nested in x
1	exclude intercept term	y ~ x − 1	force regression through the origin
0	zero intercept	y ~ x + 0	force regression through the origin
I	arithmetic variable	y ~ I(x ^ z)	model y as a function of x ^ z

where the subscripted β values are known as the *regression coefficients* and ε is a random error term. When the error term is assumed to be a $N\left(0, \sigma^2\right)$ random variable, the following three equivalent R commands fit the multiple regression model to data values contained in the equal-length vectors x1, x2, x3, and y.

```
> fit = lm(y ~ x1 + x2 + x3 + x1:x2 + x1:x3 + x2:x3 + x1:x2:x3)
> fit = lm(y ~ (x1 + x2 + x3) ^ 3)
> fit = lm(y ~ x1 * x2 * x3)
```

The object named fit will contain point estimates for the regression coefficients, interval estimates for the regression coefficients, and *p*-values associated with the appropriate hypothesis test concerning the regression coefficients. The summary function displays these values. If the three-way interaction term is not of interest, it can be excluded in any of the following three equivalent fashions.

```
> fit = lm(y ~ x1 + x2 + x3 + x1:x2 + x1:x3 + x2:x3)
> fit = lm(y ~ (x1 + x2 + x3) ^ 2)
> fit = lm(y ~ x1 * x2 * x3 - x1:x2:x3)
```

The I (inhibit interpretation) function allows the modeling of some function of a particular independent variable. Consider the cars data set with the automobile velocity speed as the independent variable and stopping distance dist as the dependent variable. A quadratic regression model that is forced through the origin (stationary cars require no distance to stop) can be fit with

```
> lm(dist ~ speed + I(speed ^ 2) + 0, data = cars)

Call:
lm(formula = dist ~ speed + I(speed^2) + 0, data = cars)

Coefficients:
    speed   I(speed^2)
  1.23903      0.09014
```

The fitted model is

$$Y = 1.23903X + 0.09014X^2 + \varepsilon$$

where X is speed and Y is stopping distance.

This concludes the brief introduction to the use of R in statistics. The `help` function, along with a statistics textbook are the best guides to learning all of the computational power that R has to offer in this area. The table below summarizes the functions introduced in this chapter.

operator or function	description
t.test	perform a t-test
ks.test	perform a Kolmogorov–Smirnov test
lm	fit a linear model
coef	extract coefficients
abline	add a line to a plot
vcov	calculate a sample variance–covariance matrix
cor.test	perform a correlation test

The next chapter re-introduces matrices, but rather than using them as simply a data structure, this time matrix operations are emphasized.

Exercises

26.1   Fit a simple linear regression model for the `Formaldehyde` data set that forces the regression line to pass through the origin.

26.2   Give a 90% confidence interval for the mean annual rainfall in the United States using the `precip` data set.

26.3   The following R code conducts a Monte Carlo simulation that results in the plotting of a histogram. Write a sentence that describes the anticipated shape of the histogram.

```
> nrep = 100000
> p = numeric(nrep)
> for (i in 1:nrep) p[i] = t.test(rnorm(25))$p.value
> hist(p)
```

26.4   The R code below conducts a Monte Carlo simulation that plots the estimated probability density function (histogram) of the p-value associated with the hypothesis test concerning the equality of the means of two standard normal populations based on $n = 3$ observations from each population.

```
> p = replicate(100000, t.test(rnorm(3), rnorm(3))$p.value)
> hist(p)
```

(a) Execute the code and comment on the results.

(b) Type `help(t.test)` to see if these commands can be modified to produce a $U(0, 1)$ distribution for the p-values.

(c) Change one of the population distributions to a $N(1, 1)$ distribution. Comment on the results.

(d) Change the population distributions from standard normal to unit exponential. Comment on the results.

26.5 Let $X_1, X_2, \ldots, X_n$ be independent and identically distributed random variables from an exponential(λ) population, where λ is a positive rate parameter. An exact $(1 - \alpha)100\%$ confidence interval for λ is given by

$$\frac{\hat{\lambda}\chi^2_{2n,\,1-\alpha/2}}{2n} < \lambda < \frac{\hat{\lambda}\chi^2_{2n,\,\alpha/2}}{2n},$$

where $\hat{\lambda} = n/\sum_{i=1}^{n} x_i$ is the maximum likelihood estimator, $x_1, x_2, \ldots, x_n$ are the observed values of the random variables $X_1, X_2, \ldots, X_n$, and the second subscript on the chi-square quantiles refers to right-hand tail probabilities. Write a function named `expon.confint` with parameters `x` and `alpha` that returns the lower and upper confidence limits of the appropriate confidence interval. The vector `x` contains the data values and the constant `alpha` ranges from 0 to 1 with a default of 0.05. Test your function by computing a 95% confidence interval for λ associated with the tiny data set of $n = 3$ observed values: $1, 2, 9$.

Chapter 27

Linear Algebra

Matrices were introduced in Chapter 5 as a data structure. In this chapter, we introduce operations on matrices. The study of matrices generally occurs in a college-level mathematics course called *linear algebra*. Familiarity with linear algebra is assumed for this chapter. Some basic facts regarding matrices are given below.

- A *matrix* is a collection, including possible repetitions, of real numbers arranged in a rectangular fashion. The elements of a matrix can be positive, negative, or zero.

- Uppercase letters are typically used to denote matrices, with subscripted lowercase letters used for their elements, for example, matrix A has elements a_{ij}. The first subscript of an element denotes the row in which the element resides and the second subscript of an element denotes the column in which the element resides.

- The *dimensions* of a matrix are the number of rows and the number of columns, in that order, for example, a 3×4 matrix has three rows and four columns.

- A generic $m \times n$ matrix A containing m rows and n columns is written as

$$A = \begin{bmatrix} a_{11} & a_{12} & \cdots & a_{1n} \\ a_{21} & a_{22} & \cdots & a_{2n} \\ \vdots & \vdots & \ddots & \vdots \\ a_{m1} & a_{m2} & \cdots & a_{mn} \end{bmatrix}.$$

- Basic arithmetic operations

  - Two matrices can be added when their dimensions are identical. The resulting matrix has the same dimensions as the original matrices and its elements are the sums of the corresponding elements of the two original matrices, for example,

$$\begin{bmatrix} 1 & 2 \\ 3 & 4 \end{bmatrix} + \begin{bmatrix} 5 & 6 \\ 7 & 8 \end{bmatrix} = \begin{bmatrix} 6 & 8 \\ 10 & 12 \end{bmatrix}.$$

  - Two matrices can be subtracted when their dimensions are identical. The resulting matrix has the same dimensions as the original matrices and its elements are the differences of the corresponding elements of the two original matrices, for example,

$$\begin{bmatrix} 1 & 2 & 0 \\ -3 & 4 & -5 \end{bmatrix} - \begin{bmatrix} 7 & -6 & 0 \\ 9 & 1 & -5 \end{bmatrix} = \begin{bmatrix} -6 & 8 & 0 \\ -12 & 3 & 0 \end{bmatrix}.$$

- The result of a scalar times a matrix is a matrix with each element multiplied by the scalar, for example,

$$3 \begin{bmatrix} 1 & 2 \\ 3 & -3 \\ 0 & -2 \end{bmatrix} = \begin{bmatrix} 3 & 6 \\ 9 & -9 \\ 0 & -6 \end{bmatrix}.$$

- Two matrices can be multiplied when the number of columns of the first matrix matches the number of rows of the second matrix. The resulting matrix has the same number of rows as the first matrix and the same number of columns as the second matrix. So multiplying an $m \times n$ matrix A with elements a_{ij} times an $n \times p$ matrix B with elements b_{ij} yields an $m \times p$ matrix C with elements

$$c_{ij} = \sum_{k=1}^{n} a_{ik} b_{kj}$$

for $i = 1, 2, \ldots, m$ and $j = 1, 2, \ldots, p$. For example,

$$\begin{bmatrix} 1 & 2 & 0 \\ -3 & 4 & -5 \end{bmatrix} \begin{bmatrix} 1 & 2 \\ 3 & -3 \\ 0 & -2 \end{bmatrix} = \begin{bmatrix} 7 & -4 \\ 9 & -8 \end{bmatrix}.$$

- The *transpose* of an $m \times n$ matrix A, typically written as A^T or A', is an $n \times m$ matrix such that the rows of A are the same as the columns of A^T.

- A *square matrix* has the same number of rows and columns.

- The *diagonal elements* of a square matrix are those elements in which the row and column indexes are equal. All other elements are *off-diagonal elements*.

- A square matrix is known as a *lower triangular matrix* if all of the entries above the diagonal are zero. A square matrix is known as an *upper triangular matrix* if all of the entries below the diagonal are zero. A matrix that is both lower triangular and upper triangular is known as a *diagonal matrix*.

- The *identity matrix I* is a square matrix with diagonal elements equal to 1 and off-diagonal elements equal to 0. For example, the 3×3 identity matrix is

$$\begin{bmatrix} 1 & 0 & 0 \\ 0 & 1 & 0 \\ 0 & 0 & 1 \end{bmatrix}.$$

- The *determinant* of a 2×2 matrix

$$A = \begin{bmatrix} a_{11} & a_{12} \\ a_{21} & a_{22} \end{bmatrix}$$

is

$$|A| = \begin{vmatrix} a_{11} & a_{12} \\ a_{21} & a_{22} \end{vmatrix} = a_{11}a_{22} - a_{21}a_{12}.$$

The determinant is also defined for larger square matrices.

- An $n \times n$ matrix A is *invertible* if there exists an $n \times n$ matrix A^{-1} such that

$$AA^{-1} = A^{-1}A = I,$$

  where I is the $n \times n$ identity matrix. The matrix A^{-1} is known as the *inverse* of A. An invertible matrix is also known as a *nonsingular* or *nondegenerate* matrix. An $n \times n$ matrix A that does not have an inverse matrix is known as a *noninvertible*, *singular*, or *degenerate* matrix.

- For an $n \times n$ matrix A, a scalar λ is known as an *eigenvalue* of A if there exists a nonzero vector x with n elements such that $Ax = \lambda x$. The vector x is known as the *eigenvector* associated with λ. The eigenvalues of A are the n solutions to the *characteristic equation*

$$|A - \lambda I| = 0.$$

  The left-hand side of this equation is a degree n polynomial known as the *characteristic polynomial*.

- A *decomposition* of a matrix is a factorization of the matrix into the product of matrices. Several different types of decompositions are useful in various applications. One such decomposition is the *LU decomposition* in which a square matrix is factored into the product of a lower triangular matrix L and an upper triangular matrix U.

The four topics introduced in this chapter are (a) elementary operations, (b) inverses and determinants, (c) eigenvalues and eigenvectors, and (d) decompositions.

27.1   Elementary operations

This section covers elementary operations on matrices, such as addition, subtraction, and multiplication. Recall from Chapter 5 that the `matrix` function can be used to create a matrix. Elements are placed in the matrix by columns by default. A 2×3 matrix A is created and the contents of a_{13} are displayed with

```
> A = matrix(1:6, ncol = 3)     # a 2 x 3 matrix
> A                             # display A
     [,1] [,2] [,3]
[1,]    1    3    5
[2,]    2    4    6
> A[1, 3]                       # the [1, 3] element of A
[1] 5
```

The second column of A can be extracted by not specifying a row as a subscript. This is placed in the vector B with the command

```
> B = A[ , 2]                   # the second column as a vector
> B                             # display B
[1] 3 4
```

But if instead you would like to extract the second column as a matrix (rather than a vector), the `drop` argument should be set to `FALSE`.

```
> C = A[ , 2, drop = FALSE]     # the second column as a 2 x 1 matrix
> C                             # display C
     [,1]
[1,]    3
[2,]    4
```

The dimensions of the matrix *A* are 2×3. The nrow and ncol functions can be used to extract the number of rows and the number of columns. The dim function extracts the dimensions of the matrix as a two-element vector.

```
> nrow(A)                       # number of rows
[1] 2
> ncol(A)                       # number of columns
[1] 3
> dim(A)                        # dimensions
[1] 2 3
> dim(B)
NULL
> dim(C)
[1] 2 1
```

The length function returns the total number of elements in a vector or matrix.

```
> length(A)                     # number of elements
[1] 6
> length(B)
[1] 2
> length(C)
[1] 2
```

The mode function returns the mode of the elements of a vector or matrix as a character string.

```
> mode(A)                       # mode of elements
[1] "numeric"
> mode(B)
[1] "numeric"
> mode(C)
[1] "numeric"
```

The row and col functions give a matrix with the same dimensions as the matrix used as an argument, but with row numbers and column numbers as elements.

```
> row(A)                        # matrix of row numbers
     [,1] [,2] [,3]
[1,]    1    1    1
[2,]    2    2    2
> col(A)                        # matrix of column numbers
     [,1] [,2] [,3]
[1,]    1    2    3
[2,]    1    2    3
```

There are built-in functions rowSums, rowMeans, colSums, and colMeans for calculating row sums, row means, column sums, and column means.

```
> rowSums(A)               # row sums of A
[1]  9 12
> rowMeans(A)              # row means of A
[1] 3 4
> colSums(A)               # column sums of A
[1]  3  7 11
> colMeans(A)             # column means of A
[1] 1.5 3.5 5.5
```

But you are not limited to just sums and means. The apply function can be used to apply any function (given in the third argument FUN) to rows (when the second argument MARGIN is 1), to columns (when the second argument MARGIN is 2), or both (when the second argument MARGIN equals c(1, 2)).

```
> apply(A, 1, max)         # row maximums
[1] 5 6
> apply(A, 2, sd)                # column standard deviations
[1] 0.7071068 0.7071068 0.7071068
```

Another way to create a matrix is with the rbind (row bind) and cbind (column bind) functions. The example below generates what is known as a "random matrix" whose elements are random variates drawn from Poisson populations. Notice that the column names are inherited from the names of the vectors that were bound together with the cbind function, but the row names are displayed generically.

```
> x = rpois(2, 1)
> y = rpois(2, 2)
> z = rpois(2, 3)
> B = cbind(x, y, z)
> B
     x y z
[1,] 3 2 4
[2,] 1 2 2
```

The matrix B can be given row names with the rownames function.

```
> rownames(B) = c("firstrow", "secondrow")
> B
          x y z
firstrow  3 2 4
secondrow 1 2 2
```

The rownames and colnames functions get and set the row names and column names as character strings. (The analogous row.names function applies to data frames.)

```
> rownames(B)
[1] "firstrow"  "secondrow"
```

So now both A and B are 2×3 matrices. A does not have any row and column names, but B does have row and column names.

```
> A
     [,1] [,2] [,3]
[1,]    1    3    5
[2,]    2    4    6
> B
          x y z
firstrow  3 2 4
secondrow 1 2 2
```

Since their dimensions match, the matrices *A* and *B* can be added and subtracted.

```
> A + B
          x y z
firstrow  4 5 9
secondrow 3 6 8
> A - B
           x y z
firstrow  -2 1 1
secondrow  1 2 4
```

Notice that the row names and column names of the sum and difference are inherited from the *B* matrix because it has row names and column names. Two can be subtracted from each element of the *A* matrix with the command

```
> A - 2
     [,1] [,2] [,3]
[1,]   -1    1    3
[2,]    0    2    4
```

The result of a matrix times (divided by) a scalar is a matrix with each element multiplied (divided by) by the scalar.

```
> 3 * A                      # multiplying by a scalar
     [,1] [,2] [,3]
[1,]    3    9   15
[2,]    6   12   18
> A / 3                      # dividing by a scalar
          [,1]     [,2]     [,3]
[1,] 0.3333333 1.000000 1.666667
[2,] 0.6666667 1.333333 2.000000
```

The reciprocal of *A* gives a matrix of the same dimension as *A* but with the element-wise reciprocals as elements. Likewise, applying the * operator to *A* and *B* gives a matrix of the same dimensions as both *A* and *B* but with elements that are the products of the associated elements of *A* and *B*. Notice that this is *not* matrix multiplication from linear algebra, which will be discussed subsequently.

```
> 1 / A                      # element-wise reciprocals
     [,1]      [,2]      [,3]
[1,] 1.0 0.3333333 0.2000000
[2,] 0.5 0.2500000 0.1666667
> A * B                      # element-wise multiplication
```

```
          x y  z
firstrow  3 6 20
secondrow 2 8 12
```

The t function calculates the transpose of a matrix.

```
> t(A)                          # the transpose of A
     [,1] [,2]
[1,]    1    2
[2,]    3    4
[3,]    5    6
> t(B)                          # the transpose of B
   firstrow secondrow
x         3          1
y         2          2
z         4          2
```

Notice that the row names and the column names get interchanged on B^T, even though they may no longer make sense. When t is called with a vector as an argument, the vector is treated as a column vector by default.

Two matrices can be multiplied when the number of columns of the first matrix matches the number of rows of the second matrix, that is, the "inner dimensions" match. The resulting matrix has the same number of rows as the first matrix and the same number of columns as the second matrix. Notice in the example below that when the 2×3 matrix A is multiplied by the 3×2 matrix B^T, the result is a 2×2 matrix whose row names are the row names of A and whose column names are the column names of B^T. R uses the %*% operator for matrix multiplication.

```
> A %*% t(B)                    # matrix multiplication
     firstrow secondrow
[1,]       29         17
[2,]       38         22
```

(The %*% is an example of an "infix" function in which the function name appears between the two arguments. This differs from the usual "prefix" function in which the function name appears before the arguments as in cor(x, y). R gives you the capability to define your own infix functions.)

There are several operations that only apply to square matrices, so we now define the 2×2 matrix P which will be used in several of the subsequent examples.

```
> P = matrix(1:4, 2, 2, byrow = TRUE)   #  2 x 2 square matrix
> P
     [,1] [,2]
[1,]    1    2
[2,]    3    4
```

The diagonal elements of a matrix are those elements in which the row and column indexes are equal. All other elements are off-diagonal elements. Although diagonal elements are typically considered for just square matrices, R also allows the versatile diag function to extract the diagonal elements of a matrix that is not square.

```
> diag(P)               # create a vector with the diagonal elements of P
[1] 1 4
> diag(A)               # create a vector with the diagonal elements of A
[1] 1 4
```

When `diag` is called with a vector containing n elements, it creates an $n \times n$ diagonal matrix with the elements of the vector along the diagonal.

```
> diag(1:5)                # create a diagonal matrix with diagonal elements 1:5
     [,1] [,2] [,3] [,4] [,5]
[1,]    1    0    0    0    0
[2,]    0    2    0    0    0
[3,]    0    0    3    0    0
[4,]    0    0    0    4    0
[5,]    0    0    0    0    5
```

This means that calling `diag` twice in succession with a matrix argument effectively zeros out all off-diagonal elements, and forces the resulting matrix to be square.

```
> diag(diag(A))            # zero out off-diagonal elements
     [,1] [,2]
[1,]    1    0
[2,]    0    4
```

Finally, the $n \times n$ identity matrix I can be generated by using a positive integer n as an argument in the `diag` function:

```
> diag(4)
     [,1] [,2] [,3] [,4]
[1,]    1    0    0    0
[2,]    0    1    0    0
[3,]    0    0    1    0
[4,]    0    0    0    1
```

There are several functions that perform matrix multiplications, which are common in linear algebra. The *cross product* of A is $A^T A$, which can be computed when the dimensions conform.

```
> crossprod(A)             # cross product A'A
     [,1] [,2] [,3]
[1,]    5   11   17
[2,]   11   25   39
[3,]   17   39   61
```

The cross product of A and B is $A^T B$.

```
> crossprod(A, B)          # cross product A'B
      x  y  z
[1,]  5  6  8
[2,] 13 14 20
[3,] 21 22 32
```

The *outer product* of A and B is the array C with dimensions `c(dim(A), dim(B))` in which each element of `C[c(xindex, yindex)]` is `FUN(A[arrayindex.x], B[arrayindex.y])`. The use of outer product extends to higher dimensions. The outer product is invoked in R as the `%o%` operator. Taking the outer product of the vectors `1:9` results in a nine-by-nine multiplication table.

```
> 1:9 %o% 1:9                # multiplication table
      [,1] [,2] [,3] [,4] [,5] [,6] [,7] [,8] [,9]
 [1,]    1    2    3    4    5    6    7    8    9
 [2,]    2    4    6    8   10   12   14   16   18
 [3,]    3    6    9   12   15   18   21   24   27
 [4,]    4    8   12   16   20   24   28   32   36
 [5,]    5   10   15   20   25   30   35   40   45
 [6,]    6   12   18   24   30   36   42   48   54
 [7,]    7   14   21   28   35   42   49   56   63
 [8,]    8   16   24   32   40   48   56   64   72
 [9,]    9   18   27   36   45   54   63   72   81
```

The display can be tightened a bit by adding single-digit row and column names to the output using the names function.

```
> x = 1:9
> names(x) = x
> x %o% x
  1 2  3  4  5  6  7  8  9
1 1 2  3  4  5  6  7  8  9
2 2 4  6  8 10 12 14 16 18
3 3 6  9 12 15 18 21 24 27
4 4 8 12 16 20 24 28 32 36
5 5 10 15 20 25 30 35 40 45
6 6 12 18 24 30 36 42 48 54
7 7 14 21 28 35 42 49 56 63
8 8 16 24 32 40 48 56 64 72
9 9 18 27 36 45 54 63 72 81
```

The outer product can also be invoked with the outer function. If the FUN argument is included, a function other than the product will be applied. For example, to raise the row to the column power, use

```
> outer(1:9, 1:9, FUN = "^")     # outer is more general
      [,1] [,2] [,3] [,4]  [,5]   [,6]    [,7]     [,8]      [,9]
 [1,]    1    1    1    1     1      1       1        1         1
 [2,]    2    4    8   16    32     64     128      256       512
 [3,]    3    9   27   81   243    729    2187     6561     19683
 [4,]    4   16   64  256  1024   4096   16384    65536    262144
 [5,]    5   25  125  625  3125  15625   78125   390625   1953125
 [6,]    6   36  216 1296  7776  46656  279936  1679616  10077696
 [7,]    7   49  343 2401 16807 117649  823543  5764801  40353607
 [8,]    8   64  512 4096 32768 262144 2097152 16777216 134217728
 [9,]    9   81  729 6561 59049 531441 4782969 43046721 387420489
```

A square matrix is lower triangular if all of the elements above the diagonal are zero. The R function lower.tri can be used to create a matrix of boolean elements associated with a lower triangular matrix. Since P is a 2×2 matrix,

```
> lower.tri(P, diag = TRUE)     # lower triangular matrix (Boolean)
```

```
     [,1]  [,2]
[1,] TRUE FALSE
[2,] TRUE  TRUE
```

returns the appropriate 2×2 matrix of `boolean` elements. Likewise, a square matrix is upper triangular if all of the elements below the diagonal are zero. The R function `upper.tri` can be used to create a matrix of `boolean` elements associated with an upper triangular matrix.

```
> upper.tri(P, diag = TRUE)    # upper triangular matrix (Boolean)
      [,1] [,2]
[1,]  TRUE TRUE
[2,] FALSE TRUE
```

Finally, in order to make P a lower triangular matrix by zeroing out all elements that fall above the diagonal, use

```
> P * lower.tri(P, diag = TRUE)    # lower triangular matrix
     [,1] [,2]
[1,]    1    0
[2,]    3    4
```

This same command applies for a square matrix of any size.

27.2 Inverses and determinants

The inverse and determinant of a square matrix can be computed in R. Consider the matrix P defined in the previous section:

$$P = \begin{bmatrix} 1 & 2 \\ 3 & 4 \end{bmatrix}.$$

The inverse of P is

$$P^{-1} = \begin{bmatrix} -2 & 1 \\ 3/2 & -1/2 \end{bmatrix}$$

because $PP^{-1} = P^{-1}P = I$, that is

$$\begin{bmatrix} 1 & 2 \\ 3 & 4 \end{bmatrix}\begin{bmatrix} -2 & 1 \\ 3/2 & -1/2 \end{bmatrix} = \begin{bmatrix} -2 & 1 \\ 3/2 & -1/2 \end{bmatrix}\begin{bmatrix} 1 & 2 \\ 3 & 4 \end{bmatrix} = \begin{bmatrix} 1 & 0 \\ 0 & 1 \end{bmatrix}.$$

The inverse of a square matrix can be found in R with the `solve` function. The inverse of P in the previous example can be computed with the command

```
> solve(P)               # inverse of P
     [,1] [,2]
[1,] -2.0  1.0
[2,]  1.5 -0.5
```

Matrix multiplication can be used to check that this is indeed the identity matrix.

```
> P %*% solve(P)         # identity matrix
     [,1]         [,2]
[1,]    1 1.110223e-16
[2,]    0 1.000000e+00
```

This matrix is tantalizingly close to the 2×2 identity matrix, but an annoying roundoff error has occurred in the upper-right element. Even when all of the elements in P and P^{-1} can be stored exactly in binary, roundoff errors can still occur. The `zapsmall` function comes to the rescue in this case, resulting in

```
> zapsmall(P %*% solve(P))
     [,1] [,2]
[1,]    1    0
[2,]    0    1
```

Our faith is renewed in the fact that the inverse was computed correctly.

The reason that the `solve` function is not named the `inverse` function will now become apparent. Matrices are useful for solving systems of linear equations. We begin with an analogy of solving a single linear equation. This will then be extended to matrices. Assume we would like to solve the equation

$$3x = 6$$

for x. The first step is to left-multiply both sides of this equation by the reciprocal (inverse) of 3, which is $1/3$:

$$(1/3)3x = (1/3)6.$$

Since $1/3$ times 3 is the identity, 1, and $1/3$ times 6 is 2,

$$1x = 2.$$

Finally, since the identity, 1, multiplied by x equals x, the equation is solved as

$$x = 2.$$

This example of solving a linear equation has been given in painstaking detail so as to highlight its generalization to matrices. Assume that A is an $n \times n$ invertible matrix whose elements are real numbers, x is an $n \times 1$ matrix whose elements are $x_1, x_2, \ldots, x_n$, and b is an $n \times 1$ matrix whose elements $b_1, b_2, \ldots, b_n$ are real numbers. Our goal is to solve the matrix equation

$$Ax = b$$

for x. The first step is to left-multiply both sides of this equation by the inverse of A, which is A^{-1}:

$$A^{-1}Ax = A^{-1}b.$$

Since A times A^{-1} is the identity matrix I,

$$Ix = A^{-1}b.$$

Finally, since the identity matrix I multiplied by x equals x, the equation is solved as

$$x = A^{-1}b.$$

This will now be applied to a numerical example in the case of $n = 2$. The R syntax is similar for larger values of n. Consider the set of linear equations with two equations and two unknowns:

$$x_1 + 2x_2 = 5$$
$$3x_1 + 4x_2 = 6$$

This set of equations can be written in matrix form as

$$\begin{bmatrix} 1 & 2 \\ 3 & 4 \end{bmatrix} \begin{bmatrix} x_1 \\ x_2 \end{bmatrix} = \begin{bmatrix} 5 \\ 6 \end{bmatrix}.$$

Recognizing the 2×2 matrix as P, which was defined earlier, this matrix equation is solved in R with the command

```
> solve(P, 5:6)          # solve a linear system
[1] -4.0  4.5
```

The first argument in `solve` is the matrix and the second argument is a vector whose elements are the values on the right-hand side of the equation. The elements of the returned vector are the solutions to the original set of equations: $x_1 = -4$ and $x_2 = 9/2$.

The determinant of a square matrix is a single number associated with the matrix. The notation associated with a determinant is to place bars around the matrix. The determinant in R is computed with the `det` function. So the determinant of the matrix P, which is written as $|P|$, is

```
> det(P)                 # calculate the determinant
[1] -2
```

A square matrix A has an inverse if and only if $|A| \neq 0$. A matrix with an inverse is called an invertible, nonsingular, or, nondegenerate matrix. As an example of a matrix that has determinant zero and no inverse, consider the matrix

$$Q = \begin{bmatrix} 1 & 2 \\ 2 & 4 \end{bmatrix}.$$

Notice that the second column is twice the first column and thus the columns are linearly dependent, as is necessary for the matrix to be singular. The determinant of Q is

$$Q = \begin{vmatrix} 1 & 2 \\ 2 & 4 \end{vmatrix} = 1 \cdot 4 - 2 \cdot 2 = 0,$$

which is confirmed in R with the commands

```
> Q = matrix(c(1, 2, 2, 4), nrow = 2)
> det(Q)
[1] 0
```

Based on the discussion above, we should not be able to compute an inverse for Q because $|Q| = 0$.

```
> solve(Q)
Error in solve.default(Q) :
  Lapack routine dgesv: system is exactly singular: U[2,2] = 0
```

The error message confirms that the matrix Q has no inverse.

The *trace* of a square matrix is the sum of its diagonal elements. A `trace` function is not built into the base package of R, but we can easily write our own using the `sum` and `diag` functions.

```
> trace = function(S) sum(diag(S))
> trace(Q)
[1] 5
```

27.3   Eigenvalues and eigenvectors

As indicated at the beginning of the chapter, the scalar value λ is an eigenvalue of an $n \times n$ matrix A if there exists a nonzero vector x with n elements such that $Ax = \lambda x$. The vector x is known as the eigenvector associated with λ. The eigenvalues of A are the n solutions to the characteristic equation

$$|A - \lambda I| = 0.$$

The left-hand side of this equation is a degree n polynomial known as the characteristic polynomial. Define the matrix A as

$$A = \begin{bmatrix} 1 & 2 \\ 4 & 3 \end{bmatrix}.$$

The characteristic polynomial is

$$|A - \lambda I| = \left| \begin{bmatrix} 1 & 2 \\ 4 & 3 \end{bmatrix} - \lambda \begin{bmatrix} 1 & 0 \\ 0 & 1 \end{bmatrix} \right| = \begin{vmatrix} 1 - \lambda & 2 \\ 4 & 3 - \lambda \end{vmatrix} = (1 - \lambda)(3 - \lambda) - 8 = \lambda^2 - 4\lambda - 5.$$

So the characteristic equation is

$$\lambda^2 - 4\lambda - 5 = 0.$$

The left-hand side of this equation can be factored:

$$(\lambda - 5)(\lambda + 1) = 0.$$

Solving for λ gives the eigenvalues $\lambda = 5$ and $\lambda = -1$. Now we consider how to calculate the associated eigenvector in R. The equation $Ax = \lambda x$ for the first eigenvalue, $\lambda = 5$, is

$$\begin{bmatrix} 1 & 2 \\ 4 & 3 \end{bmatrix} \begin{bmatrix} x_1 \\ x_2 \end{bmatrix} = 5 \begin{bmatrix} x_1 \\ x_2 \end{bmatrix}$$

or

$$x_1 + 2x_2 = 5x_1$$
$$4x_1 + 3x_2 = 5x_2.$$

Any (x_1, x_2) pair satisfying $x_2 = 2x_1$ solves this set of equations. Hence there are an infinite number of eigenvectors associated with the eigenvalue $\lambda = 5$. The `eigen` function in R computes the eigenvalues and places them in a vector sorted in decreasing order. It also calculates the associated eigenvectors as columns of a matrix. The eigenvectors are normalized to unit length. For the matrix A, the normalized eigenvector associated with $\lambda = 5$ is $(-1/\sqrt{5}, -2/\sqrt{5})$ and the normalized eigenvector associated with $\lambda = -1$ is $(-1/\sqrt{2}, 1/\sqrt{2})$.

```
> A = matrix(c(1, 2, 4, 3), 2, 2, byrow = TRUE)
> eigen(A)                # eigenvalues and eigenvectors of A
$values
[1]  5 -1

$vectors
           [,1]        [,2]
[1,] -0.4472136 -0.7071068
[2,] -0.8944272  0.7071068
```

The eigenvalues can be extracted with the $ extractor as

```
> eigen(A)$val           # eigenvalues of A
[1]  5 -1
```

Likewise, the associated eigenvectors can be extracted with the $ extractor as

```
> eigen(A)$vec           # eigenvectors of A
           [,1]        [,2]
[1,] -0.4472136 -0.7071068
[2,] -0.8944272  0.7071068
```

Numerical errors can arise when working with matrices, so we now check to see if the original equation associated with eigenvalues and eigenvectors, that is, $Ax = \lambda x$, is satisfied for $\lambda = 5$. The left-hand side of the equation is calculated with

```
> A %*% eigen(A)$vec[ , 1]
          [,1]
[1,] -2.236068
[2,] -4.472136
```

The right-hand side of the equation is calculated with

```
> eigen(A)$val[1] * eigen(A)$vec[ , 1]
[1] -2.236068 -4.472136
```

Since both vectors match (to seven-digit accuracy), we have faith in the first eigenvalue/eigenvector combination. We should check the second eigenvalue/eigenvector combination in the same fashion.

27.4   Decompositions

As mentioned at the beginning of the chapter, it is often of value to factor a matrix into the product of matrices. These factorings are known as *decompositions*. Each of the many types of decompositions finds application in a particular type of problem. We illustrate three types of decompositions below, leaving it to the reader to determine the meaning and applications of the particular type of decomposition. We will use the matrix

$$R = \begin{bmatrix} 5 & 1 \\ 1 & 3 \end{bmatrix}$$

to illustrate some of the decompositions.

```
> R = matrix(c(5, 1, 1, 3), 2, 2)
```

The Cholesky decomposition of R is

```
> chol(R)                # Cholesky decomposition
          [,1]       [,2]
[1,] 2.236068 0.4472136
[2,] 0.000000 1.6733201
```

The singular value decomposition of R is

```
> svd(R)                    # singular value decomposition
$d
[1] 5.414214 2.585786

$u
            [,1]          [,2]
[1,] -0.9238795 -0.3826834
[2,] -0.3826834  0.9238795

$v
            [,1]          [,2]
[1,] -0.9238795 -0.3826834
[2,] -0.3826834  0.9238795
```

The QR decomposition of *R* is

```
> qr(R)                     # qr decomposition
$qr
            [,1]        [,2]
[1,] -5.0990195 -1.568929
[2,]  0.1961161  2.745626

$rank
[1] 2

$qraux
[1] 1.980581 2.745626

$pivot
[1] 1 2

attr(,"class")
[1] "qr"
```

The condition number of a matrix, which is a measure of the "condition" of a matrix, is calculated with the kappa function.

```
> kappa(R)                  # condition number
[1] 2.011905
```

If the condition number is close to one, the inverse and decompositions of the matrix can be computed with accuracy. The larger the condition number gets, the more that the matrix is "ill-conditioned," and numerical procedures for computing the inverse and decompositions are prone to numerical error.

   This ends the discussion of the functions in R that are capable of performing calculations on matrices. We end this chapter with an example that combines Monte Carlo simulation with linear algebra. When the elements of a matrix are random variables, the matrix is known as a *random matrix* or a *stochastic matrix*. If the elements of a 3×3 matrix are independent $U(0, 1)$ random variables with positive diagonal elements and negative off-diagonal elements, use Monte Carlo simulation to estimate the probability that the matrix has a positive determinant.

The R commands below assign nrep to the number of replications of the simulation, which in this case is 100,000. Next, count, which counts the number of times that the determinant is positive, is initialized to zero. Within the for loop, m holds the random matrix. Whenever the determinant of m is positive, count is incremented.

```
> nrep = 100000
> count = 0
> for (j in 1:nrep) {
+    m = matrix(-runif(9), 3, 3)
+    diag(m) = abs(diag(m))
+    if (det(m) > 0) count = count + 1
+ }
> print(count / nrep)
```

After a call to set.seed(4), five runs of this simulation give

0.04897   0.04992   0.05034   0.05041   0.05004.

We can report that the probability the random matrix has a positive determinant is 0.050, with some doubt about the trailing digit. More replications would be required to achieve additional precision.

This concludes the discussion of linear algebra in R. The table below summarizes the functions introduced in this chapter.

operator or function	description
row	a matrix of row numbers
col	a matrix of column numbers
rowSums	calculate row sums
rowMeans	calculate row means
colSums	calculate column sums
colMeans	calculate column means
rownames	get or set row names
colnames	get or set column names
t	transpose
%*%	matrix multiplication
diag	extract diagonal; construct diagonal matrix
crossprod	cross product
%o%	outer product
outer	outer product
lower.tri	lower triangular matrix
upper.tri	upper triangular matrix
solve	solve a system of linear equations; find inverse
det	determinant
eigen	calculate eigenvectors and eigenvalues
chol	Cholesky decomposition
svd	singular value decomposition
qr	qr decomposition
kappa	calculate condition number

The final chapter considers packages, which open up nearly endless functionality in R.

Exercises

27.1   If A is an $n \times m$ matrix, what are the dimensions of $\left(A^T A\right)^{-1}$, where the T superscript denotes transpose and the -1 superscript denotes inverse?

27.2   Write the R commands that construct a 3×3 one-step transition matrix named `taxi`, with row and column labels, given below. If `taxi` is considered a from–to matrix with entries interpreted as probabilities, compute and interpret `taxi %*% taxi`.

```
        airport city suburbs
airport    0.0  0.3    0.7
city       0.6  0.1    0.3
suburbs    0.4  0.2    0.4
```

27.3   Let A be the 2×3 matrix

$$A = \begin{bmatrix} -1 & 1 & 3 \\ 0 & 2 & 4 \end{bmatrix}.$$

Calculate the value of AA^T by hand, then execute R commands to verify your result.

27.4   Consider the 3×3 random matrix A

$$A = \begin{bmatrix} u_{11} & -u_{12} & -u_{13} \\ -u_{21} & 2 \cdot u_{22} & -u_{23} \\ -u_{31} & -u_{32} & 3 \cdot u_{33} \end{bmatrix},$$

where u_{ij} are mutually independent $U(0, 1)$, random variates. Use Monte Carlo simulation to estimate the probability that the determinant of the inverse of A is positive. Replicate this experiment enough times so that you are sure of your answer to at least two-digit accuracy.

27.5   Look up the definition of a *Hilbert matrix* on the world wide web. Write an R function named `Hilbert` with a single argument n, which is a positive integer greater than one, that returns an $n \times n$ Hilbert matrix. Test `Hilbert` with the R command

```
> Hilbert(4)
```

which should return the matrix

$$\begin{bmatrix} 1 & 1/2 & 1/3 & 1/4 \\ 1/2 & 1/3 & 1/4 & 1/5 \\ 1/3 & 1/4 & 1/5 & 1/6 \\ 1/4 & 1/5 & 1/6 & 1/7 \end{bmatrix}.$$

27.6   Write and execute R code that solves the following set of linear equations by inverting the appropriate matrix.

$$\begin{aligned} 3x_1 - 2x_2 + 4x_3 - 5x_4 &= 16 \\ 2x_1 - 7x_2 - 2x_3 + 2x_4 &= -4 \\ 8x_1 - 4x_2 + 3x_3 - 4x_4 &= 18 \\ 5x_1 - 3x_2 - 4x_3 - 9x_4 &= 6 \end{aligned}$$

27.7 Write an R function named `mult.table` with a single argument n, a positive integer, which prints an n by n multiplication table. Test your function with the R command `mult.table(12)`.

27.8 Write an R function named `complex.det` with a single argument n, a positive integer, which prints the determinant of an n by n matrix containing complex numbers whose real part is the row number and imaginary part is the column number. For example, when n equals 3, `complex.det` returns the determinant of

$$
\begin{bmatrix}
1+i & 1+2i & 1+3i \\
2+i & 2+2i & 2+3i \\
3+i & 3+2i & 3+3i
\end{bmatrix}.
$$

(a) For $n = 2$ calculate the determinant by hand and by `complex.det(2)` and see that the two match.

(b) Calculate the value of the determinant for $n = 3$ using `complex.det`.

27.9 Write an R function named `antiidentity` with a single integer-valued argument n that returns an $n \times n$ matrix with diagonal elements of 0 and off-diagonal elements of 1.

27.10 Write an R command that creates a 5×5 matrix with elements that are the row number raised to the column number power, that is, the (i, j) element is i^j, for $i = 1, 2, \ldots, 5$ and $j = 1, 2, \ldots, 5$.

27.11 The 5×5 matrix named x has integer elements. Write a single R command that assigns a matrix named y to a 3×5 matrix consisting of three different rows of x selected at random from x and placed in y in a random order.

Chapter 28

Packages

All of the R commands encountered thus far are part of the "base" distribution of R. But this is just the tip of a very large iceberg. An R "package" consists of functions and data sets that extend R's functionality in a particular direction, for example, advanced statistical procedures or advanced graphical capability. (A package is sometimes referred to as a "library.") This chapter covers the important topics of identifying packages based on their capability, loading packages (with the library command), and installing packages (with the install.packages command) in R. The topics that are introduced in this chapter are broken out by these two types of packages: (a) base packages, and (b) contributed packages. It is a fairly simple process to gain access to one of these two types of packages in R.

28.1 Base packages

When you first downloaded R, it took a few minutes because R is a relatively large language. This is partly due to the large number of built-in functions and data sets. But it is also due to the fact that there are a number of base packages installed in the downloaded version of R. Most of these packages are not active when you initiate an R session. Only about a half-dozen packages are active, for example, the base package, which contains the sqrt function, the graphics package, which contains the plot function, and the stats package, which contains the t.test function. The previous 27 chapters have surveyed the capability of these active packages. The first line associated with any of the R documentation returned by the help function, for example, help(sqrt), reveals the package associated with a particular function. The sessionInfo() command lists the packages that are loaded (attached) into your current R session.

There are two types of packages: base packages, which are downloaded with R, and contributed packages, which have not been downloaded. This first section concerns base packages. A call to the library function, which will be illustrated subsequently, brings a package from the inactive to the active state by loading the package into the current R session.

Begin by listing the names of all of the packages that are downloaded with the base distribution of R. Calling the library function with no arguments displays an alphabetical list and brief description of the R packages that the R Core Development Team decided to place in the base distribution of R. There are currently two or three dozen such packages, spanning a wide range of applications. The packages in this group are likely to change over time as R evolves. When you enter R for the first time, only a subset of these packages have been attached.

```
> library()                    # display base packages
stats                          The R Stats Package
survival                       Survival Analysis
```

The lengthy output has been shortened to show only two of the packages, stats and survival, which will be illustrated in this section.

A package that arises in many statistical applications is known as the stats package. The stats package is already pre-loaded when you start up R. To display some documentation that highlights the capability of the stats package, type

```
> library(help = "stats")      # information on the stats package
```

The range of applications in the stats package is very wide, including analysis of variance, regression, nonparametric tests, factor analysis, kernel density function estimation, goodness-of-fit tests, forecasting, optimization, and root finding. Some of this capability was illustrated in Chapter 26. Only one application area is illustrated here: time series analysis. A function named ts.eda (for "time series exploratory data analysis") will be written in a similar fashion to the eda (exploratory data analysis) function from Chapter 21. This function can be applied to a time series in order to get a first look at the structure of the time series. The R commands below define a 2×2 array of plots that would be of interest to an analyst who was interested in an initial look at the time series. Details on these functions can be found in any book on time series analysis. The first plot is simply the time series over time using the ts.plot function. The second plot is the autocorrelation function of the time series using the acf function. The third plot is the partial autocorrelation function of the time series using the pacf function. Finally, the fourth plot is the estimated spectral density function (also known as the periodogram) of the time series using the spectrum function.

```
> ts.eda = function(x) {       # time series exploratory data analysis
+    par(mfrow = c(2, 2))       # a two row, two column display of graphics
+    ts.plot(x)                 # time series plot
+    acf(x, plot = TRUE)        # autocorrelation function
+    pacf(x, plot = TRUE)       # partial autocorrelation function
+    spectrum(x, plot = TRUE)   # estimated spectral density function
+ }
```

The ts.eda function is applied to the AirPassengers data set with the R command

```
> ts.eda(AirPassengers)        # call ts.eda for AirPassengers time series
```

Recall that the built-in AirPassengers data set from the base package contains the total number of international airline passengers (by month, in thousands) between 1949 and 1960. The results of the call to ts.eda are a pop-up window containing the four plots, which follows. This data set is typical of many economic data sets in that it increases over time and contains a strong cyclic component, both of which are apparent from the first plot. The autocorrelation function in the second plot contains horizontal dashed lines that indicate whether spikes are statistically significant. The number of lags at which spikes are plotted is determined internally in the acf function. This graph shows significant positive autocorrelation at low lags. The partial autocorrelation function also has horizontal dashed lines that indicate whether spikes are statistically significant. Most of these spikes are not statistically significant or marginally significant, except for the spike at lag 12, which is associated with the fact that the data values are collected monthly. Finally, the periodogram that is generated by the spectrum function indicates frequencies associated with the data set. These plots are consistent with what is expected of a time series with these particular characteristics.

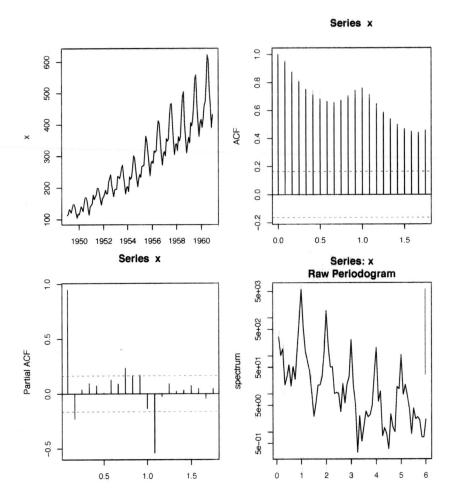

Now consider a base package that was installed with R when it was downloaded, but has not yet been attached. We begin with the process of making the R code in the survival package active. First, to illustrate what happens when a package is attached (becomes active), type aml to see if an object named aml currently exists.

```
> aml                    # aml does not exist
Error: object 'aml' not found
```

It does not. Next call the library function using the argument survival to attach the R code contained in the survival package.

```
> library(survival)   # attach survival package
Loading required package: splines
```

R attaches in the survival package, but since one or more functions in the survival package requires R code from the splines package, it gets attached in as well. You might be interested in more information than the two-word description of the survival package as "survival analysis" given earlier. The help facility in R works in largely the same fashion as before. For example, to find out more about the `survival` package, type

```
> ??survival        # help on survival package
```

Similarly, help on a particular function or built-in data set in the survival package is found in the usual fashion. For example, to get help on the `Surv` function that is a part of the `survival` package, type

```
> ?Surv             # help on Surv
starting httpd help server ... done
```

The lengthy output is again suppressed. We now move to a specific task that can be accomplished with the aid of the `survival` package. We would like to analyze the built-in data set named `aml`, which is built into the `survival` package. We begin by typing the name of the object `aml`, which, prior to attaching in the `survival` package, did not exist. That has changed with the `survival` package being attached. Now typing `aml` results in a data set (stored as a data frame) that has been attached with the `survival` package.

```
> aml               # leukemia data set (the time column is remission time)
   time status          x
1     9      1 Maintained
2    13      1 Maintained
3    13      0 Maintained
4    18      1 Maintained
5    23      1 Maintained
6    28      0 Maintained
7    31      1 Maintained
8    34      1 Maintained
9    45      0 Maintained
10   48      1 Maintained
11  161      0 Maintained
12    5      1 Nonmaintained
13    5      1 Nonmaintained
14    8      1 Nonmaintained
15    8      1 Nonmaintained
16   12      1 Nonmaintained
17   16      0 Nonmaintained
18   23      1 Nonmaintained
19   27      1 Nonmaintained
20   30      1 Nonmaintained
21   33      1 Nonmaintained
22   43      1 Nonmaintained
23   45      1 Nonmaintained
```

Typing `?aml` brings up a help page on the data set `aml`.

```
> ?aml              # information on leukemia data set
```

The help page reveals that `aml` stands for acute myelogenous leukemia. The object `aml` is a data frame containing three columns. The first column, `time`, contains the remission time or right censoring time (in weeks) for each of the 23 patients with acute myelogenous leukemia. The second column, status, is 1 if a physician observed a recurrence of the leukemia, and 0 if the patient is lost to the study (for example, left town, died in an accident, or the leukemia was still in remission at the end of the study), constituting a right-censored observation. The third column, x, is a character string that can assume either Maintained (for the first 11 patients) or Nonmaintained (for the last 12 patients). These two groups were established to see if the standard course of chemotherapy should be extended (the Maintained group) for additional cycles beyond the standard course of treatment.

We would like to plot the Kaplan–Meier product–limit estimate of the survivor function associated with the aml data set. Although the details associated with the estimate are not important here, the survivor function gives the probability of survival as a function of time. The survfit function from the survival package will be used to calculate the estimator. The call to the help page

```
> ?survfit.formula    # information on survfit.formula
```

gives help on the use of the survfit function. The commands below create an object named km that holds the Kaplan–Meier product–limit estimate of the survivor function. The "formula" given in the call to survfit, which is Surv(time, status) ˜ x, indicates that survival is being considered a function of x, with time and status as the failure times and indicator of censoring status, respectively. Typing km shows a summary of the estimate broken down by x.

```
> km = survfit(Surv(time, status) ˜ x, data = aml)  # 1 obs. 0 right-censored
> km                  # display km
Call: survfit(formula = Surv(time, status) ˜ x, data = aml)

              records n.max n.start events median 0.95LCL 0.95UCL
x=Maintained       11    11      11      7     31      18      NA
x=Nonmaintained    12    12      12     11     23       8      NA
```

The estimated median remission time for the Maintained group is 31 weeks; the estimated median remission time for the Nonmaintained group is 23 weeks. The summary function provides specifics on the Kaplan–Meier product–limit estimate broken out by the two groups, Maintained then Nonmaintained. Each line in the summary corresponds to an observed remission time.

```
> summary(km)        # summary of the km estimate
Call: survfit(formula = Surv(time, status) ˜ x, data = aml)

             x=Maintained
 time n.risk n.event survival std.err lower 95% CI upper 95% CI
    9     11       1    0.909  0.0867       0.7541        1.000
   13     10       1    0.818  0.1163       0.6192        1.000
   18      8       1    0.716  0.1397       0.4884        1.000
   23      7       1    0.614  0.1526       0.3769        0.999
   31      5       1    0.491  0.1642       0.2549        0.946
   34      4       1    0.368  0.1627       0.1549        0.875
   48      2       1    0.184  0.1535       0.0359        0.944

             x=Nonmaintained
 time n.risk n.event survival std.err lower 95% CI upper 95% CI
    5     12       2   0.8333  0.1076       0.6470        1.000
    8     10       2   0.6667  0.1361       0.4468        0.995
```

12	8	1	0.5833	0.1423	0.3616	0.941
23	6	1	0.4861	0.1481	0.2675	0.883
27	5	1	0.3889	0.1470	0.1854	0.816
30	4	1	0.2917	0.1387	0.1148	0.741
33	3	1	0.1944	0.1219	0.0569	0.664
43	2	1	0.0972	0.0919	0.0153	0.620
45	1	1	0.0000	NaN	NA	NA

In order to create a plot of the Kaplan–Meier product–limit estimates of the survivor function for each of the two groups, the plot function is called in the usual fashion.

```
> plot(km, lty = 1:2, xlab = "time (weeks)", ylab = "survival probability")
> legend(80, 0.7, c("Maintained", "Nonmaintained"), lty = 1:2)
```

A legend is added with the legend function in the usual fashion. The plot shown below indicates that the probability of survival is slightly higher in the Maintained group. Whether this difference between the two groups is statistically significant is another question that can be answered using the functions in the survival package, although it will not be addressed here. The log-rank test is commonly used to test for a difference between survivor functions for data sets containing right-censored observations.

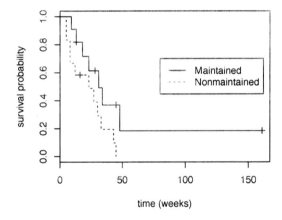

Now consider a second application in the survival package. Typing the name of the object named ovarian, which is also an object in the survival package, reveals the following data set.

```
> ovarian                # ovarian cancer data set
  futime fustat     age resid.ds rx ecog.ps
1     59      1 72.3315        2  1       1
2    115      1 74.4932        2  1       1
3    156      1 66.4658        2  1       2
4    421      0 53.3644        2  2       1
5    431      1 50.3397        2  1       1
6    448      0 56.4301        1  1       2
7    464      1 56.9370        2  2       2
8    475      1 59.8548        2  2       2
```

```
9     477    . 0 64.1753    2  1        1
10    563      1 55.1781    1  2        2
11    638      1 56.7562    1  1.       2
12    744      0 50.1096    1  2        1
13    769      0 59.6301    2  2        2
14    770      0 57.0521    2  2        1
15    803      0 39.2712    1  1        1
16    855      0 43.1233    1  1        2
17   1040      0 38.8932    2  1        2
18   1106      0 44.6000    1  1        1
19   1129      0 53.9068    1  2        1
20   1206      0 44.2055    2  2        1
21   1227      0 59.5890    1  2        2
22    268      1 74.5041    2  1        2
23    329      1 43.1370    2  1        1
24    353      1 63.2192    1  2        2
25    365      1 64.4247    2  2.       1
26    377      0 58.3096    1  2        1
```

A call to the help page for this data set with

```
> ?ovarian              # information on ovarian cancer data set
```

reveals that this data comes from a randomized trial comparing two treatments for $n = 26$ patients with ovarian cancer. So ovarian is a data frame, just like aml, that is a part of the survival package. The columns of ovarian are:

- futime, survival or censoring time (in days);

- fustat, the censoring status (1 for a failure, 0 for a right-censored observation);

- age, in years (to an astounding six digit accuracy!);

- resid.ds, an indicator variable indicating whether residual disease present (1 for no, 2 for yes);

- rx, the treatment group (1 or 2);

- ecog.ps, ECOG performance status (1 or 2, 1 is better).

One of the traditional models used in the analysis of a data set of this nature is known as the *Cox proportional hazards model*, which can be used to screen covariates (age, resid.ds, rx, and ecog.ps in this example) for statistical significance. In other words, do any of these four covariates significantly impact survival from ovarian cancer? The coxph function can be used to fit the Cox proportional hazards model. Using age and rx as the covariates in a linear model, for example, can be accomplished with the R command below that sets the object coxmod to the fitted Cox proportional hazards model.

```
> coxmod = coxph(Surv(futime, fustat) ~ age + rx, data = ovarian)
> coxmod              # cox proportional hazards model
Call:
coxph(formula = Surv(futime, fustat) ~ age + rx, data = ovarian)
```

```
      coef exp(coef) se(coef)      z      p
age  0.147     1.159   0.0461   3.19 0.0014
rx  -0.804     0.448   0.6320  -1.27 0.2000

Likelihood ratio test=15.9  on 2 df, p=0.000355  n= 26, number of events= 12
```

The object `coxmod` contains the fitted coefficients in the model (given in the `coef` column of the summary) and the *p*-values (given in the p column of the summary) associated with a statistical hypothesis test to determine whether the coefficient associated with `age` and `rx` differs significantly from 0. The *p*-value of 0.0014 for `age` indicates that age is a statistically significant covariate in surviving ovarian cancer. The sign of the coefficient 0.147 for `age` indicates that older patients are at higher risk than younger patients if the statistical model is correct. This is consistent with intuition because younger patients tend to have stronger immune systems to fend off disease. On the other hand, the *p*-value of 0.2 for the `rx` covariate indicates that the treatment group is not a statistically significant covariate. The last line in the summary reports the results of a likelihood ratio test that has been conducted. The formula given inside of the call to the `coxph` function allows you to experiment with different combinations of covariates, nonlinear models, and interactions between covariates.

28.2 Contributed packages

In addition to the base packages that are downloaded with R, there are thousands of contributed packages that have been written and maintained by benevolent R users. These contributed packages can be stored locally or remotely in a storage location that is typically referred to as a *repository*. Typing the R command `available.packages()` lists the R packages in the CRAN (which stands for comprehensive R archive network). These are stored in a manner so that they are easy to load into your R session. One way to find these contributed packages is to use a search engine on the character string "CRAN task views." This is equivalent to clicking on "task views" on the main R website: `http://cran.r-project.org`. The CRAN task views contains a list of several dozen areas in which packages exist, for example, Bayesian inference, computational econometrics, empirical finance, experimental design, genetics, graphics, and time series analysis. Clicking on one of these areas of interest reveals a list of packages which are maintained by the individual(s) who wrote the code. If you click, for example, on graphics, you will find dozens of packages on graphics. One of these packages is named `vioplot`, which is short for "violin plot." This is a combination of a box plot and a kernel density function estimator. To load the contributed package named `vioplot` requires two steps. First, use the `install.packages` function, which will prompt you to select a nearby mirror to install the package.

```
> install.packages("vioplot")  # select a mirror and install
```

Next, the package must be loaded into the current R session in the usual fashion with the `library` function.

```
> library(vioplot)             # load in vioplot package (or use packages tab)
Loading required package: sm
Package 'sm', version 2.2-5.4: type help(sm) for summary information
```

The `vioplot` package consists of a single function named, not surprisingly, `vioplot`. To find out more information about the `vioplot` function, type

```
> ?vioplot                     # information on vioplot
```

Finally, to see a violin plot on the data set `precip`, which consists of average annual precipitation amounts (in inches) in 70 U.S. cities, type

```
> vioplot(precip)             # violin plot: boxplot & kernel density function
```

The violin plot shows the sample median, the interquartile range, and a mirror-image kernel density estimate of the population probability density function.

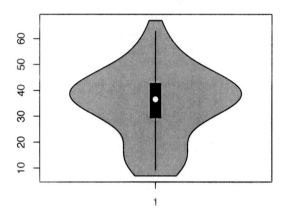

This concludes the discussion of packages. The table given next summarizes the functions introduced in this chapter.

function	description
sessionInfo	display attached packages
library	list attached packages or load packages
install.packages	install contributed packages
ts.plot	plot a time series
acf	compute and plot a sample autocorrelation function
pacf	compute and plot a sample partial autocorrelation function
spectrum	compute and plot a spectral density function (periodogram)
survfit	compute and plot survival functions
coxph	fit the Cox proportional hazards model to survival data
vioplot	plot a violin plot

This completes the brief introduction to the R language. There are numerous other facets of the language that could have been explored in more detail, for example,

- using an integrated development environment (IDE), such as `RStudio`,

- writing your own package,

- dealing with dates in their various formats using the contributed package `lubridate`,

- benchmarking to compare the speeds of various types of R code,

- interfacing with other computer languages, such as C and C++,

- more graphical capability, including the popular contributed package `ggplot2`,

- more on the thousands of packages that have not been introduced here, and

- R's internal storage mechanisms for objects.

In an effort to keep the size of this book manageable, these important topics are left to a more advanced and more encyclopedic treatment of the R language. This book is enough to get you started with the R language. Enjoy R!

Exercises

28.1   Find a function in a package of your choice. Execute the `example` function to illustrate how a particular function in this package works.

Index

CPSIA information can be obtained
at www.ICGtesting.com
Printed in the USA
FFOW01n2359270418
46365950-48047FF

9 780982 917480